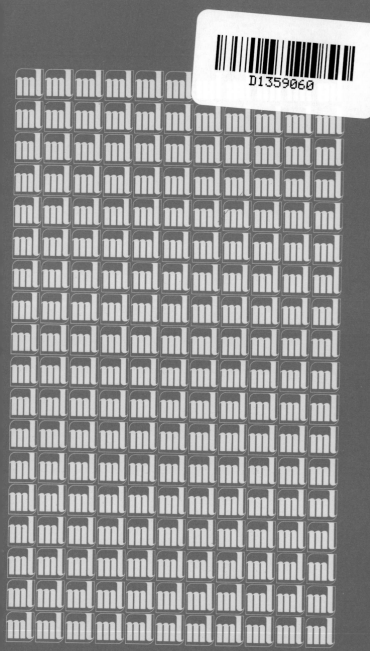

THE COMPLETE GREEK TRAGEDIES

VOLUME VI

EURIPIDES II

HELEN

HECUBA

ANDROMACHE

THE TROJAN WOMEN

ION

RHESUS

THE SUPPLIANT WOMEN

THE COMPLETE GREEK TRAGEDIES

VOLUME VI

EURIPIDES II

HELEN

HECUBA

ANDROMACHE

THE TROJAN WOMEN

ION

RHESUS

THE SUPPLIANT WOMEN

Edited by David Grene *and* Richmond Lattimore

THE MODERN LIBRARY · NEW YORK

THE MODERN LIBRARY
is published by
RANDOM HOUSE, INC.

CONTENTS

THE COMPLETE GREEK TRAGEDIES

VOLUME VI

EURIPIDES II

HELEN

HECUBA

ANDROMACHE

THE TROJAN WOMEN

ION

RHESUS

THE SUPPLIANT WOMEN

HELEN

Translated and with an Introduction by

RICHMOND LATTIMORE

CHARACTERS

Helen
Teucer
Chorus of Greek captive women
Menelaus
Portress
Servant of Menelaus
Theonoë
Theoclymenus
Follower of Theoclymenus
Slave of Theonoë
Castor
Polydeuces } *as divine*

Because those who are unfamiliar with this play will find that it contains surprises, it is suggested that they read the text first and the introduction afterwards. The introduction is accordingly printed after the play.

HELEN

SCENE: *Egypt, near the Canobic mouth of the Nile and before the gates of the royal house. The tomb of King Proteus is down stage. Helen discovered sitting against the tomb.*

Helen

These are the waters of the Nile, stream of sweet nymphs.
The river, fed with melting of pale snows, and not
with rain, rises to flood the flats of Egypt. Here
Proteus, while yet he lived, was lord over the land,
at home in Pharos, king in Egypt; and his bride   5
was Psamathe, one of the daughters of the deep,
wife once to Aeacus, later sundered from him,
who bore two children to him in the house, a boy
called Theoclymenus (because his father showed
the gods love in his lifetime) and a fine girl they named   10
Ido (her mother's image) when she was a child;
but when she came to nubile age they changed her name
to Theonoë, for she understands all things that are,
all things to be, that divination alone can tell.
Nereus, her forefather, granted her this privilege.   15

Nor is my own country obscure. It is a place
called Sparta, and my father was Tyndareus: though
they tell a story about how Zeus took on himself
the shape of a flying swan, with eagle in pursuit,
and came on wings to Leda my mother, and so won   20
the act of love by treachery. It may be so.

3

They called me Helen. Let me tell you all the truth
of what has happened to me. The three goddesses came
to remote Ida, and to Paris, for him to judge
their loveliness, and beauty was the cause. These were   25
Hera, the Lady of Cyprus, and the Daughter of Zeus.
But Aphrodite, promising my loveliness
(if what is cursed is ever lovely) to the arms
of Paris, won her away. Idaean Paris left
his herds for Sparta, thinking I was to be his.   30

But Hera, angry that she was not given the prize,
made void the love that might have been for Paris and me
and gave him, not me, but in my likeness fashioning
a breathing image out of the sky's air, bestowed
this on King Priam's son, who thinks he holds me now   35
but holds a vanity which is not I. See, next,
how further counsels of Zeus add to my misery.
He loaded war upon the Hellenic land and on
the unhappy Phrygians, thus to drain our mother earth
of the burden and the multitude of human kind.   40
Also, he would advertise the greatest Hellene prince.
The Phrygians fought for me (except it was not I
but my name only) held against the spears of Greece.
I myself was caught up by Hermes, sheathed away
in films of air, for Zeus had not forgotten me,   45
and set down by him where you see me, in the house
of Proteus, chosen because, most temperate of men,
he could guard my honor safe for Menelaus. So
here am I; but meanwhile my ill-adventured lord
assembled an armament to track me down the trail   50
of my abduction, and assaulted Ilium's towers.
Because of me, beside the waters of Scamander, lives
were lost in numbers; and the ever patient I
am cursed by all and thought to have betrayed my lord
and for the Hellenes lit the flame of a great war.   55

Why do I go on living, then? Yet I have heard
from the god Hermes that I yet shall make my home

4

in the famous plain of Sparta with my lord, and he
shall know I never went to Ilium, had no thought
of bed with any man. Here, while yet Proteus looked   60
upon this sun we see, I was safe from marriage. Now
that he is dead and hidden in the dark, his son
pursues me for my hand, but I, remembering
my first husband, cling a suppliant here upon
the grave of Proteus, for help to keep my love intact.   65
Thus, though I wear the name of guilt in Greece, yet here
I keep my body uncontaminated by disgrace.

(*Enter Teucer, who does not at first see Helen.*)

Teucer

What master holds dominion in these lowering halls?
The scope of wall is royal, and the massive pile
bespeaks possession by the Lord of Gold and Death.   70
(*seeing Helen*) Ah!
O gods, what do I see before me. Do I see
the deadly likeness of that woman who destroyed
all the Achaeans and me? May the gods spurn you for
looking so much like Helen's copy. Were I not   75
footfast on alien ground, with my true-winging shaft
I would have killed you, for looking like the child of Zeus.

Helen

Poor wretch, whoever you are, whatever cause has driven
you here, why must *her* sorrows turn your hate on *me?*

Teucer

I was wrong so to give way to anger more   80
than it became me. Hellas hates the child of Zeus.
Therefore forgive me, lady, for what I have said.

Helen

But who are you? From what country have you journeyed
    here?

5

Teucer
Lady, I am one of those Greek unfortunates.

Helen
It is no wonder you hate Helen then. But tell   85
me who are you. Where from? Whose son you should be
called.

Teucer
My name is Teucer, and the father who gave me life
is Telamon. The land of Salamis nursed my youth.

Helen
And what has brought you to this valley of the Nile?

Teucer
I am an exile, driven from my father's land.   90

Helen
You must be unhappy. Who was it who forced you out?

Teucer
Telamon, my father. Who could be nearer to my love?

Helen
But why? Such action means catastrophe for you.

Teucer
Aias my brother died at Troy. This meant my doom.

Helen
Surely it was not by your hand he lost his life?   95

Teucer
His death came when he hurled himself on his own sword.

Helen
In frenzy? Could a sane man see such an act through?

Teucer
You have heard of one they call Achilles, Peleus' son.

6

Helen
> Yes.
> He came once to ask for Helen's hand; so we are told.

Teucer
> He was killed. His armor caused a quarrel among his
>   friends.   100

Helen
> But how could all this have brought Aias any harm?

Teucer
> Someone else won the armor, and he killed himself.

Helen
> But has this suffering of his damaged your life?

Teucer
> Yes, if only because I did not die with him.

Helen
> I see. Tell me, were you at famous Ilium, then?   105

Teucer
> I helped sack it. That act has been my own ruin.

Helen
> And the city has been set afire? It is all gone?

Teucer
> You could no longer tell for sure where the walls stood.

Helen
> Helen, poor wretch! The Phrygians have perished for
>   your sake.

Teucer
> The Achaeans also; for great evil has been done.   110

Helen
> How long is it now since the city was destroyed?

7

Teucer
Seven years have almost circled with their crops since
then.

Helen
How much time in addition did you spend at Troy?

Teucer
Moon after moon, until it came to ten full years.

Helen
And then you got the woman of Sparta?

Teucer
Yes we did. 115
Menelaus seized her by the hair and dragged her off.

Helen
Did you see the poor woman, or have you only heard?

Teucer
I saw her with my own eyes, as I see you now.

Helen
Think. Could this be only an impression, caused by
God?

Teucer
Speak of some other matter, please. No more of her. 120

Helen
You *do* believe your impression is infallible.

Teucer
These eyes saw her. When the eyes see, the brain sees
too.

Helen
So. Then by now Menelaus and his wife are home.

8

Teucer
    They are not in Argos, nor where the Eurotas runs.

Helen
    You speak them evil, and, ah, you tell of evil for them.   125

Teucer
    The rumor is that he has vanished with his wife.

Helen
    Then all the Argives did not cross for home together?

Teucer
    They did, but a storm split them and drove them variously.

Helen
    Among what waves, where on the open sea?

Teucer
                          Just as
    they cut across the middle of the Aegean main.   130

Helen
    And after this, none knows of Menelaus' return?

Teucer
    No one does; and in Greece he is reported dead.

Helen
    Then I am undone.
                    Is Thestius' daughter still alive?

Teucer
    You mean by this Leda? No, she is dead and gone.

Helen
    It could not have been the shame of Helen that caused
    her death?   135

9

Teucer
> They say so; that she fastened the noose on her fair
> throat.

Helen
> Tyndareus' sons, then; are they alive, or are they not?

Teucer
> Dead, not dead. There are two interpretations here.

Helen
> Which one prevails? How much sorrow must I endure?

Teucer
> Men say that they have been made stars and are divine. 140

Helen
> Fair told when thus told; but what is the other account?

Teucer
> That for their sister's shame they died by their own
> hands.
> Enough words now. I should not have to suffer twice.
> But for the matter of my errand to this house
> of kings, it was my wish to see Theonoë 145
> the prophetess. Be you my representative
> and help me learn from her how I should steer the wings
> of my ship with best wind for the sea-girt land
> of Cyprus, where Apollo prophesied that I
> should found and name New Salamis from my island
> home. 150

Helen
> Sail, friend. Your course will show itself; but you must
> leave this country and escape before you have been seen
> by the son of Proteus, ruler of this land. He now
> has gone with hounds, hopeful of killing beasts of chase.
> He slaughters every Greek he lays his hand upon, 155
> but why he does this, you must not try to find out,
> as I am silent. For how could my speech help you?

Teucer

    All you have said was good, my lady, and may the gods
grant you the grace your kindness has deserved. You wear
the bodily shape of Helen, but you have a heart   160
that is not hers. Wide is the difference. May she
die miserably, never see Eurotas' stream
again.

    But may you, lady, always prosper well.

                    (Exit. Helen is left alone.)

Helen

    Here, with a song of deep wretchedness for the depth of
        my sorrows,
what shall be the strain of my threnody, what singing
        spirit   165
supplicate in tears, in mourning, in sorrow? Ah me.
You who go winged women in form
young and maiden, daughters of earth,
O Sirens, if you would only come   170
to attend my mourning
with Libyan harp, with pipes,
with lyres, with tears of your own to give
the singing of all my unhappiness.
With passion for passion, sorrow for sorrow,
melody matching
my dirges, given
by Persephone   175
of the dead, she in turn shall be given
in her halls of night the sweet of my sorrow
in consecration
of those who are dead and gone from us.

                   (Enter the Chorus, singing.)

Chorus

    I was down by the shining blue
water, and on the curl of the grass   180

11

there in the golden glare of the sun
laid out the colored wash
in the bed of the young rushes
to dry. There I heard my lady
and the pitiful sound as she cried out,
the voice of sorrow, lament without lyres,   185
a sharp voice of pain, of mourning
as cries aloud for grief some nymph,
a naiad, caught
in the hills for all her flight, gives voice
to pain, as under the rock hollows
she cries out
on Pan and his captured marriage.   190

Helen

Hear me,
spoil of the savage oar blade,
daughters of Greece, hear;
from Achaea a mariner
came, yes came, and tears on my tears he loaded.   195
The wrecked city of Ilium
is given up to the teeth of fire,
all through me and the deaths I caused,
all for my name of affliction. So
Leda has taken her life within   200
the strangling noose, for the thought of shame
in those sorrows that have been mine.
My lord is lost, he is gone, far driven
over the sea. And the twin-born glory
of the house of my father, Castor   205
and Polydeuces his brother, vanished,
vanished away; the plain where their horses
trampled, their running-field, desolate
down by the reeds of Eurotas   210
where the young men rode and ran.

Chorus

Ah me,

12

so sorrowful was that destiny,
lady mine, that befell you,
a life better unlived
given to you, yes given, when Zeus blazed in the bright
air, in the snowflash of the swan's   215
wing to beget you upon your mother.
What grief is there you have not known?
What in life have you not lived through?
Your mother is lost and gone:
the twins, beloved children of Zeus,   220
are blessed in fortune no longer. Your eyes
are kept from the sight of your country,
while through the cities of men there goes
the rumor, divine lady, that gives
you up to barbarian lusts. And now   225
your husband, lost on the tossing sea,
is gone from life. You can come no more
to bless the halls of your father, bless
the brazen house of Athene.

Helen

What man of the Phrygians was it
or was it one from Hellenic soil   230
who cut down the dripping pine timbers
fatal to Ilium?
This was the timber that Priam's son
shaped into that accursed ship
which, driven by outland oars, brought him
to the hearth where I lived; he came   235
after my ill-starred beauty,
after my love's capture.
And she, the treacherous goddess,
the murderous queen of Cyprus,
drew death down on the Danaid men
cruel in all her working.   240
Then Hera, goddess of grandeur,
queen of the golden throne, who lies
in the arms of Zeus, sent down to me

13

Hermes, fleet son of Maia.
I was picking fresh flowers
gathering them into my robe, to take
to Athene there in her brazen house   245
when he caught me away through the bright
air to this unprofitable
country, poor me, made a prize of war
for Priam's sons and the Hellenes
while upon my name
where Simois runs has descended   250
a false fame and a vanity.

Chorus

You have your sorrows, I know it well. But it were best
to hear your life's constraints as lightly as you may.

Helen

Women and friends, what is this destiny on which   255
I am fastened? Was I born a monster among mankind?
[No woman, neither in Greece nor yet in Barbary,
is hatched from the white envelope that contains young
     birds,
yet thus Leda bore me to Zeus, or so they say.]
And so my life is monstrous, and the things that happen   260
to me, through Hera, or my beauty is to blame.
I wish that like a picture I had been rubbed out
and done again, made plain, without this loveliness,
for so the Greeks would never have been aware of all
those misfortunes that now are mine. So I would keep   265
what was not bad, as now they keep the bad of me.
He who sees from the gods a single strain of luck,
all bad, has a sad lot, but can endure it still.
More complex is the sorrow in which I am involved.
I have done nothing wrong and yet my reputation   270
is bad, and worse than a true evil is it to bear
the burden of faults that are not truly yours. Again,
the gods have torn me from my father's land and made
me live among barbarians. I have no kin

14

and therefore live a slave although my birth was free. 275
All Barbary is slave except a single man.
There was one anchor to my hope; the thought of how
my husband might come some day and deliver me,
but gone is that hope now, for he is dead and gone.
My mother is dead, I am her murderer. I know 280
that is unfair, but such unfairness I must take.
My daughter, pride of the household and my own pride,
is growing to gray years unmarried. And the sons
of Zeus, or so men call them, the Dioscuri,
no longer live. So all my luck is turned to grief 285
and for all purposes I am dead, yet live in fact.
But worst of all is, if I ever should win home
I must be crushed by scandal, for men think that I
am that Helen whom Menelaus went to Troy
to bring. If my husband were alive, I could be known 290
by him through signs which no one else could recognize.
But this fails now. It cannot be that he lives still.
Why do I go on living then? What course is left?
Shall I choose marriage as my means to get away
from hardship? Live with a barbarian husband? Sit 295
to a rich table? No, for when a hateful lord
lives with a wife, then all the body is hateful too.
Death is best. But to die in some unseemly way?
[When one hangs by the neck, it is ugly
and is thought a bad sight for the slaves to look upon. 300
Death by the knife is noble and has dignity
and the body's change from life to death is a short time.]
Such is the depth of my unhappiness, that while
for other women beauty means their happiness
it is my very beauty that has ruined me. 305

Chorus

Helen, you should not be so sure that that stranger
who came, whoever he is, has spoken all the truth.

Helen

But he said plainly that my husband had been lost.

Chorus
Many things can be said and yet prove to be false.

Helen
And much that contradicts the critic may be true.   310

Chorus
You push yourself to believe the worst and not the best.

Helen
Yes, I am frightened, and so led by fright to fear.

Chorus
How does your favor stand with those inside the house?

Helen
All here are friends, except the man who hunts my love.

Chorus
Do you know? I think you should . . . leave your place
      at the tomb. . . .   315

Helen
What advice is it you so hesitantly give?

Chorus
Go to the house, and ask the daughter of the sea's
nymph, ask Theonoë, who understands all things,
about your husband, whether he still lives, or if
he is lost from daylight. Then, when you are well in-
      formed   320
be happy, or be sorry, as the chance deserves.
Now, when you really know nothing, where is the use
in hurting yourself as you do now? Do what I say.
Give up the shelter of this tomb. Speak with the girl.
Why look further, when in this very house you have   325
a source of knowledge that will tell you all the truth?
I volunteer to go inside the house with you
and help you ask the maiden for her prophecies.
It is right for women to stand by a woman's cause.

16

Helen

    Friends, I accept your argument. 330
    Go, then, go inside the house
    so that there you may ask
    what new trials await me now.

Chorus

    I will, nor hesitate. Urge not.

Helen

    O pitiful day. 335
    Unhappy I, unhappy, oh what
    tale of tears shall I be told?

Chorus

    Do not be prophetic of grief.
    Do not, dear, anticipate sorrow.

Helen

    My poor husband, what has happened to him? 340
    Do his eyes see the light,
    the sun's chariot and four horses, the stars in course,
    or among dead men under ground
    takes he the long period? 345

Chorus

    For the future which is yet
    to come, lean to the better hope.

Helen

    I call upon you by name, I invoke,
    river pale by the washed reeds,
    Eurotas; if this tale 350
    of my lord's death that has come to me
    is true—and where was the story not clear?—
    then I will bind my throat
    fast in the hanging noose of death,
    or with the deadly stroke that cuts
    the throat open and bleeding 355

drive the iron with my own hand hard into my body,
a sacrifice to the trinity
of goddesses, and to Priam's son
who held the hollows of Ida
long ago when he tended his herds.

Chorus
    From somewhere may defense emerge   360
    against evils: the turn of your fortune.

Helen
    Ah, Troy, the unhappy,
    for things done that were never done
    you died, hurt pitifully. The gifts
    the Lady of Cyprus gave me brought
    showers of tears, showers of blood, pain   365
    on pain, tears upon tears, suffering.
    Mothers who saw their children die,
    maidens who cut their long hair
    for kinsmen who were killed beside the waters
    of Phrygian Scamander.
    Hellas too has cried, has cried   370
    aloud in lamentation,
    beaten her hands against her head
    and with the nails' track of blood
    torn her cheeks' softness.
    Blessed long ago in Arcadia, maiden Callisto,   375
    who shared the bed of Zeus, who were made into
    a four-foot beast, how happy was your lot beside
    my mother's; for all the bear's shaggy bulk
    is made gentle by the soft eyes,
    and the metamorphosis took away   380
    your sorrows. Artemis drove from her dances
    the doe of the golden horns, Titanian daughter of
        Merops,
    for her loveliness. But by body's beauty
    ruined the castle of the Dardanians, ruined
    all the perished Achaeans.   385

*(Exeunt all into the house. Enter Menelaus, in
tattered clothing.)*

Menelaus
Ah Pelops, racer of chariots and horses long
ago with Oinomäus in the Pisa field,
how I could wish that, when you were constrained to
     make
an offering to the gods, you had then left this life
for theirs, before you had sired my father, Atreus;   390
who by his marriage with Aërope begot
Agamemnon and myself, Menelaus, two renowned
brothers; for here I do not boast, yet I believe
we marshalled the greatest of armadas against Troy
although we led them not as tyrants, not by force,   395
but the young men of Greece willingly served with us.
Those who are no more living can be numbered now,
and those who, gratefully escaping from the sea,
brought home again the names of all the dead. But I,
battered and driven over the gray swell of the open   400
sea, have been wandering ever since I stormed the towers
of Ilium, trying to win back to my own land
whereto the gods debar my right of homecoming.
I have now sailed to all the friendless, desolate
approaches of Libya; always, as I make near home,   405
the wind buffets me back again, nor ever fills
favorable my sail to bring me home again.
     And now, hapless and shipwrecked, with my friends
          all lost,
I am driven upon this shore. My ship shattered against
the rocks, and broke up into wreck and flotsam there.   410
Of all the ship's various parts the keel held out,
and on it, by some unexpected chance, I managed
to save myself and Helen, whom I seized from Troy.
What this land is I do not know, nor yet the name
of its people; I was too embarrassed to be seen   415
in public, could not ask, but tried to hide away
my ragged state in shame for my bad luck. For when

a great man falls upon evil chance, the strangeness of it
makes him feel worse than the man accustomed to hard
    times.
But the need is too much for me, for we have no food   420
nor any clothing for our skin, as you may guess
by the kind of ship's flotsam in which I wrap myself.
The robes and all the shining wraps I had before
are lost at sea with all my treasures. Deep inside
a cave I hid the wife who was the cause of all   425
my evil fortunes, and constrained those friends who still
are left alive, to keep her safe for me. So now
I am here, all by myself, to see if I can raise
some provisions to take to the friends I left behind.
I saw this house with its expanse of masonry   430
and the grand gates as of some fortunate man, and so
came here. Seafarers always hope for charity
from the houses of the rich. Those who themselves are
    poor
would not be able to help them, though the wish were
    there.
O-ay! Who is the porter here? Will he come out   435
and take the message of my griefs to those inside?

(Enter Portress, from the house.)

Portress

Who is at the gates? Go away, will you, from the house?
Do not keep standing here before the courtyard doors
and bothering the masters. It will mean your death.
You are a Greek, and Greeks are not allowed in here.   440

Menelaus

Quite so, granny, just as you say, and fair enough.
Very well, I will do what you say, only let me talk.

Portress

Out with you. I have orders, stranger, never to let
anyone come from Greece to stay around this house.

20

Menelaus
Ah! Keep your hands off me, and stop pushing me.   445

Portress
That is your fault. You are not doing what I say.

Menelaus
Now go inside and take this message to your master.

Portress
I shall smart for it if I take a message from you.

Menelaus
I am a shipwrecked foreigner of high degree.

Portress
Go on then to some other house instead of this.   450

Menelaus
No, I am going in; do as I tell you to.

Portress
I tell you, you are bothersome. We'll throw you out.

Menelaus
Ah, where are all my armies now, which won such fame?

Portress
You may have been a great man at home. You are not
     one here.

Menelaus
God, what a loss of station, and now undeserved.   455

Portress
Your eyes are wet with tears. Tell me, why are you sad?

Menelaus
Thinking of all my happiness in times gone by.

Portress
Go then, bestow those tears upon your own people.

21

Menelaus
>   Tell me first, what is this country, what king's house is
>   this?

Portress
>   This is the house of Proteus; Egypt is the land.   460

Menelaus
>   Egypt? What an unhappy chance to have sailed here.

Portress
>   What do you find wrong with the glories of the Nile?

Menelaus
>   Nothing wrong. It is my own bad luck that makes me
>   sad.

Portress
>   There are many men who have bad luck, not only you.

Menelaus
>   Is there some master of the house you could name to me?   465

Portress
>   This is his tomb you see here. Now his son is king.

Menelaus
>   Where would he be then? In the house, or gone some-
>   where?

Portress
>   He is not in; and above all else he hates Hellenes.

Menelaus
>   What have we done to him that I should suffer for it?

Portress
>   It is because Zeus' daughter, Helen, is in this house.   470

Menelaus
>   What? What is this you are telling me? Say it again.

22

Portress

I mean Tyndareus' daughter who lived in Sparta once.

Menelaus

Where did she come from? What is the explanation of
    this?

Portress

She came from Lacedaemon and made her way here.

Menelaus

When? Has my wife I left in the cave been carried off?   475

Portress

She came, friend, before the Achaeans sailed for Troy.
So go away from here quietly. The state of things
inside is such that all the great house is upside down.
You came at the wrong time, and if my master catches
you, all the hospitality you will find is death.   480
I myself like the Greeks, in spite of those harsh words
I gave you. I was afraid of what the master might do.

(*The Portress goes back into the house and closes the
door.*)

Menelaus

What am I to think or make of this? She tells me now
of present difficulties grown from those gone by,
since, while I come bringing my wife, lost once by force,   485
from Troy, and she is guarded for me in the cave,
all the while some other woman with the same name
as my wife has been living in this house. She said
that this one was by birth the child of Zeus. Can it be
there is some man who bears the name of Zeus and lives   490
beside the banks of the Nile? There is one Zeus; in
    heaven.
And where on earth is Sparta except only where
Eurotas' waters ripple by the lovely reeds?
Tyndareus is a famous name. There is only one.

And where is there another land called Lacedaemon   495
or Troy either? I do not know what to make of it.
I suppose it must be that in the great world a great many
have the same name, men named like other men, cities
like cities, women like women. Nothing to wonder at
in this.
      I will not run away for the servant's threats.   500
There is no man whose heart is so uncivilized
that when he has heard my name he will not give me
    food.
Troy is renowned, and I, who lit the fire of Troy,
Menelaus, am not unknown anywhere in all
the world. I will wait the master of the house. I have   505
a choice of courses. If he is a savage man
I will hide myself and make for where I left the wreck,
but if he gives way and is gentle, I shall ask
for what the present circumstances make me need.
Of all the evils in my distressed plight, this is   510
the worst, that I, myself a king, should have to ask
other kings for sustenance. But so it has to be.
For the saying is not mine, but it was wisely said,
that nothing has more strength than dire necessity.

(*Enter the Chorus and Helen from the house.*)

Chorus
    Before I came back I heard from the maid   515
    prophetic all she divined for the house
    of kings: how Menelaus is not
    lost yet nor sunk in the dim,
    shining cave of the under-earth,
    but still over the sea's surges   520
    hard driven he cannot win
    to the harbors of his own land,
    in hardship, wandering
    for want of food, with his friends all gone
    all across the wide world he keeps   525
    his foot hard for the oarsman's stroke
    since ever he sailed from Troy land.

Helen

So, here am I, come back to the shelter of the tomb
once more. I have heard Theonoë's words, and they were
    good,
and she knows everything. She says my husband lives   530
still in the light and looks upon the day-star; yet
he is driven sailing back and forth along the sea
on endless crossings, hardened by the wanderer's life,
but when his work is ended and over, he will come.
One thing she did not tell me, whether when he comes   535
he will be safe. I carefully did not ask her this,
I was so happy to hear that he is safe so far.
She said also that he was in this country, near
at hand, a shipwrecked castaway with few friends left.
When will you come? And if you come, how dear to me!   540

(*As she speaks this line, she turns to face Menelaus, whom
    she has not seen until now. She gives a little scream.*)

Who is it, who are you? Does this mean I am waylaid
by the machinations of Proteus' godless son? What shall
I do? Not run like a racing filly, like the god's
bacchanal, to the tomb with flying feet? This man
is savage by his look and hunts me for his prey.   545

Menelaus

You, who now race in such an agony of fear
to reach the grave-mound and the uprights where the
    fires
are burned, stay! Why this flight? Know when I saw
    your face
it struck me with amazement and with unbelief.

Helen

We are set upon, my women. This man bars my way   550
to the tomb. His purpose is to catch me, and then give
me over to that tyrant whose embrace I shun.

Menelaus

I am no thief, nor any servant of bad men.

25

Helen
And yet the clothes that cover you are poor and mean.

Menelaus
Stay your swift feet from running, put aside your fear.　　555

Helen
Very well, I will stand, since I have reached my goal.

Menelaus
Who are you? I look, lady, upon your face: whose face?

Helen
And who are you? The same question for both of us.

Menelaus
Never have I seen a form so like another form.

Helen
Oh gods!—it is divine to recognize your own.　　560

Menelaus
Are you a Hellene woman or a native here?*

Helen
Hellene. But tell me who you are. I would know too.

Menelaus
You are more like Helen, my lady, than any I know.

Helen
You are like Menelaus, too. What does it mean?

Menelaus
The truth. You have recognized that most unhappy man.　　565

Helen
Oh, you are come at long last here to your wife's arms.

* The line is not in the manuscripts of this play. Markland has supplied it from the parody of this scene in Aristophanes' *Thesmophoria-zusae.*

Menelaus

Wife? What wife do you mean? Take your hands off my
clothes.

Helen

The wife Tyndareus, my own father, gave to you.

Menelaus

O Hecate of the lights, send better dreams than this.

Helen

I am no dream of the crossway goddess. You see me.　　　570

Menelaus

I am only one man and could not have two wives.

Helen

And who might be this other mate whose lord you are?

Menelaus

Whom the cave hides, whom I brought here from the
Phrygian land.

Helen

I am your wife. There is no other in my place.

Menelaus

Am I in my right senses? Are my eyes at fault?　　　575

Helen

When you look at me, do you not think you see your
wife?

Menelaus

Your body is like her. Certainty fails me.

Helen

　　　　　　　　　Look and see.
What more do you want? And who knows me better
than you?

27

Menelaus
In very truth you are like her. That I will not deny.

Helen
What better teacher shall you have than your own eyes?   580

Menelaus
It is they that fail me, since another is my wife.

Helen
It was an image of me. I never went to Troy.

Menelaus
And what artificer makes bodies live and breathe?

Helen
The air: from which the work of gods shaped you a bride.

Menelaus
And which of the gods made her? This is past all wit.   585

Helen
Hera, to palm on Paris, so he should not have me.

Menelaus
How could you be here and in Troy at the same time?

Helen
My name could be in many places where I was not.

Menelaus
Let me go. I had pain enough when I came here.

Helen
And will you leave me, for that empty shadow's arms?   590

Menelaus
You are like Helen, so, at least, happy farewell.

Helen
Lost, lost! I won my husband, and must lose him still.

Menelaus
I trust my memory of great hardships more than you.

Helen
Ah me, was any woman more wretched ever? They
who stand closest forsake me. I shall never find   595
my way to Greece, land of my fathers, ever again.

(*Enter Servant of Menelaus. He does not see, or does
not notice, Helen until he has told his story.*)

Servant
Menelaus, I have been wandering all over this land
of barbarians looking for you and find you now
at last. The friends you left behind sent me for you.

Menelaus
What is it? Have the barbarians robbed or plundered
you?   600

Servant
A strange thing, stranger in itself than the telling of it.

Menelaus
Tell me. You must bring some surprise, for haste like this.

Servant
I tell you: all your thousand toils were toiled in vain.

Menelaus
This is old weeping for old sorrows. What is new?

Servant
Your wife is gone, swept up and away and out of sight   605
into the hollows of the high air. Sky veils her now.
She left the secret cave where we were keeping her
with only this said to us: "Wretched men of Troy
and all you Achaeans who, day after day, went on
dying for me beside Scamander, by Hera's craft,   610
you thought Paris had Helen, when he never did.

Now I, having kept the duty of destiny, stayed out
the time I had to stay, go back into the sky,
my father. All for nothing Tyndareus' daughter has
heard evil things said of her, who did nothing wrong."   615
   Oh, daughter of Leda, hail! Were you here all this
       time?
I was in the act of telling him, fool that I was,
how you had left our caverns for the stars and gone
on wings away. I will not let you mock at us
like this again. It was enough hardship that you,   620
your husband, and his helpers gave us there in Troy.

Menelaus

I see it, I see it! All the story that she told
has come out true. O day of my desires, that gave
you back into my arms to take and hold again!

Helen

Oh, dearest of men to me, Menelaus, time has grown   625
old, but the joy that now is ours is fresh and new.
I have my husband again, all my delight, sweet friends,
my arms circle him now,
beloved, light and a flame in dark that has been so long.

Menelaus

And I hold you. And we have so much to say about   630
the time between, I do not know where to begin.

Helen

I am so happy, all my hair is rising
with shivering pleasure, and the tears burst. Husband
and love, I have your body here close in my arms,
happiness, mine again.   635

Menelaus

O sweetest face, there is nothing left to wish for.
This is my bride, daughter of Zeus and Leda,
she whom the maidens of white horses, girl of your
   kindred

brought me by candle-light, to bless me, to bless   640
me long ago, but it was a god who took you away
from my house, and drove you
away, where your fate was the stronger.
But evil turned to good brought us together again,
my wife, lost so long. Now may my luck be good.   645

Chorus

May it be good, surely. All my prayer is as your prayer.
Where there are two, one cannot be wretched, and one
    not.

Helen

My friends, dear friends, I will no longer
weep and grieve for the past.
I have my husband, I have him. Long I waited for him.   650
all the years of Troy, waited for him to come.

Menelaus

You have me, I have you. But the suns of ten thousand
    days
were hard to win through to God's gladness here at the
    end.
My happiness has its tears in it; but there is more
sweetness here than the pain.   655

Helen

What shall I say? Who ever could hope that this would
    be,
to have you so unhoped-for here against my breasts?

Menelaus

Or I to hold you, when I thought you had gone away
to Idaean Troy and to those pitiful towers.
In gods' name, tell me how you were taken from my
    house.   660

Helen

Ah, a bitter cause that you open here,
and ah, a bitter story you waken for me.

31

Menelaus
Speak. The gods gave this; we must even hear it out.

Helen
I spit away that story, the story that I must tell.

Menelaus
Tell it still. There is pleasure in hardship heard about.   665

Helen
It was not to the bed of a young barbarian man
borne on the beating of oars,
borne on the beating of desire for a lawless love.

Menelaus
No, but what spirit, what destiny robbed home of you?

Helen
The son of Zeus, of Zeus, my lord,   670
brought me here to the Nile.

Menelaus
Strange, strange! Who sent him? There is danger in this
    tale.

Helen
I have wept for this, my eyes are wet with tears.
It was the wife of Zeus destroyed me.

Menelaus
Hera? What need had she to make it evil for us?   675

Helen
Ah, there was danger for me in the bathing there and
    the springs
where the goddesses made bright
their bodies; there the judgment was begun.

Menelaus
And Hera made the judgment mean this evil for you?

32

Helen

So she might take away from Paris. . . .

Menelaus

How? Speak. 680

Helen

Me. Cypris had promised him me.

Menelaus

Oh, cruel.

Helen

Cruel, cruel. So I was driven to Egypt.

Menelaus

She gave him the image in your place. So you tell me.

Helen

But you in your house, my mother, ah, the sorrows of
you,
the hurt that happened.

Menelaus

Tell me. 685

Helen

My mother is gone. Ill starred in marriage for my sake
and for my shame she caught the noose to her neck.

Menelaus

Ah. But Hermione our daughter, does she live?

Helen

Wedless, childless, my dear, she grieves
for my marriage that was none. 690

Menelaus

Oh, Paris, you sacked my house from top to bottom, and
yet
it killed you too, and in their thousands killed
the bronze armored Danaans.

33

Helen

It was the god who cast me away from my city, from you,
out of the land of my fathers, star-crossed and cursed   695
when I left my house, when I left my bed; but I left them
    not
for any shameful love.

Chorus

If now for the rest of fortune you are fortunate,
in time to come, it is enough to heal the past.

Servant

Menelaus, let me into your happiness as well.   700
I begin to understand it, but am not yet clear.

Menelaus

Indeed, my father. Share in what we have to say.

Servant

Is she not mistress of sorrows for the men in Troy?

Menelaus

She is not. We were swindled by the gods. We had
our hands upon an idol of the clouds.

Servant

                    You mean   705
it was for a cloud, for nothing, we did all that work?

Menelaus

The hand of Hera, the hate of the three goddesses.

Servant

This woman who stands here with us is your real wife?

Menelaus

Herself. It is I who tell you this. You must believe.   710

Servant

My daughter, the way of God is complex, he is hard
for us to predict. He moves the pieces and they come

somehow into a kind of order. Some have bad luck
while others, scatheless, meet their evil and go down
in turn. None can hold fortune still and make it last.   715
You and your husband have had your turn of trouble
    now.
Yours was a story, but he fought with the spear, and all
his hard fighting was fought for nothing. Now his luck
has turned, and the highest blessings fall into his hands.
You never shamed your aged father, never shamed   720
your divine brothers, nor did what you were rumored to.
It all comes back to me, your marriage long ago,
and I remember the torch I carried as I ran
beside your four-horse chariot, where you, a bride,
rode from your noble house beside the master here.   725
He is a poor thing who does not feel as his masters do,
grieve in their grief, be happy in their happiness.
I, though I wear the name of lackey, yet aspire
to be counted in the number of the generous
slaves, for I do not have the name of liberty   730
but have the heart. Better this, than for a single man
to have the double evil of an evil spirit
and to be named by those about him as a slave.

Menelaus

Come then, old friend, you who have had your share of
    work
in the hard stands beneath the shield and at my side,   735
share now the blessings of my fortune too, and go
to take the news back to those friends I left behind
how you have found our state here, how our luck holds
    now;
tell them, too, to wait by the sea-shore, follow from there
the progress of those trials of strength I see in store   740
for me, and if we can steal my wife out of this place
they must see to it that, joining our fortunes all in one,
we get clear of these natives, if we have the strength.

Servant

It shall be done, my lord.

35

Only, now I am sure
how rotten this business of prophets is, how full of lies. 745
There never was any good in burning things on fires
nor in the voices of fowl. It is sheer idiocy
even to think that birds do people any good.
Calchas said nothing about this, he never told
the army when he saw his friends die for a cloud, 750
nor Helenus either, and a city was stormed in vain.
You might say: "No, for God did not wish it that way."
Then why consult the prophets? We should sacrifice
to the gods, ask them for blessings, and let prophecy go.
The art was invented as a bait for making money, 755
but no man ever got rich on magic without work.
The best prophet is common sense, our native wit.

(*Exit.*)

Chorus
My own opinion about prophets marches with
that of this old man. If you have the gods for friends
you have a better thing than prophecy in your house. 760

Helen
So. All has been peaceful here where I have been. But
tell
me, my poor husband, how you survived Troy. I know
there is no good in learning, but when you love you feel
a fascination in even the sorrows of those you love.

Menelaus
Your single question, one approach, ask me so much. 765
Why must I tell you how the Aegean wore us out,
of the Euboean wrecking-fires Nauplius set,
of Crete, of the Libyan cities we were driven upon,
of Perseus' eyrie? I could never satisfy
you telling of troubles. Telling would only burden me 770
who am so tired already, and be double pain.

Helen
What you have said was better than my question. Still,

36

leave out the rest and tell me only this. How long
have you been wandering battered on the waves of the
sea?

Menelaus

The years at Troy were ten, and to this add the time   775
I was at sea, where I filled the circles of seven years.

Helen

Too long, unhappy husband, all too long a time
to live through, and survive it, and come here to die.

Menelaus

To die! What will you tell me now? You have broken me.

Helen

Make your escape, get clear of this place with speed, or
else   780
you must be killed by the man who is the master here.

Menelaus

What have I done to deserve treatment such as this?

Helen

You have come unlooked-for to prevent my marrying.

Menelaus

You mean someone here is trying to marry my wife?

Helen

He meant to force my favors; and I must endure.   785

Menelaus

In his own private strength, or by some lordship here?

Helen

The man is Proteus' son and master of the land.

Menelaus

Now I understand the puzzle of the portress' speech.

Helen
  At what outlandish doors have you been standing now?

Menelaus
  These. And like any beggar I was driven away.   790

Helen
  You were not asking for charity? Oh, my shame.

Menelaus
  The action was that, but I did not call it so.

Helen
  It seems, then, you know all about his courting me.

Menelaus
  I know; what I do not know is whether you held him
    off.

Helen
  Hear it then: all my love is kept untouched for you.   795

Menelaus
  What will make me sure of this? (but how sweet, if
    true!).

Helen
  Do you see where I sat in suffering beside this tomb?

Menelaus
  The marks, yes, of your suffering. What was your plan?

Helen
  I took a suppliant's place here to escape his bed.

Menelaus
  For lack of an altar, or is it a foreign custom here?   800

Helen
  It saved me, as well as the gods' temples could have
    done.

Menelaus
　Is there no way for me and my ship to take you home?

Helen
　A sword waits for you, rather than a love-bed with me.

Menelaus
　Thus I would be the most unhappy man alive.

Helen
　Take flight, and do not be ashamed. Escape from here.　805

Menelaus
　And leave you? It was for your sake I captured Troy.

Helen
　But better so than that my love should mean your death.

Menelaus
　Cowardly counsel, unworthy of the siege of Troy.

Helen
　You would kill the king, I suspect. It cannot be done.

Menelaus
　You mean he has a body that no steel can pierce?　810

Helen
　You will see. The bold are helpless without cleverness.

Menelaus
　Shall I then quietly give him my hands to tie?

Helen
　You are desperate. What we need now is strategy.

Menelaus
　I would rather die in action than die passively.

Helen
　There is a single hope for escape, a single way.　815

Menelaus
What way? Bribery? Daring and force? Or argument?

Helen
What if the tyrant never learns that you are here?

Menelaus
Who will tell him? He will not know me by himself.

Helen
He has an ally, strong as a god, inside the house.

Menelaus
Has Rumor come and taken a secret place inside?   820

Helen
No, it is his sister, whom they call Theonoë.

Menelaus
The name is ominous, surely. Tell me what she does.

Helen
She knows everything. She will tell her brother you are
     here.

Menelaus
That would be death. I have no way to lie concealed.

Helen
But if we threw ourselves on her mercy, worked on her?   825

Menelaus
To do what? What is the hope you lead me gently to?

Helen
That she will *not* tell her brother you are in the land.

Menelaus
If we won her over, could we get ourselves out of here?

Helen
With her help, easily. Without her knowledge, no.

Menelaus
> Best for woman to approach woman. You do this.   830

Helen
> She will not leave until my arms have embraced her
> knees.

Menelaus
> But look now. What if she will not listen to us?

Helen
> You must die, and I be married by force, and sorrowful.

Menelaus
> But treacherous still. By force, you say. Only an excuse.

Helen
> No, then. I have sworn a sacred oath, by your own head.   835

Menelaus
> You mean that you will die and never change your mate?

Helen
> Die by the sword that kills you, and be laid to rest
> beside you.

Menelaus
> I accept it. Take my hand on this.

Helen
> I take it, swear to forsake the daylight when you die.

Menelaus
> And I swear, when I lose you I shall take my life.   840

Helen
> How, in such death, shall we make men know how we
> died?

Menelaus
> I will kill you on this grave-mound, then kill myself.

But come, first we shall dare a great action for your sake
and for your marriage. If he wants you, let him come.
I will not shame my glories of the Trojan War   845
nor take the common blame of Hellas when I come
    home,
I who made Thetis lose Achilles, I who looked
on Telamonian Aias in his suicide
and saw Nestor made childless. Shall I then not dare
count death as worth the dying for my lady's sake?   850
Oh, I must. If there are gods and if they are wise,
when a man falls high-hearted in the close of war
they make the earth lie light upon him in the grave,
but fling the cowards out on the hard stones of earth.

Chorus

Oh gods, I pray you, let the race of Tantalus   855
turn fortunate at last, and let their troubles end.

Helen

Unhappy me! My destiny is luckless still.
Menelaus, we have no chance left. Theonoë
the diviner is coming out now, for the house sounds
to the unbarring of the doors. Run! Only where   860
to run? What use? Whether or not she is here, she
    knows
that you are here. Poor husband, it is ruin now.
Saved from the savages of Troy, you have come here
once again to be driven on a savage sword.

(Enter Theonoë from the house, attended by women
    who carry torches and a sacred image. Each of
        her instructions is to a single attendant.)

Theonoë

Lead the way. Carry torches, let them shine, and bring   865
the image, gift of the solemn sky, from its inward room
so we may take and breathe the purity of this air.
You: if anyone with unhallowed foot has stepped
and fouled the way, treat it with purifying flame,

then quench the blaze so I can make my way through. Then   870
when we have rendered my devotion to the gods
take the fire back inside to burn upon the hearth.

Helen, what of my prophecies? Are they not true?
Here is your husband Menelaus, plain before
my eyes, with his ships lost, and with your image gone.   875
Poor man, with what dangers escaped you have come here,
nor even yet know whether you shall go home or must
stay here. This very day before the seat of Zeus
there shall be argument among the gods about
your case. Hera, who was your enemy before   880
is now your friend, desires that you go home with Helen
here, so that Greece may learn how Aphrodite's gift
to Alexander of a bride was a false gift.
Cypris would wreck your homecoming, so none shall know
the truth of how she bought the name of beauty for   885
false payment, Helen's marriage—which was no real thing.
The decision rests with me, to do as Cypris wills
and tell my brother you are here, destroy you so,
or take the side of Hera, save your life, and hide
your coming from my brother, though his orders were   890
to tell him, when your journey home brought you this way.

Which of you will go tell my brother that this man
is here? Thus will my future be made safe for me.

    (Helen flings herself at the feet of Theonoë.)
Helen
   Maiden, I throw myself as suppliant against
your knees, and kneel in a forlorn posture, for the sake   895
of my own self and for this man. I have found him
at last, and finding him am like to see him die.
Do not then tell your brother that my husband here

43

has come to my most loving and beloved arms,
but save us, I implore you. You must not betray   900
your duty and your good name for a brother's sake
to buy him wicked pleasures he does not deserve.
God hates violence. He has ordained that all men
fairly possess their property, not seize it. So
the rich man who is wicked must be left in peace.   905
There is the sky, which is all men's together, there
is the world to live in, fill with houses of our own
nor hold another's, nor tear it from his hands by force.
For me it was hard, and yet it was a blessed thing,
that Hermes gave me to your father to keep safe   910
for my husband, who is here and who would have me
    back.
How can he take me back when he is dead? And how
could your father duly give the living to the dead?
Consider now your father's case, the case of God.
Would the divine power, and would the dead man, wish
    to see   915
what belongs to another given back, or would they not?
I think they would. You must not give a greater weight
to a wild brother than to an honorable father.
If you, who are a prophetess and lead men through
the ways of God, spoil the just actions of your father   920
and uphold the right of an unrighteous brother, then
knowing the ways of God is a disgraceful thing.
Shame to know past and future, not know right and
    wrong!
Save me from my misfortunes, from hardships where I
submit. It is an accidental gift of grace.   925
There is no man living but Helen is his hate,
notorious through all Hellas as having betrayed
my husband, to live in the golden houses of the East.
But if I go to Greece and reach Sparta again
and they hear, and see, how it was by the arts of gods   930
that they were ruined, that I never betrayed my loves,
they will restore me to my reputation once
again. My daughter—nobody will take her now—

44

shall be given by me. I shall escape the shabby life
I lead here, and live on my own money in my own house.   935
If Menelaus lay dead and murdered on the pyre,
I should have loved him from my distance, with my
    tears.
But he is here, alive. Must he be taken from me?

No maiden, no. I kneel here as your suppliant.
Give me your grace in this, and let your ways be like   940
your upright father's ways, for it is the brightest fame
of children, when they have a father who was good,
if they can match the character that gave them birth.

Chorus

The words you have spoken since we spoke are pitiful
and you have pathos too. Yet still, I long to hear   945
what Menelaus has to argue for his life.

Menelaus

I cannot bring myself to fall before your feet
nor to make my eyes wet with tears. Such abjectness
would be the greatest shame upon the tale of Troy.
Yet I have heard, or read, how even stately men   950
have found it in them to let tears burst from their eyes.
I waive this privilege of honor—if privilege
of honor it is. Courage is better.
                              Rather, thus:
if you think best to save a man, an outlander,
who asks with right to have his wife given back to him,   955
give her, and save me too. If you do not think it best,
it does not mean new misery for me but the old
continued; and it means you are an evil woman.
But what I think is worthy and right for me to say,
and what will take your heart beyond all else, I shall   960
say here before your father's monument, in grief.

Aged sir, here indwelling in the stony tomb,
give her back to me. What I ask is my own wife

45

whom Zeus had brought here, so you could keep her safe
    for me.
I understand now you will never give her back   965
since you are dead. But she must not deign that the
    invoked
and so much honored father underground shall hear
despiteful speech against him. All is in her hands.

Hades of the downworld, I invoke your aid as well.
You have taken many dead men, fallen before my sword,   970
because of this woman. You are paid your price in full.
Now bring these bodies to life again and yield them back,
or force this maiden to outpass her father's fame
for right dealing, and give me back the bride of my love.
If you Egyptians take my wife away from me,   975
I will tell you what will happen then, as she did not.
For your attention, maiden: we are bound by oath.
First I shall find your brother and we two shall fight.
He will be killed, or I. There is no more to say.
But if he lacks the courage to stand up to me,   980
and tries to starve and snare two suppliants at the tomb,
I have decided to kill her, then thrust the blade
of this two-edged sword into my own heart, upon
the back of this grave mound before us, where the blood
will splash and drip upon the grave. There we shall lie   985
two corpses, side by side, upon the marble tomb,
to shame your father, to hurt you, forevermore.
Your brother will not marry her. Nobody else
will marry her. I shall take her away with me,
away to the dead, if I am not to bring her home.   990

Why do I say this? Turning to woman and to tears
I should be pitied, but I should get nothing done.
Kill me, if you think best. You will not kill your shame.
But better, be persuaded by my arguments;
for so you would be just, and I should have my wife.   995

Chorus
    It is yours to pass judgment on their arguments,

maiden. Judge then, and judge so all will be well
    pleased.

Theonoë
My nature is to deal fairly; so is my wish.
I have myself to think of, and my father's name
is not to be defiled. I must not give my brother   1000
such pleasures as will leave me with my honor gone.
The sanctity of justice is a powerful thing
in my own nature. This is Nereus' heritage.
I have it, Menelaus; I will try to keep
it always. And, since Hera wishes to help you,   1005
my vote shall be as Hera votes. And as for Love
(may Love not be offended!) that means nothing here.
My aim is to remain a maiden all my life.
As for reproaches on my father and this tomb,
the same tale must apply to me. I should do wrong   1010
not to restore her. For my father, had he lived,
would have given her back to you, and you to her.

    For all men, in the world below and in the world
above must pay for acts committed here. The mind
of those who have died, blown into the immortal air,   1015
immortally has knowledge, though all life is gone.
I must not strain this matter to great length. I shall
be quiet about your supplication, and shall not
let my good counsels help my brother toward his lust.
Really, I serve him so, though I seem not to do,   1020
if I can make him good, not dissolute any more.
Now it will rest upon yourselves to find a way.
I shall have nothing to do with it, but shall withdraw
and be silent. Begin by praying to the gods, and ask
the Lady of Cyprus to let Helen now come home,   1025
and ask Hera to hold steadfastly that good will
toward you, and toward your husband, which shall save
    you both.

My father, you are dead, but while I have the strength
your name of goodness shall not change to a vile name.

(Exit, attended.)

Chorus

The unrighteous are never really fortunate.   1030
Our hopes for safety depend upon our doing right.

Helen

We are safe, Menelaus, as far as the maiden is con-
    cerned.
Now it is yours to propose measures, so that we
can make a plan between us to escape from here.

Menelaus

Listen then: you have lived some time in this house   1035
and have been familiar with the attendants of the king.

Helen

Yes, but why did you mention it? Does it mean you
    hope
to accomplish something that will help the two of us?

Menelaus

Would you be able to persuade those who have charge
of the chariots? Would they perhaps give us one?   1040

Helen

I could persuade them. But what course? How shall we
    run
the plains of this strange land where we do not know
    our way?

Menelaus

Hopeless, as you say. . . . Come, then, hide me in
    the house
and I kill the king with my own blade. Shall we do
    this?

Helen

No. His sister could no longer keep the secret   1045
of your presence here, if it were to mean her brother's
    death.

48

Menelaus
But we have no ship in which to make a safe escape.
The ship we had is at the bottom of the sea.

Helen
I know! Even a woman might have one clever thought.
Are you willing, though not dead, to be reported dead? 1050

Menelaus
Unlucky omen. But if it does us any good
I consent. You may say that I am dead, though I am
    not.

Helen
Then we shall use the pitiful customs of women,
the dirges and cutting of hair to the unhallowed god.

Menelaus
Where is there any help toward our escape in this? 1055
I think there is some trick lurking behind your words.

Helen
Yes. I will say that you have died at sea, and ask
the king to let me bury you in effigy.

Menelaus
Suppose he grants it? Even so, without a ship,
how shall we save our bodies by this funeral? 1060

Helen
I shall ask him for conveyance, so your burial
fineries may be submerged and gathered in the sea's
    arms.

Menelaus
Well spoken, except for one thing. He will merely say
you must bury him on land. Where, then, is your
    excuse?

49

Helen

But I shall tell him that in Greece it is not allowed   1065
to bury ashore those who have met their death at sea.

Menelaus

Right again; so you correct it. Then I too shall sail
in the same boat, and with you let the offerings down.

Helen

By all means, yes, you are to be there. Bring with you
those mariners of yours who escaped from the shipwreck.   1070

Menelaus

Thus once I get possession of the anchored ship
there will be fighting, man to man, sword against
sword.

Helen

You shall be in charge of all thenceforward. Only let
the wind blow fair in our sail. Let the ship run!

Menelaus

It shall. The gods will end my troubles now at last.   1075
Who will you say has told you the story of my death?

Helen

You. And you tell him you sailed with Atreus' son, and
that
you were the sole survivor, and you saw him die.

Menelaus

This fishing-net of rags I wear upon myself
will be most authentic evidence of my spindrift state.   1080

Helen

It is timely now, though your ship was untimely lost.
The misery of time since might turn now to good.

Menelaus
　　Should I then go inside the house with you, or sit
　　here and wait quietly for you beside the tomb?

Helen
　　Stay here. So, if he uses violence on you   1085
　　this tomb, and then your own sword, will be your
　　　　defense.
　　I shall go in the house and cut my curls and change
　　the white clothing that I wear for black, and drag
　　my nails across my cheek leaving a red furrow there.
　　I must. Great hazard. I see two ways the scales can tip. 1090
　　I may be caught in treachery, then I must die.
　　Or I shall save your life, and we shall both go home.
　　O queen and goddess, given to the arms of Zeus,
　　Hera. We are two pitiful people. Grant us wind
　　from work. We ask, and lift our arms straight toward
　　　　that sky   1095
　　where your home is, among the splendors of the stars.
　　And you, whose beauty's cost was my brute marriage,
　　　　you
　　Dione's daughter, Cyprian, oh destroy me not.
　　It is enough, that filth you rolled me in before
　　when you gave barbarians not my body but my name. 1100
　　But if you wish to kill me, let me only die
　　in my own country. Why this thirst for evil things?
　　Why do you work in passions, lies, devices full
　　of treachery, love-magics, murder in the home?
　　Were you only temperate, in all else you are found
　　　　sweet   1105
　　to us beyond all other gods. This I confess.

　　　　　　　　　　　　　　　　(*Exit into the house.*)
Chorus
　　To you, who deep forested, choired in the growth
　　of singing wood hide nested,
　　to you I utter my outcry,
　　to you, beyond all other birds sweet in your singing,

O nightingale of the sorrows   1110
come, with brown beak shaken,
to the beat of your melody, come
with song to my sad singing
as I mourn for the hard sorrows
of Helen, for all the suffering,
all the tears of the daughters of Troy   1115
from spears held by Achaeans,
all from the time when with outland oar he swept over
the water-flats, came, came, and his coming was sorrow
in marriage for Priam's people, moving
from Lacedaemon, from you, Helen: Paris, dark lover   1120
brought there by Aphrodite.

And there were many Achaeans who by the spear
and by the stone's smash have died
and are given, in vain, to Hades.
For these, unhappy wives have cut their long hair.
The chambers of their love are left forsaken.   1125
Many Achaeans besides
the man of the single oar drowned
off waterswept Euboea
when he lit his wreck fires, blazed
the false flares, and crashed them to death
on Aegean rocks at Caphereus.   1130
And the harborless mountains of Malea in the storm
          wind
were death, when he fled from our land, with the prize
          of his outland
glory; prize, no prize, but war,
the Greek cloud shape his ship carried off,   1135
the divine image of Hera.

What is god, what is not god, what is between man
and god, who shall say? Say he has found
the remote way to the absolute,
that he has seen god, and come   1140
back to us, and returned there, and come

back again, reason's feet leaping
the void? Who can hope for such fortune?
Yourself were born, Helen, daughter to Zeus.
Winged in the curves of Leda there   1145
as bird he childed you.
Yet even you were hallooed through Greece
as traitress, faithless, rightless, godless. No man's
thought I can speak of is ever clear.
The word of god only I found unbroken.   1150

> (*Helen returns and joins Menelaus.*)

Mindless, all of you, who in the strength of spears
and the tearing edge win your valors
by war, thus stupidly trying
to halt the grief of the world.
For if bloody debate shall settle   1155
the issue, never again
shall hate be gone out of the cities of men.
By hate they won the chambers of Priam's city;
they could have solved by reason and words
the quarrel, Helen, for you.   1160
Now these are given to the Death God below.
On the walls the flame, as of Zeus, lightened and fell.
And you, Helen, on your sorrows bear
more hardships still, and more matter for grieving.

> (*Enter Theoclymenus, from the country,*
> *attended by hunters.*)

Theoclymenus
Tomb of my father, greeting! It was even for such   1165
addresses, Proteus, I caused you to be buried here
at the entrance, and in passing in and out of doors
I, Father, Theoclymenus your son, greet you.

You, my serving men, take the dogs and the hunting-
     nets
inside the king's palace, put them away.
                              Now I   1170
have found many hard things to say against myself.

Do we not chastise evildoers with death? And yet
even now they tell me there has been a Greek man
    seen
who has openly come here but has escaped the guards,
to spy on us, or watching for the chance to steal   1175
Helen away. Let him be caught, and he is dead.
Ah,
I have come too late, it seems. The whole thing has
    been done
and the daughter of Tyndareus, leaving empty her
    place
in the tomb's shelter, is carried away out of the land.
Hallo! Unbar all bolts and let the horses out   1180
from their mangers, men, and get the chariots out and
    ready.
Let it not be for lack of effort that the bride
I would win is stolen secretly from my domain.

No, wait. I see the two that I am after, here
beside the palace still, they have not yet escaped.   1185
Why have you changed from your white clothes, and
    put on black
and wear them? Why have you put the iron to your
    head
and shorn away the glory of your lovely hair?
And why are your cheeks wet with the fresh tears? For
    whom
do you weep? Is it compulsion of dreams in the night   1190
that makes you sorrow so, or have you heard from
    home
some rumor, and the grief of it has wrecked your heart?

Helen

My lord—for now at last I name you in such terms—
my life is ruined. There is nothing left for me.

Theoclymenus

What has happened? What is the disaster that has
    struck you down?   1195

Helen
My Menelaus—how shall I say it? He is dead.

Theocylmenus
I cannot take pleasure in what you tell me, though it is my fortune. How do you know? Did Theonoë tell you?

Helen
She says so. Also, one who was with him when he died.

Theoclymenus
There is someone here then, with an authentic report? 1200

Helen
Yes, here. May he go where I too desire to go.

Theoclymenus
Who is he? Where is he? Tell me, let me get this clear.

Helen
That man you see there, sitting abject under the tomb.

Theoclymenus
By Apollo! The rags of clothing he is in!

Helen
I think my husband has looked thus. I pity both. 1205

Theoclymenus
Who is this man? Where from? Where did he come ashore?

Helen
He is a Greek, an Achaean who sailed with my husband.

Theoclymenus
What manner of death does he say that Menelaus died?

Helen

The most pitiful; washed down in the running sea.

Theoclymenus

Where in our remote waters was he sailing then?   1210

Helen

He was driven against Libya's harborless cliffs.

Theoclymenus

How was this man his oarsmate, and yet did not die?

Helen

Sometimes the baser have more fortune than their
betters.

Theoclymenus

He is here, a castaway. Where did he leave his ship?

Helen

Where I wish he had perished, and Menelaus had not.   1215

Theoclymenus

But Menelaus has perished. In what boat did he come?

Helen

Sailors came on him and picked him up, or so he says.

Theoclymenus

Where is that evil that was brought to Troy instead of
you?

Helen

The cloud image? You mean that? Gone into the sky.

Theoclymenus

O Priam, O Troy, how you were brought down in vain!   1220

Helen

I too, with Priam's children, shared this luckless
chance.

Theoclymenus
    Did he leave your husband unburied? Is he beneath
        ground?

Helen
    Not buried yet. And oh, my grief!

Theoclymenus
                        Was it for this
    you cut away the long curls of your yellow hair?

Helen
    He is dear to me. Whoever is with me now is dear.   1225

Theoclymenus
    This is real. Sorrow has distracted her to tears.

Helen
    It could easily happen that your own sister might die.

Theoclymenus
    Oh, no. How?
                    Will you go on making this tomb your home?

Helen
    Why do you make fun of me? Let the dead man be.

Theoclymenus
    Yet you showed faith to him when you avoided me.   1230

Helen
    That is all past. You may make the wedding arrange-
        ments now.

Theoclymenus
    It has been long in coming, but I still am glad.

Helen
    Do you know what we should do? Let us forget the
        past.

Theoclymenus
What terms? Grace should be given in return for grace.

Helen
Let us make peace between ourselves. Forgive me all.   1235

Theoclymenus
My quarrel with you is cancelled. Let it go with the
wind.

Helen
But by your knees I ask of you, if you are my friend—

Theoclymenus
What is it that your suppliant arms would wrest
from me?

Helen
I desire your permission to bury my dead lord.

Theoclymenus
How? Are there graves for the lost? Would you bury a
shadow?   1240

Helen
There is a Greek custom for those who die at sea.

Theoclymenus
What is it? Pelops' people are knowing in such things.

Helen
To hold a burial ceremony in empty robes.

Theoclymenus
Do it, then. Raise a mound on my land, where you
wish.

Helen
It is not thus we bury our drowned mariners.   1245

Theoclymenus
How, then? I cannot keep up with Greek usages.

Helen
We take all the dead should be given out to sea.

Theoclymenus
What shall I give you for your dead, then?

Helen
                                This man knows.
I am inexperienced. All my luck was good before.

Theoclymenus
So, friend, you have brought me news that I am glad
    to hear.   1250

Menelaus
Not good hearing for me, nor for the dead.

Theoclymenus
                                Tell me,
how do you bury those who have been drowned at sea?

Menelaus
As lavishly as a man's substance lets him do.

Theoclymenus
For this woman's sake tell me without minding the
    cost.

Menelaus
First, there must be a blood-victim for the undergods.   1255

Theoclymenus
What beast? Only tell me, and I will do your will.

Menelaus
Decide yourself. Whatever you give will satisfy.

Theoclymenus
  Among us outlanders, it would be a bull or horse.

Menelaus
  Give such then, only give nothing which is malformed.

Theoclymenus
  Our herds are rich. We have no lack of good victims. 1260

Menelaus
  Coverings are given too for the body, though none is
    there.

Theoclymenus
  That will be done. Is anything else customary?

Menelaus
  Brazen armor; for Menelaus loved the spear.

Theoclymenus
  What we shall give will be worthy of Pelops' clan.

Menelaus
  We need also other fair produce of the earth. 1265

Theoclymenus
  What will you do? How will you sink all this in the
    sea?

Menelaus
  A ship must be there, also rowers to man the oars.

Theoclymenus
  How far distant is the ship to be from the land?

Menelaus
  Out where the breakers can barely be seen from ashore.

Theoclymenus
  Tell me, why does Greece keep this custom? For what
    cause? 1270

Menelaus
So the waves cannot wash pollution back ashore.

Theoclymenus
You shall have a fast-running Phoenician ship, with
oars.

Menelaus
That would be excellent. Menelaus would like it so.

Theoclymenus
Do you need her too? Can you not do it by yourself?

Menelaus
A man's mother must do this, or his wife, or children.   1275

Theoclymenus
You mean it is her duty to bury her husband?

Menelaus
It is duty's part not to rob the dead of their due.

Theoclymenus
She may go. A wife kept dutiful is to my own
advantage. Go in, and bring the funeral robes of state.
And if you act so as to please her, I shall send   1280
you from my country with no empty hands, to bear
a good report of me; you shall have clothing, not
this ragged state, and food, enough to bring you home
again; for now I see you are in hard case.

And you, my dear, do not wear yourself away in longing   1285
for the impossible. Menelaus has met his fate,
and your dead husband shall not come to life again.

Menelaus
You see your task, young woman; it is to love and serve
the husband you have, and let the other husband go.
In the circumstances, this is the best that you can do.   1290
But if I come through safe to Hellas, I shall put

61

an end to former scandals that were said of you.
Only be now the wife that you were meant to be.

Helen

It shall be so. My husband shall have no complaint
of me. You will be there, and you will know the truth.   1295
Come in the house, poor wanderer, you shall have your
    bath
and a change of clothing. Kindnesses I have for you
shall not be put off. If I give all you should have
from me, in all the better spirit you will do
the things my dearest Menelaus has deserved.   1300

        (*Exit Helen, Menelaus, and Theoclymenus*
                   inside the house.)

Chorus

Long ago, the Mountain Mother
of all the gods, on flashing feet,
ran down the wooded clefts
of the hills, crossed stream-waters in spate
and the sea's thunderous surf beat   1305
in wild desire for the lost girl
not to be named, her daughter,
and the cry of her voice keened high to break
through mutter of drums and rattles.
And as the goddess harnessed   1310
wild beasts to draw her chariot
in search of the daughter torn away
from the circling pattern of dance where she
and her maidens moved, storm-footed beside
the mother, Artemis with her bow,   1315
stark eyed, spear-handed Athene
attended. But Zeus, from his high place
in the upper sky shining ordained
a different course to follow.

For when the wandering and the swift
course of the mother was done, the far,   1320
the toilsome, the vain search

62

for her daughter's treacherous capture,
she crossed the place where the mountain nymphs
keep watch in the snows of Ida,
and there cast the blight of her grief   1325
across the stone and snow of the hill forests.
Earth, green gone from her fields, would give
food no more in the sown lands,
and generations were wasted.
For the flocks she shot out no longer   1330
tender food from the curling leaves.
The cities of men were starving,
the sacrifice to the gods was gone,
no offerings flamed on the altars. She,
turned cruel by grief for her daughter, dried   1335
the springs that gush from deep in the ground,
and there were no jets of bright water.

But now, as those festivals the gods
share with the race of men died out,
Zeus spoke, to soften the ruinous
rages of the Great Mother: 1340
"Go, stately Graces, and go
Muses, to Deio angered
thus for the sake of the maiden.
Change with wild singing the strain of grief
in her, and with choral and dancing."   1345
It was then that the loveliest
of the immortals took the death-
voice of bronze and the skin-strung drums:
Aphrodite. The goddess smiled
and drew into her hands   1350
the deep sounding flute
in delight with its music.

You had no right in this. The flames you lit
in your chambers were without sanction.
You showed, child, no due reverence   1355
for this goddess' sacrifice.

63

You won the great mother's anger.
The dappled dress in the deer skin
is a great matter, and the ivy wound
green on the sacred hollow reed   1360
has power; so also the shaken,
the high, the whirled course of the wheel
in the air; so also the dances,
the wild hair shaken for Bromius,
the goddess' nightlong vigils.   1365
It is well that by daylight
the moon obscures her.
All your claim was your beauty.

                              (*Enter Helen from the house.*)

Helen

Friends, all that happened in the house was favorable.
The daughter of Proteus keeps our secret. Though she
    knows   1370
my husband is here, and though her brother questioned
    her,
she told him nothing, rather she told him he was dead
and buried, out of the sunlight. She did this for me.
My lord has gained a capture, fair and fortunate.
He took the armor that is to be sunken in the sea   1375
and fitted the shield-handle upon his powerful arm
and wears it so, with the spear held in his right hand,
as if working to help grace the dead man. Yet still
first he practiced, with the armor on him, for a fight
as one who would raise a monument on a whole world   1380
of outlanders once we embark in the oared boat;
then I took off the wreck-stained clothes he wore, and
    gave
him new, and made him fine again, and bathed his
    body
at last in fresh water drawn from the stream.
                              But see,   1385
this prince, who now thinks that he has a marriage
    with me

64

in his hands' reach, is coming from the house. Do me
the favor of silence. We want you on our side. Control
your lips, be kind, and some day, if we ever save
ourselves from here, we shall attempt to save you too.

(*Enter Theoclymenus, followed by Menelaus,
and leading a group of serving men who
carry the funeral properties.*)

Theoclymenus

Men, go on to your work as the stranger told you to   1390
and take with you the funeral offerings to the sea.
Helen, if what I say to you does not seem wrong,
stay here, as I ask you. Your duty to your husband,
     whether
you go, or stay, will have been done in any case.
I am afraid longing for him will seize you, make   1395
you fling your body down into the tossing sea
stunned with delights remembered from him before. I
     know
how much, too much, you mourned for him when he
     was not here.

Helen

O my new husband, how can I help holding dear
the memory of my first marriage, all the love   1400
and closeness of it? I have loved him well enough
to die when he died. But what grace would he have
     known
in death from my death? Only let me go, myself
in person, and give his dead body what it deserves.
So may the gods grant you what I would wish to have   1405
them grant you, and this stranger, who is helping here.
For your kindness now to Menelaus and to me
you shall have me in your house, as wife, to the degree
that you deserve, since all this is in fortune's gift.
Now give your orders to the man who will provide   1410
the ship for your conveyance. For my sake do this.

65

Theoclymenus
> Go then, get ready a Sidonian fifty-oar
> galley, have master-rowers aboard, give it to her.

Helen
> Is not this man to be in charge of the funeral ship?

Theoclymenus
> Certainly. My sailors are hereby ordered to obey him.   1415

Helen
> Give the order again so they will be quite clear.

Theoclymenus
> Again, and still a third time, if you wish me to.

Helen
> For your good, and for my good in the things I plan.

Theoclymenus
> Now, do not waste yourself with too much weeping.

Helen
>   No.
> Today will show the quality of my love for you.   1420

Theoclymenus
> Remember, the dead are nothing. This is wasted work.

Helen
> It is matters there of which I speak; and matters here.

Theoclymenus
> You will find me as good a man as Menelaus.

Helen
> I ask no more. I need only the favoring time.

Theoclymenus
> That is in your power, as long as you are kind to me.   1425

Helen

   I shall not need teaching to love those I ought to love.

Theoclymenus

   Shall I go too and see the expedition along?

Helen

   Oh no. My lord, you must not do slave's work for your
      slaves.

Theoclymenus

   Very well. I shall pass the rituals of the Pelopidae.
   My house needs no lustration, since it was not here   1430
   that Menelaus died. Therefore, one of you go
   and tell my vassals to take the wedding images
   inside my palace. All my country must be loud
   with singing for congratulation and with strains
   of marriage for Helen and me, to bless our state.   1435
   Go now, my stranger guest, and give all this to the arms
   of the sea, in honor of him who was her husband once,
   then make haste back to my house again, and bring my
      wife,
   so that you may be my guest at our wedding feast,
   and then go home—or stay and prosper here with me.   1440

                         (*Exit into the house.*)

Menelaus

   O Zeus, renowned as father and wise among the gods,
   look down upon us. Grant us surcease from our pain,
   and as we grate the shoal-rocks of catastrophe
   reach us your hand, touch only with your fingertips
   and we are there, triumphant, where we wish to be.   1445
   Our past has been our share of troubles, all our share.
   I have heard, O gods, much said of you. I have heard
      good,
   and hard things also. I do not deserve bad luck
   forever, but to walk with upright stride. Grant me
   this one grace. It will make me happy all my life.   1450

         (*Helen and Menelaus go out at the side.*)
                         67

Chorus

 Phoenician queen out of Sidon, O
 lady of oars swift in the splashing water,
 dear mother of oared ships
 after whose lead in the dance move
 the dolphins, when the open sea   1455
 sleeps in stopped winds: may she,
 Galaneia, who is called lady of calms,
 and the Great Sea's green daughter
 so speak: "Set wide the sails on the masts,
 leave them free to the salt airs,   1460
 but take in your hands the pinewood oars,
 mariners, oh mariners,
 as you convey Helen home
 to kind haven upon the shores of Perseus."
 So, Helen, might you find again   1465
 the Daughters of the White Horses there by the river,
 or before the temple of Pallas
 come back at last to the dances
 or the revels for Hyacinthus
 and the night-long festival   1470
 established by Phoebus after
 his whirled throw of the discus
 in games: for the Laconian land
 a day of sacrifices
 by ordinance of him, son of Zeus;   1475
 come back to the girl you left
 in your house, Hermione,
 for whose marriage the pine-flares have not shone yet.

 Oh, that we might fly in the air
 winged high over Libya
 where the lines of the migrant   1480
 birds, escaping the winter rain,
 take their way, following
 the authority of their leader's
 whistle. And he flying into the rainless, the wheat-
   burdened flat   1485

places, screams his clear call.
O flying birds with the long throats, who
share the course of the racing clouds,
go to the midmost Pleiades.
Go to Orion of the night,   1490
cry like heralds your message
as you light down on Eurotas,
that Menelaus has taken the town
of Dardanus and will come home.

May you riding down through the bright   1495
air, swift on your horses,
sons of Tyndareus, come
down the stormy courses of your stars' flaring,
oh, dwellers in the sky,
saviors of Helen, come   1500
cross close on the green swell and the dark-skinned back
     of the rollers
and the gray splash of the breaking sea,
bringing from Zeus those winds that blow
sweet airs for the mariners: 1505
and cast away from your sister the shame
spoken, of her barbarian loves,
shame that was hers for punishment
out of the quarrel on Ida, though
she never went to the land of Troy,   1510
not to the towers of Phoebus.

(Enter a servant of Theoclymenus, from the sea.)
Servant *(shouting)*
    My lord, the worst of news from our house. We have
      just learned.

(Enter Theoclymenus from the house.)

    Fresh news, strange news and bad. Hear it from me at
      once.

Theoclymenus
    What is it?

Servant

Your work is wasted for a wife who is not
yours. Helen is gone away, out of our land.   1515

Theoclymenus

How gone? On wings, or do her feet still tread the
    earth?

Servant

Menelaus carried her away. For that was he.
He came himself, and brought the news of his own
    death.

Theoclymenus

This is disgraceful. But still I cannot quite believe.
What sort of transport carried him away from here?   1520

Servant

Precisely what you gave your guest. He took your men
and left you. There you have it in a single word.

Theoclymenus

How? I must understand this, and I cannot yet
credit it that a single arm could overpower
so many sailors, all those who were sent with you.   1525

Servant

After Zeus' daughter left the palace here, and you,
and was escorted to the sea, there as she placed
her tiny feet, she mourned aloud, most cleverly,
for that husband who was by her side, by no means
    dead.
Now as we came to your shipyards and your arsenal
we hauled down a Sidonian ship of the first class   1530
with fifty rowing benches to accommodate
the oars. And now our various duties were assigned.
One took his place at the mast, another at the bench,
hands on his oar, another had charge of the white sails, 1535
the steersman sat to the tiller and the steering gear.

Now as we were hard at it, there came down to the
    shore
certain Greek men who had sailed with Menelaus once
and who had been watching for just this. They wore
    the rags
of shipwreck. Fine-looking men, but in a filthy state.   1540
The son of Atreus saw them as they came, and made
a false pretense of pity for our benefit,
with: "Poor castaways, what ship? It must once have
    been
Achaean, cracked up now, and so we see you here.
Will you help bury Atreus' fallen son? His wife,   1545
Tyndareus' daughter, buries him in effigy.
This is she." They then let fall some fictitious tears
and took aboard what was to be sunk in the depths
for Menelaus. We had our suspicions here,
and there were words among us, how these newcomers   1550
were very numerous. Nevertheless we held our peace.
We had orders from you and kept them. You had said
your guest was to have full command. That ruined all.
Now all the cargo was light and easily picked up
and stowed inside the ship, except the bull, who stood   1555
and baulked at going up on the steep slanted plank,
but bellowed aloud, and with arched back and head
    low down
rolled his eyes round the circle past his lowered horns
forbidding all to touch him. Helen's husband raised
his voice, and cried: "Oh, you who captured Ilium,   1560
come, do it the Greek way, can you not? Hoist the
    bull's
weight on the strength of your young shoulders, heave
    him in
over the prow. You, draw your sword and prod him on.
For he shall be our sacrifice to the dead man."
They at his order went and laid hands on the bull   1565
and heaved him up and forced him on the rowing deck,
and Menelaus, rubbing its forehead and its skin,
persuaded him, without harness, to go inside the ship.

At last, when all was got aboard and stowed away,
Helen, with dainty steps, put her feet through the rungs   1570
of the ladder, and took possession of the central bench,
with Menelaus, the supposed dead man, by her side,
and left and right along the bulkheads all took place,
man ranked on man in order (but the Greeks had
    swords
hidden away beneath their garments).

                     Then we all   1575
whitened the water at the bosun's shout of "Row!"
Now when we had reached a point where we were not
    remote
from the land, nor near it either, then our steersman
    asked:
"Shall we make further out, my friend, or is this far
enough to suit you? What we do is yours to say."   1580
He said: "This will do." Then, with a sword in his
    right hand,
crept to the prow, and braced himself to strike the bull,
and where he stood, there were no dead men in his
    mind,
but as he cut the throat he prayed: "Lord of the sea,
Poseidon in the depth, and you, chaste Nereids,   1585
convey me safe to Nauplia's strand, convey my wife
who left it, but was chaste." And as he spoke, the blood
rained on the water, favoring the stranger's prayer.
One of us said then: "There is treacherous sailing here.
We must make back. You, give the order for right oar,   1590
and you, reverse the rudder." But now Atreus' son
stood from the slaughtered ox and hailed his company:
"Oh, flower of all the land of Greece, why longer wait
to smash these savages, cut them down and throw them
    off
the ship into the water." Then your bosun called   1595
aloud upon your seamen to resist: "Come on!
Get anything to fight with. Take the end of a spar;
break up a bench and use it, or an unshipped oar,

and smash the heads of these foreigners, who turned
    on us."
Both sides sprang to their feet then. We laid hands
    upon   1600
whatever ship's lumber we could find. But they had
    swords.
The ship ran blood; but there was Helen cheering them
on from the stern: "Where is the glory of Troy? Come
    on,
show it on these barbarians." Then all fought hard,
and some went down, some kept their feet, but a man
    down   1605
was a man dead. Menelaus had his armor on
and watched where his companions had the worst of it
and there rallied them, with his sword in his right hand,
so that men, to escape, dived overboard. He swept
the rowing benches clean of your mariners, then went   1610
to the rudder and made the helmsman steer the ship
    for Greece,
and they got the mast up, and a wind came, favoring
    him.

They are gone from your country. I myself, escaping
    death,
let myself into the water where the anchor hung,
and as I was failing, one of the fishermen at his lines   1615
pulled me out and set me ashore so I could bring
this message to you. Man's most valuable trait
is a judicious sense of what not to believe.

                             (*Exit.*)

Chorus
I never would have thought Menelaus could be here
unknown, my lord, to you and us. Yet so it was.   1620

    (*As Theoclymenus speaks the next lines, he starts to
        rush into the house but is met at the door by an-
        other servant, an attendant of Theonoë, who
        struggles to keep him from going in.*)

Theoclymenus

Oh, I have been duped and tricked with women's artful
treacheries.

Now my bride has escaped away, and if they could be
overhauled

I would make all haste to catch the ship that carries
those foreigners.

But at least I can take vengeance on the sister who
betrayed

me, who saw Menelaus in my house and did not tell me
so.   1625

She shall never again deceive another with her
prophecies.

Servant

Hallo, you there, master, where are you going? Is it
death you mean?

Theoclymenus

I am going where justice takes me. Out of my way and
stand aside.

Servant

It is a monstrous thing to rush to. I will not let go my
hold.

Theoclymenus

You, a slave, will overpower your master?

Servant

                                        Yes. I mean
you well.   1630

Theoclymenus

No good to me, unless you let me go.

Servant

                                    But that I will not
do.

74

Theoclymenus
Let me kill my hateful sister.

Servant

No, not hateful. Dutiful.

Theoclymenus
She betrayed me.

Servant

It was just betrayal. What she did **was**
right.

Theoclymenus
Giving my bride away to others.

Servant

Others had more right
than you.

Theoclymenus
Who has right over what is mine?

Servant

The man her father
gave her to.   1635

Theoclymenus
Fortune gave her then to me.

Servant

And fate took her away
again.

Theoclymenus
You are not to judge what I do.

Servant

If I am in the right, I
must.

75

Theoclymenus
Then I am no longer ruler, but am ruled.

Servant
For right, not wrong.

Theoclymenus
You desire to die, I think.

Servant
Then kill me, but you shall not kill
your sister while I have the power to stop you. Slaves,
if they are true,   1640
find no glory greater than to perish for their masters'
sake.

> (*As Theoclymenus is about to overpower and stab
> the servant, the Dioscuri, Castor and Polydeuces,
> appear above the palace.*)

Castor
Lord of this land, Theoclymenus, hold hard the rage
that carries you off your true course. We are the twins
called Dioscuri, sons of Zeus, whom Leda once
gave birth to, with that Helen who has fled your house. 1645
That marriage over which you rage was not to be,
nor has the daughter of the divine Nereid done
you wrong, Theonoë your sister, but she kept
the righteous orders of my father and the gods.
It had always been ordained that for the present time   1650
she was to be a dweller in your house. But when
Troy was uptorn from its foundations, and she lent
the gods her name for it, this was no more to be,
for now she must be once more married with her own,
and go home, and live with her husband. Therefore,
hold   1655
your hand, nor darken your sword with a sister's blood.
Believe it was in thoughtful care that she did this.
We would have saved our sister long ago, since Zeus
had made us into gods and we had power, except

that we were weaker still than destiny, and less   1660
than all the gods, whose will was that these things
    should be.

This is for you. Henceforward, let my sister hear.
Sail with your husband, sail on. You shall have fair
    wind.
We, your twin brothers, guardian divinities,
shall ride the open water and bring you safely home.   1665
And when your life turns its last course and makes an
    end,
you shall be called, with the two sons of Zeus, divine,
have your libations, and with us be entertained
as honored guests by mortals. Zeus has willed it so.
And where the son of Maia first defined your place   1670
when he caught you up from Sparta on the skyward
    way,
stealing you, so that Paris might not have you, where
the island stretches to guard Acte, shall your name
be know as *Helen*, meaning Captive, for mankind
hereafter; because you were stolen from your house.   1675
For Menelaus, who has wandered much, the gods
have granted a home upon the island of the blest.
For Heaven never hates the noble in the end.
It is for the nameless multitude that life is hard.

(*The Dioscuri disappear.*)

Theoclymenus
   O sons of Leda and of Zeus, I will forego   1680
the quarrel I had with you for your sister's sake.
Nor do I wish to kill my sister now. Then let
Helen go home, if so the gods would have it. Know
that you are born of the same blood from which was
    born
the best and the most faithful sister in the world.   1685
Go then rejoicing for the great and noble heart
in her. There are not many women such as she.

(Exit. The chorus begin to go off.)

Chorus

Many are the forms of what is unknown.
Much that the gods achieve is surprise.
What we look for does not come to pass;　　　　　1690
God finds a way for what none foresaw.
Such was the end of this story.

INTRODUCTION TO *HELEN*

The Legend

The variant, according to which Helen never went to Troy, is not found here for the first time. Hesiod, in his lost works, apparently told the story of how it was a phantom-image, and not the Spartan queen herself, who was stolen away by Paris and recovered after a long war by Menelaus and the Achaeans. Better known in antiquity was the work of Stesichorus, the sixth-century West-Greek lyricist and successor to Hesiod. He, it seems, had said certain hard things about Helen, and as a result he lost his sight, which returned only after he had composed his Palinode, or Apology, from which we have his lines

> That story is not true.
> You never went away in the benched ships.
> You never reached the citadel of Troy.

"That story" is, of course, the standard version as told by Homer; the corrected version of Stesichorus, as we learn elsewhere, substituted the phantom for Helen herself.

We do not know where Stesichorus (and Hesiod) said that Helen did go, if not to Troy. We might gather from the lines above that she went nowhere at all. But Herodotus, whose work was published in full not much more than a decade (maybe much less) before our play, had told a different story, which he claimed to have heard from the priests of Hephaestus in Memphis, Egypt. According to these, Paris did steal Helen away, but adverse winds forced him ashore on the Egyptian coast. There Proteus, King of Egypt, was deeply shocked to hear of what was going on; he sent Paris about his business, and confiscated Helen, whom he held in safekeeping

79

until her husband should come to claim her. Meanwhile
Menelaus and Agamemnon gathered together a Greek armada,
sailed to Troy, and demanded Helen. The Trojans protested
that they did not have her, she was in Egypt. The Greeks did
not believe this. They besieged the city and finally captured it,
only to learn that the Trojans had been telling the truth all
the time. Menelaus accordingly went to Egypt, collected
Helen, and (after disgracing himself and Greece by an illicit
sacrifice involving two Egyptian boys) sailed home (Herodotus 2. 112-20).

Euripides, plainly, has combined these two versions, and
perhaps drawn on other earlier writers as well. He uses the
phantom-image, but has Helen herself supernaturally transported to Egypt. The image has its Homeric precedent in the
image Apollo made of Aeneas, for Achaeans and Trojans to
fight over, while Aeneas himself was transported away through
the air (*Iliad* 5. 443-53, and compare 21. 595-605); so also, in
the *Iliad*, Paris, Agenor, and Aeneas once again were divinely
spirited away alive, and set down elsewhere; and so, too, in another play, Euripides himself tells how Iphigenia was caught
up and transported away to the very ends of the earth, there
to live as a lonely Greek princess among barbarians awaiting
delivery by means of a long lost relative whom she herself
thought was dead.

Despite these precedents, the play which Euripides presented undoubtedly struck most of his audience with a pleas-
urable thrill of surprise. Although he used the Herodotean
variant, he contrived, through the old idol-story, to remove
that stain of dishonor which the Egyptian version had re-
attached to Helen. And he exploited fully the factor common
to both legends: the tragic futility of that utterly unnecessary
Trojan War.

Date and Occasion

Helen was produced in 412 B.C., written therefore during
the winter which immediately followed the tragic end (tragic
for Athens at least) of the great Sicilian expedition. With

that defeat there disappeared, once for all, the strange Athenian dream of conquering the entire west. There remained the war at home, where Sparta now held a strong position. But Sparta had seldom, perhaps never, for all these years been pushing the war against Athens with complete conviction; and perfectly patriotic citizens might well hope, and urge, that the fratricidal war be ended, that Athens should save as much out of the wreck as possible, before things got even worse. It was a year later that Aristophanes, in his greatest and funniest peace-play, made a strapping and genial Spartan wench ably second Athenian Lysistrata in her program to save the Greek world, and *Lysistrata* ends with a lyric in Laconian dialect honoring Helen of Sparta. In his play, Euripides too is conciliatory toward Sparta, not only in his kindly treatment of the Spartan hero and heroine, elsewhere maligned (*Andromache, Trojan Women, Orestes*), and his flattering terms in allusion to Sparta, but also in his sweeping condemnation of war, *all* war, under which the war in hand is necessarily subsumed (ll. 1151-57).

Such may be a part of the political motivation, but the times seem to have generated personal and artistic motives as well. The sordid state of the world between 431 and 403 B.C., which has its effect in tragedies like *Hecuba* and *The Trojan Women*, also drove Euripides to escape from his own conscience with a new type of play, which may best be described as romantic comedy. Using the theme of the lost one found, a variation of the foundling story (employed also in such bitter comedies as *Alcestis* and *Ion*) he indulges himself in an illusion of optimism in *Iphigenia in Tauris* and *Helen*.

The Play

What we have, therefore, is a light, elegant romance written not only deftly but with wit. The dominant theme is paradox, illusion, surprise, all to be summed up in the relation of Helen to that other self, the idol who is not, but in some way is, Helen herself. Triumphantly, the heroine emerges with all the attributes Homer gave her—the charm, the wit, the self-importance and self-pity—above all, the inescapable loveliness (featuring, we guess, a most accomplished actor in a ravishing mask and with a voice that fairly demanded an extra allowance of solo lyrics); but adding to all these, in perfect harmony, the virtues of Penelope. To her, enters her minor Odysseus, Menelaus. The plot saves him from the low character he wore in *Andromache* and is to wear again in *Orestes* and *Iphigenia in Aulis*. No doubt his heroic leg may be pulled a little in the scene where the Portress (a manly woman, typical of Egypt, straight out of Herodotus) faces him down; but Euripides saw the pathos in situations where a great man's strength is worn away by circumstance, in this case sheer fatigue and starvation, and the hero in rags and tatters is so standard a Euripidean figure that we should not suspect farce. Better to take this play neither too seriously nor too lightly. It is romance, but not without recognition of realities, even realities new to tragedy. In *Andromeda*, a part of the same set of plays, Euripides dealt with young love, rarely considered worth bothering about in early Greek literature; in *Helen*, he realizes that there can be real, exciting love between two middle-aged people who are married to each other. Doubtless, all these elements are there in the *Odyssey*; nevertheless, what Euripides gives us here is his own, as he saw and experienced it, in the form of one of his most compact and elegant dramas.

HECUBA

Translated and with an Introduction by

WILLIAM ARROWSMITH

INTRODUCTION TO *HECUBA*

Along with Croesus, Oedipus, and Priam, the figure of Hecuba, the *mater dolorosa* of Troy transformed by suffering into
the "bitch of Cynossema," survives in classical imagination as
a supreme example of the severest degradation the reversal of
human fortune can inflict. From Euripides on, through Ovid,
medieval literature, and Dante to the "mobled queen" of
Hamlet's players, the image persists with extraordinary purity,
untampered with, almost unchanged. What Euripides may
have taken from his own presumptive source, the lost epic on
the sack of Troy by the eighth-century Arctinus of Miletus,
we have no way of knowing; but between Euripides and
Ovid,[1] very little has been lost, and between Euripides and
Dante so little has been lost that the essential experience of
the Greek *Hecuba* is still vivid in two compressed tercets of
the *Inferno:* [2]

1. *Metamorphoses* xiii. 407 ff.
2. Canto xxx, ll. 16-21: "Hecuba, sad, miserable and captive, after
she had seen Polyxena slain, and, forlorn, discerned her Polydorus on
the shore of the sea, barked like a dog, out of her senses: to such a
degree had the sorrow wrung her soul."

> Ecuba, trista, misera e cattiva,
>   poscia che vide Polïssena morta,
>   e del suo Polidoro in su la riva
>
> del mar si fu la dolorosa accorta,
>   forsennata latrò sì come cane:
>   tanto il dolor le fe' la mente torta.

Whether this persistence of the image derives from the myth or the play hardly matters; but the purity with which it persists argues, I suppose, as much the power of the original play as the authority of Ovid who transcribed it for later literature. Ovid is normally nothing if not fickle with his sources, but in this case he was working with a celebrated play and a myth so standardized in its Euripidean version as to prove intractable. But either through Greek or, via Ovid, through Latin, the Euripidean Hecuba has left to subsequent literatures an authoritative and compelling image of human suffering under the reversal of fortune.

To a large degree this authority was quickened by the high esteem and even popularity which the *Hecuba* enjoyed for more than two thousand years. Admired, much quoted and echoed in antiquity, it became one of the favorite plays of the Byzantine schoolbooks, was translated by Erasmus into Latin, and was finally almost canonized as a model of tragedy by the French classical dramatists. But in the nineteenth century the *Hecuba*, in a peripety as sudden and undeserved as that of its protagonist, fell into a profound disfavor, which has never been withdrawn; indeed, it is still commonly cited by handbooks, those tidy morgues of leached opinion, as one of the feeblest, if not the feeblest, of surviving Greek plays. The cause of this demotion—one which overtook the bulk of Euripides' plays as well—was twofold: first, the persistent misconception, based on too humble or too literal a reading of Aristotle, that Sophoclean structure provides the ideal norm of Greek tragic structure; second, a killing misunderstanding of the political experience of the play and what the logic of political necessity does to the characters. The consequence of the first has been to snarl Euripides' meaning by hopelessly disfiguring his form, while the second has operated to cut off our access to a range and power of experience which Euripides, alone of the Greek tragedians, shares with the twentieth century.

But the *Hecuba*, if it is not a great play, is at least a moving and a powerful one, a taut, bitter little tragedy of the interrelationships between those who hold power and those who

suffer it. And, far from lacking unity or formal coherence—
though its unity is anything but Aristotelian—it is in fact a
tightly constructed tragedy, driving home with great economy and control its central tragic idea. Superficially, the action is episodic; like the *Heracles*, it consists of two separate
actions joined together without causal connection. Over both
actions—the slaughter of Polyxena by the Greeks and the discovery of the body of Polydorus which leads to Hecuba's
atrocious revenge on Polymestor—the figure of the suffering
Hecuba loosely presides, giving at least the feel of unity to the
various episodes as they occur. Carefully, if not elaborately,
her progress, from grief to despair, toward the final atrocity is
traced under the rhythm of the descending blows, each one
heavier than the last; but the emphasis is not so much on the
psychology of the change within Hecuba as the way in which,
confronted by her tormentors, she is forced to yield, one by
one, her values, her self-respect, and the faith which makes
her human. If what she suffers dehumanizes her, Euripides'
emphasis is centered at least as much on *what* she suffers, its
rationale, its cost, its significance, as on the anguish of the suffering itself. And, for this reason, though Hecuba provides a
convenient focus for the play, whose episodes and values con-
verge around her, her figure does not suffice to give the play
unity or to make of it a tragedy of character.

Like so many Euripidean plays, the *Hecuba* is not the
tragedy of an individual but a group tragedy, its apparently
random and disconnected episodes bound together by a single
overriding idea, forced up in ever more inclusive complexity
by the development of the action. Uniting the *Hecuba*, under-
lying Hecuba's transformation, and joining persecutors and
persecuted alike in a common tragedy is a bleak logic of political necessity, a concern that brings the *Hecuba* close to the
Trojan Women and Thucydides' Melian Dialogue. Those
characters who urge that necessity leaves them no choice are
as corrupted by their own logic as those who, like Hecuba and
the Chorus, suffer it. Confronted by the fact of power which
makes her helpless, Hecuba, like the Melians, can only plead
honor, decency, the gods, the moral law (*nomos*); when these

appeals fail, what is civilized in her fails with them, and she takes a revenge so hideously brutal that we know, even before Polymestor, himself brutalized by suffering, predicts her transformation into the "bitch of Cynossema," that her humanity has been destroyed. Blow by blow, her hold on her humanity weakens: it is this loss of purchase that explains her sophistic approval of pure persuasion and her appeal to Agamemnon to repay his nights with Cassandra. In the end, she passes beyond the reach of judgment, for no moral judgment is pertinent when the denial of justice has destroyed her human and moral skills alike. At the same time, Hecuba's tormentors are corrupted by their commitment to their own logic: Odysseus involved in private dishonor for public reasons; Agamemnon emptying the meaning of human justice by enforcing justice only when his reputation is threatened.

But there is more to it than that. Necessity—what it is, when it arises, what it entails in action—is not easy to know, especially from the point of view of those who hold power. But just because necessity is hard and because the justification it gives—in politics, in love, in war—is unanswerable, it is the justification most frequently debased. And in the *Hecuba*, which is a tragedy and not a melodrama, it is this difficult and tragic aspect of necessity which interests Euripides. Hecuba is not tormented by the calculating cruelty of two vicious politicians but is a victim of men in the process of corruption by a power whose real necessities they understand no better than their own real motives. For what they do they claim the justification that they cannot act otherwise. In actuality, they do not act from necessity, but the excuse of necessity cloaks their fear. And just as Thucydides, by setting his Melian Dialogue on the strategically unimportant island of Melos, undercuts the Athenian generals' justification of necessity, so Euripides, by introducing Talthybius to pity Hecuba and to describe the soldiers' admiration for Polyxena's courage, undercuts the whole force of Odysseus' and Agamemnon's arguments, all based on the mistaken premise of the insensitivity of the mass to moral considerations. In the disparity between the facts and their arguments justice withers, while the callous shifting of responsibility from those in power to the mass dooms political life by depriving it of either trust or the illusion of moral action.

Within this binding framework of necessity, the characters are presented with severe economy. Hecuba herself is not so much character as an image of character in the process of annihilation. Odysseus is a demagogue by conviction (and hence all the more dangerous), decisive in action, alive to compassion but not to the point of allowing it to affect considerations which, because they are political, he thinks are beyond the reach of morality. Agamemnon, less arrogant than Odysseus, is weak, vacillating for the same reason that Odysseus is decisive, and enormously sensitive to the figure he cuts. But both alike, confident in their crude estimate of their necessities and driven by the same fear, compound the tragedy, forfeiting to their own power their freedom of moral action and as enslaved by their misguided notion of their necessities as Hecuba by her real necessity. Polymestor, alone of the characters in the play, has no necessity; he acts from crude greed and is a stark picture of barbarian viciousness. Opposite him, as virtuous as he is corrupt, stands Polyxena, almost too noble to be true. But Euripides' point is surely that it is only extreme youth and extreme innocence which can afford the illusion of total commitment. Like so many of Euripides' self-sacrificing young heroes, her death, futile in itself, exposes, by the quality of its commitment, the dense ambiguity of the moral atmosphere for those who cannot die.

What, finally, of justice and the gods? To this question the *Hecuba* makes no answer; if the action proves anything, it proves precisely the impossibility of making an answer. In the collision of their powers and necessities and purposes, men and women suffer; their appeals to *nomos* and the gods may be answered or not. Thus, at the close of the play, Polymestor predicts Agamemnon's death in Argos, and so hints at justice from heaven. But it is the very lag between crime and heaven's punishment of it, the apparent carelessness of the gods in the face of human anguish, that indicts any firm answer. Stubbornly, bleakly, rightly, the play refuses to annul the honesty of its experience on behalf of the time-honored theodicy, hinting merely that if there are powers beyond man, their justice is so alien, so slow, so indifferent, as to make impossible even the hope of communication or understanding. But man continues to demand justice and an order with which he can live, and it is the nobility of this demand, maintained against the whole tenor of his experience, in the teeth of the universal indifference and the inconsistency of fortune, that in Euripides makes man tragic. His suffering is limited only by his hope; take away his hope, as Hecuba's was taken, and he forfeits his humanity, destroyed by the hideous gap between his illusion and the intolerable reality.

The Date

The date of the *Hecuba* is uncertain, but the play may be reasonably assigned to the year 425-424. At least line 173 of the play is parodied by Aristophanes in the *Clouds* (423 B.C.) and line 462 refers to the establishment of the Delian Games by the Athenians in 426. The background of the Archidamian War helps to explain the choral emphasis on the tragic waste of war, as well as the concern of the play with the logic of imperial necessity. It is my personal conviction that the *Hecuba* was one of three tragedies for which the extant *Cyclops* was performed as the satyr-play. The connections in theme, treatment, and character are extremely close, especially in the blinding of Polymestor and Polyphemus.

CHARACTERS

Ghost of Polydorus
Hecuba
Chorus of captive Trojan women
Polyxena
Odysseus
Talthybius
Maidservant of Hecuba
Agamemnon
Polymestor, king of Thracian Chersonese
Sons of Polymestor

For Marshall Van Deusen

HECUBA

SCENE: *The shore of the Thracian Chersonese. Pavilioned tents, the quarters of the Trojan women, stand in the background. The time is just before dawn. Enter above, ex machina, the ghost of Polydorus.*

Polydorus

Back from the pit of the dead, from the somber door
that opens into hell, where no god goes,
I have come,
            the ghost of Polydorus,
son and last surviving heir of Hecuba
and Priam, king of Troy.
                        My father, fearing
that Troy might fall to the assembled arms of Hellas,   5
had me conveyed in secret out of danger
sending me here to Thrace, to Polymestor,
who rules this fertile plain of Chersonese
and curbs with harsh power a nation of horsemen.
With me my father sent a sum of gold,   10
intending that, if Troy should someday fall,
his living sons might be provided for.
Being the youngest, I was chosen, still too small
and slight to carry arms or throw a spear.
But as long as Troy's great ramparts stood proud   15
and unbreached, so long as our towers held intact
and Hector, my brother, prospered in the fighting,
I flourished under the care of my father's friend,
a green shoot thriving under his watchful eye.   20
But when Troy fell and Hector died,

and picks and shovels rooted up our hearth,
and there, by the altar that Apollo's hands once built,
Priam fell, butchered by Achilles' son,
then my father's friend took off his mask,
and moved by nothing more than simple greed,   25
murdered me and threw my body to the sea.
Here, pounded by the surf, my corpse still lies,
carried up and down on the heaving swell of the sea,
unburied and unmourned.
                Disembodied now,
I hover as a wraith over my mother's head,   30
riding for three long days upon the air,
three hopeless days of suffering and fear
since she left Troy and came to Chersonese.
Here on the shore of Thrace, in sullen idleness
beside its ships, the whole Achaean army waits   35
and cannot sail. For Achilles' ghost appeared,
stalking on his tomb, wailing, and stopped the ships
as they stood out for sea on the journey home.
He demanded my sister Polyxena as prize,   40
the blood of the living to sweeten a dead man's grave.
And he shall have her, a prize of honor and a gift
bestowed upon him by his friends. On this day
destiny shall take my sister down to death.
And you, poor Mother, you must see   45
your two last children dead this day,
my sister slaughtered and my unburied body
washed up on shore at the feet of a slave.
These were the favors I asked of the gods below—
to find my mother and be buried by her hands—   50
and they have granted my request.
                Now I go,
for there below I see my mother coming,
stumbling from Agamemnon's tent, still shaken
by that dream in which she saw my ghost.

(Enter Hecuba from the tent. At the entrance she
crumbles to the ground, and stretches out her

hands to the three or four Trojan women
who stand beside her in the tent.)

—O Mother,   55
poor majesty, old fallen queen,
shorn of greatness, pride, and everything but life,
which leaves you slavery and bitterness
and lonely age.
          Some god destroys you now,
exacting in your suffering the cost
for having once been happy in this life.

Hecuba

          O helplessness of age!
          Too old, too weak, to stand—
          Help me, women of Troy.   60
          Give this slave those hands
          you offered to her once
          when she was queen of Troy.
          Prop me with your arms   65
          and help these useless
          stumbling legs to walk.

          O star of morning,
               light of Zeus
               shining in the night!
          What apparition rose,
what shape of terror stalking the darkness?   70

          O goddess Earth,
               womb of dreams
               whose dusky wings
trouble, like bats, the flickering air!

          Beat back that dream I dreamed,
that horror that rose in the night, those phantoms of
     children,
my son Polydorus in Thrace, Polyxena, my daughter!   75
          Call back that vision of horror!

93

O gods who protect this land,
preserve my son, save him,
the last surviving anchor of my house,   80
still holding in the snows of Thrace,
still warded by his father's friend!

Disaster I dreamed,
terror on terror!
Never has my heart   85
so shivered with fear!

O Helenus, I need you now,
interpreter of dreams!
Help me, Cassandra,
help me read my dreams!
I saw a little doe, a dappled doe, torn from between my
    knees,   90
cruelly ripped away, mangled by a wolf with blood-red
    nails!

And then fresh terror rose:
I saw Achilles' ghost
stalk upon his tomb, howling,
demanding a prize
from the wretched women of Troy.   95

O gods, I implore you,
beat back this dream,
preserve my children!

(*Enter chorus of captive Trojan women.*
They speak individually.)

Chorus
—We come to you in haste,
  Hecuba.
—   We left the tents . . .
—where the lost assigned us.   100
—Slaves, torn from home
  when Troy was burnt and sacked
  by the conquering Greeks!

—We bring you painful news. 105
—We cannot lighten your load.
—We bring you worse to bear.
—Just now, in full assembly,
 the Greek decree came down.

—They voted your daughter must die . . .
—to be slaughtered alive
—on the tomb of Achilles!

—The sails had been unfurled,
 and the fleet stood out to sea,
 when from his tomb Achilles rose, 110
 armor blazing, and held them back,
 crying:
 "Ho, Argives, where do you sail,
 leaving my grave unhonored?" 115
—Waves of argument broke loose,
 dividing Greek from Greek.
 If one man spoke for death,
 another spoke against it.

—On your behalf spoke Agamemnon, 120
 lover of your daughter,
 poor, mad Cassandra.

—Then the two sons of Theseus,
 twin shoots of Athens, rose and spoke,
 but both with one intent— 125
 to crown Achilles' grave
 with living blood, asking
 if Cassandra's love meant more
 than the courage of Achilles.

—And so the struggle swayed, 130
 equally poised—
—   Until *he* spoke—
 that hypocrite with honeyed tongue,
 that demagogue Odysseus.

95

And in the end he won,
asking what one slave was worth   135
when laid in the balance
with the honor of Achilles.

—He wouldn't have the dead
descending down to Hades
telling tales of Greek
ingratitude to Greeks
who fell for Hellas
on the foreign field of Troy.   140

—And he is coming here
to tear your daughter from your breast
and wrench her from your arms.

—Go to the temples!
—   Go to the shrines
—Fall at Agamemnon's knees!   145
—Call on Heaven's gods!
—Invoke the gods below!
—Unless your prayers prevent her death,
  unless your pleas can keep her safe,
  then you shall see your child,   150
  face downward on the earth
  and the stain in the black earth spread
    as the red blood drops
  from the gleaming golden chain
  that lies broken at her throat.

Hecuba
  O grief!
        What can I say?
  What are the words for loss?   155

  O bitterness of age,
  slavery not to be borne,
  unendurable pain!
  To whom can I turn?   160

Childless and homeless,
my husband murdered,
my city stained with fire. . . .
Where can I go?
What god in heaven,
what power below
will help me now?
O women of Troy,   165
heralds of evil,
bringers of loss,
this news you bring is my sentence of death.
Why should I live? How live in the light
when its goodness is gone,
when all I have is grief?
Bear me up,
poor stumbling feet,   170
and take me to the tent.

(*She stumbles painfully to Agamemnon's tent and
then cries out in terror to Polyxena within.*)

O my child!
          Polyxena,
step from the tent!
Come and hear the news
your wretched mother brings,
this news of horror   175
that touches your life!

(*Enter from the tent Polyxena, a
beautiful young girl.*)

Polyxena
    That terror in your voice!
    That cry of fear
    flushing me forth
    like a bird in terror!

Hecuba
    O my child! My baby. . . .   180

97

Polyxena
Again that cry! Why?

Hecuba
I am afraid for you—

Polyxena
Tell me the truth, Mother.
No, I am afraid. Something
in your face frightens me.   185

Hecuba
O my child! My child—

Polyxena
You *must* tell me, Mother.

Hecuba
A dreadful rumor came.
Some Greek decree   190
that touches your life—

Polyxena
Touches my life how?
For god's sake, Mother,
speak!

Hecuba
        —The Greeks,
in full assembly,
have decreed your death,
a living sacrifice   195
upon Achilles' tomb.

Polyxena
O my poor mother!
How I pity you,
this broken-hearted life
of pain!
        What god

could make you suffer so,
impose such pain,
such grief in one poor life?   200
Alive, at least
I might have shared
your slavery with you,
my unhappy youth
with your embittered age.
But now I die,
and you must see my death:—
butchered like a lamb   205
squalling with fright,
and the throat held taut
for the gashing knife,
and the gaping hole
where the breath of life
goes out,

      and sinks
downward into dark
with the unconsolable dead.   210

It is *you* I pity,
Mother.

      For *you* I cry.
Not for myself,

        not for this life
whose suffering is such
I do not care to live,
but call it happiness to die.   215

Coryphaeus
    Look, Hecuba. Odysseus is coming here
himself. There must be news.

      (Enter Odysseus, attended by several soldiers.)
Odysseus

        By now, Hecuba,
I think you know what decision the army has taken
and how we voted.

But let me review the facts.
By majority vote the Greeks have decreed as follows: 220
your daughter, Polyxena, must die as a victim
and prize of honor for the grave of Achilles.
The army has delegated me to act as escort.
Achilles' son will supervise the rite
and officiate as priest.
                              There matters rest.
You understand your position? You must not attempt   225
to hold your daughter here by force, nor,
I might add, presume to match your strength with mine.
Remember your weakness and accept this tragic loss
as best you can.
                        Nothing you do or say
can change the facts. Under the circumstances,
the logical course is resignation.

Hecuba

                              O gods,
is there no end to this ordeal of suffering,   230
this struggle with despair?
                              Why do I live?
I should have died, died long ago.
But Zeus preserved me, saved me, kept me alive
to suffer, each time to suffer worse
than all the grief that went before.
                                    Odysseus,
if a slave may put her question to the free—
without intent to hurt or give offense—   235
then let me ask you one brief question now
and hear your answer.

Odysseus

                        Ask me your question.
I can spare you the time.

Hecuba

                        Do you remember once
how you came to Troy, a spy, in beggar's disguise,   240

smeared with filth, in rags, and tears of blood
were streaming down your beard?

Odysseus

           I remember
the incident. It left its mark on me.

Hecuba

But Helen penetrated your disguise
and told me who you were? Told *me* alone?

Odysseus

I stood, I remember, in danger of death.

Hecuba

And how humble you were? How you fell at my knees   245
and begged for life?

Odysseus

        And my hand almost froze on your
    dress.

Hecuba

And you were at my mercy, *my* slave then.
Do you remember what you said?

Odysseus

          Said?
Anything I could. Anything to live.

Hecuba

And I let you have your life? I set you free?

Odysseus

Because of what you did, I live today.   250

Hecuba

Then can you say your treatment now of me
is not contemptible? To take from me
what you confess you took, and in return

do everything you can to do me wrong
and ruin me?

O gods, spare me the sight   255
of this thankless breed, these politicians
who cringe for favors from a screaming mob
and do not care what harm they do their friends,
providing they can please a crowd!

Tell me,
on what feeble grounds can you justify   260
your vote of death?

Political necessity?
But how? And do your politics require
the shedding of human blood upon a grave,
where custom calls for cattle?

Or is it vengeance
that Achilles' ghost demands, death for his death,
and exacts of her? But what has she to do
with his revenge? Who ever hurt him less
than this poor girl? If death is what he wants,   265
let Helen die. He went to Troy for *her*;
for *her* he died.

Or is it merely looks
that you require, some surpassing beauty in a girl
whose dying loveliness might appease the hurt
of this fastidious ghost? Then do not look
for loveliness from us. Look to Helen,
loveliest of lovely women on this earth
by far—lovely Helen, who did him harm   270
far more than we.

So much by way of answer
to the justice of your case.

Now, Odysseus,
I present my claim for your consideration,
my just demand for payment of your debt
of life.

You admit yourself you took my hand;
you knelt at my feet and begged for life.

But see—

*(Hecuba kneels at the feet of Odysseus
and takes his hand.)*

now I touch you back as you touched me.   275
I kneel before you on the ground and beg
for mercy back:
              Let her stay with me.
Let her live.
              Surely there are dead enough
without her death. And everything I lost
lives on in her. This one life   280
redeems the rest. She is my comfort, my Troy,
my staff, my nurse; she guides me on my way.
She is all I have.
              And you have power,
Odysseus, greatness and power. But clutch them gently,
use them kindly, for power gives no purchase
to the hand, it will not hold, soon perishes,
and greatness goes.
              I know. I too was great
but I am nothing now. One day   285
cut down my greatness and my pride.
                        But I implore you,
Odysseus, be merciful, take pity on me!
Go to the Greeks. Argue, coax them, convince them
that what they do is wrong. Accuse them of murder!
Tell them we are helpless, we are women,
the same women whom they tore from sanctuary   290
at the altars. But they pitied us, they spared us then.
Plead with them.
              Read them your law of murder. Tell
    them how
it applies to slave and free without distinction.
But go.
       Even if your arguments were weak,
if you faltered or forgot your words, it would not matter.
Of themselves that power, that prestige you have
would guarantee success, swelling in your words,

and borrowing from what you are a resonance and force   295
denied to less important men.

Coryphaeus

Surely
no man could be so callous or so hard of heart
he could hear this mother's heartbroken cry
and not be touched.

Odysseus

Allow me to observe, Hecuba,
that in your hysterics you twist the facts.

First,
I am not, as you fondly suppose, your enemy,   300
and my advice, believe me, was sincerely and kindly
    meant.
I readily admit, moreover, the extent of my debt—
everything I am today I owe to you.
And in return I stand ready and willing
to honor my debt by saving your life. Indeed,
I have never suggested otherwise.

But note:
I said *your* life, not your daughter's life,
a very different matter altogether.
I gave my word that when we captured Troy   305
your daughter should be given to our best soldier
as a prize upon request. That was my promise,
a solemn public commitment which I intend to keep.
Besides, there is a principle at stake
and one, moreover, in whose neglect or breach
governments have fallen and cities come to grief,
because their bravest, their most exceptional men,
received no greater honor than the common run.
And Achilles deserves our honor far more than most,
a great man and a great soldier who died greatly   310
for his country.

Tell me, what conduct could be worse
than to give your friend a lifetime of honor and respect

104

but neglect him when he dies?
                         And what then,
if war should come again and we enlist our citizens
to serve? Would we fight or would we look to our lives,   315
seeing that dead men get no honor?
                         No:
for my lifetime give me nothing more than what I need;
I ask no more. But as regards my grave,
I hope for honor, since honor in the grave
has eternity to run.   320
                    You speak of pity,
but I can talk of pity too. Pity us,
pity our old people, those old men and women
no less miserable than yours, the wives and mothers
of all those brave young men who found a grave
in the dust of Troy.
                    Endure; bear your losses,   325
and if you think me wrong to honor courage
in a man, then call me callous.
                    But what of you,
you foreigners who refuse your dead their rights
and break your faith with friends? And then you wonder
that Hellas should prosper while your countries suffer   330
the fates they deserve!

Coryphaeus

                This is what it means
to be a slave: to be abused and bear it,
compelled by violence to suffer wrong.

Hecuba

                    O my child,
all my prayers are lost, thrown away   335
on the empty air!
                So try your powers now.
Implore him, use every skill that pity has,
every voice. Be like the nightingale,
touch him, move him! Fall at his knees,

beg him for life!
Even he has children too   340
and may pity them in you.

Polyxena

I see your hand,
Odysseus, hidden in the folds of your robes and your
    face
averted, lest I try to touch your hand or beard
and beg for life.
Have no fear. You are safe
from me.
I shall not call on Zeus who helps   345
the helpless.
I shall not beg for life.
No:
I go with you because I must, but most
because I wish to die. If I refuse,
I prove myself a coward, in love with life.   350
But why should I live?
I had a father once,
king of Phrygia. And so I started life,
a princess of the blood, nourished on lovely hopes
to be a bride for kings. And suitors came
competing for the honor of my hand, while over the
    girls
and women of Troy, I stood acknowledged mistress,
courted and envied by all, all but a goddess,   355
though bound by death.
And now I am a slave.
It is that name of slave, so ugly, so strange,
that makes me want to die. Or should I live
to be knocked down to a bidder, sold to a master   360
for cash? Sister of Hector, sister of princes,
doing the work of a drudge, kneading the bread
and scrubbing the floors, compelled to drag out
endless weary days? And the bride of kings,
forced by some low slave from god knows where   365

to share his filthy bed?
Never.
With eyes still free, I now renounce the light
and dedicate myself to death.
Odysseus,
lead me off. For I see nothing in this life
to give me hope, and nothing here at all   370
worth living for.
As for you, Mother,
do nothing, say nothing now to hinder me.
Help me instead; help me to die, now,
before I live disgraced.
I am a novice   375
to this life of shame, whose yoke I might endure,
but with such pain that I prefer to die
than go on living.

Coryphaeus
Nobility of birth
is a stamp and seal, conspicuous and sharp.   380
But true nobility allied to birth
is a greatness and a glory.

Hecuba
I am proud of you,
my child, so very proud, but anguish sticks
in this nobility.
If your Achilles
must have his victim, Odysseus, if you
have any care for your own honor left,   385
then let her live. Let me take her place
upon the tomb; kill *me*, be merciless
to *me*, not her. For I gave birth to Paris
whose arrows brought Achilles down.

Odysseus
The ghost
demanded this girl's blood, not yours,   390
old woman.

Hecuba

> Then let me die with her at least,
and we shall be a double drink of blood
for earth and this demanding ghost below.

Odysseus

Her death will do. One victim is required,   395
no more.

Hecuba

> I *must* die with her! I *must!*

Odysseus

Must? A strong word, Hecuba. It was my impression
I was the master here.

Hecuba

> I shall stick to her
like ivy to the oak.

Odysseus

> Take my advice, Hecuba.
For your own good, do not.

Hecuba

> Never, never   400
will I let her go.

Odysseus

> While I, for my part,
refuse to leave her here.

Polyxena

> Mother, listen.
And you, Odysseus, be gentle with a mother's love.
She has reasons for despair.
> Poor Mother,
do not struggle with those stronger than you.
Is this what you want—to be thrown down in the dust,   405
this poor old body bruised, shouldered away,

hustled off by younger and stronger arms?
They will do it. No, this is not for you.
O Mother, Mother,
                          give me your hand,
and put your cheek to mine for one last kiss   410
and then no more. For the last, last time
I look upon this gleaming circle of the sun
and speak the last words I shall ever say.
O Mother, Mother,
                          now I go below—

Hecuba
    Leaving me to live, a slave in the light—   415

Polyxena
    Unmarried to my death, no wedding-songs for me—

Hecuba
    The song of mourning for you, wretchedness for me—

Polyxena
    To lie in the dark with Hades, far from you—

Hecuba
    O gods, where can I go? Where shall I die?

Polyxena
    I was born to freedom and I die a slave.   420

Hecuba
    Fifty children I once had, and all are dead.

Polyxena
    What message shall I take to Priam and Hector?

Hecuba
    Tell them this: I am the queen of sorrow.

Polyxena
    O sweet breasts that nourished me!

Hecuba
So wrong, so wrong! So young to die! 425

Polyxena
Farewell, Cassandra! Mother, farewell—

Hecuba
Let others fare well. I never shall.

Polyxena
Goodbye, Polydorus, my brother in Thrace—

Hecuba
If he lives at all—for all I have is loss.

Polyxena
He lives. He shall close your dying eyes. 430

Hecuba
I died of sorrow while I was still alive.

Polyxena
Shroud my head, Odysseus, and lead me out.
Even before I die, my cries have broken
my mother's heart, and she has broken mine.
O light of day!
        I still can cry the light 435
in that little space of life I have to live
before I die upon Achilles' tomb!

      (*Odysseus shrouds Polyxena and leads her out.*
            Hecuba collapses to the ground.)

Hecuba
I am faint—my legs give way beneath me—
Polyxena!
      Touch your mother, give me your hand,
reach me! Do not leave me childless!
                O gods, 440
to see there, in her place, Helen of Sparta,
sister of the sons of Zeus, whose lovely eyes
made ashes of the happiness of Troy!

Chorus

    O wind of ocean,
    wind that blows on the sea
    and drives the scudding ships,   445
    where are you blowing me?
    Where shall I be slave?
    Where is there home for me?
    There in distant Doris,   450
    in Phthia far away
    where men say Apidanus runs,
    father of waters,
    river whose lovely flowing
    fattens the fields?

    There in the islands?   455
    The salt sea churning, borne on by oars,
    to days of mourning in the house,
    there where the primal palm
    and the bay broke out their leaves
    for lovely Leto   460
    in honor of her son?
    There shall I sing
    with the maidens of Delos,
    praising Artemis,
    the bow and fillets of gold?   465

    Or there where Athene drives
    her chariot of burnished gold?
    There in Athens, yoking
    the horses on the goddess' robe,
    stitching cloth of saffron
    with threads of every color,   470
    sewing the Titans there,
    killed by stabbing fire,
    the thunderbolts of Zeus?

    O my children!   475
    My father, my mother!
    O city, ruined land,

ashes and smoke, wasted,
wilderness of war!
I live, but live a slave,   480
forced to a foreign land,
torn westward out of Asia
to a marriage that is death!

(Enter Talthybius.)

Talthybius

Women of Troy, where can I find Hecuba,   485
your onetime queen?

Coryphaeus

There she lies, Talthybius,
in the dust at your feet, her head buried in her robes.

Talthybius

O Zeus, what can I say?
That you look on man
and care?
Or do we, holding that the gods exist,
deceive ourselves with unsubstantial dreams   490
and lies, while random careless chance and change
alone control the world?
This was the queen
of fabulous Troy. This was once the wife
of Priam the great.
And now, childless, old,   495
enslaved, her home and city wrecked by war,
she lies there on the ground, her proud head
fouled in the dust.
I too am old,
an old man, and life is precious now,
but I would rather die than sink as low
as this poor woman has fallen now.
Rise,
lady. Lift your head to the light; raise
that body blanched with age.   500

112

Hecuba

Who are you
who will not let me lie? Who disturbs
my wretchedness? Why?

Talthybius

I am Talthybius,
herald of the Greeks, lady. I bring you a message
from Agamemnon.

Hecuba

Have the Greeks decreed my death?   505
Tell me that, and you are welcome, herald.
No other news could please me now.

Talthybius

No, not that.
I come on behalf of the army and the sons of Atreus   510
to bid you bury your daughter. She is dead.

Hecuba

Is that your news, herald?

I cannot die?
You came to tell me *this*?

O gods, my child!
My poor child! Torn from my arms! Dead!
Dead. All my children died with you.
How did you put her to death? With honor and respect,   515
or did you kill her savagely, with cold brutality?
Tell me. Let me hear it all, everything,
no matter how it hurts.

Talthybius

There is a cost
in telling too, a double price of tears,
for I was crying when your daughter died,
and I will cry again while telling you,   520
lady. But listen.

The whole army of the Greeks,

113

drawn up in ranks, was present at the execution,
waiting and watching while Polyxena was led
by Achilles' son slowly through the center of the camp
and up the tomb. I stood nearby, while behind her
came a troop of soldiers purposely appointed   525
to prevent her struggles.
                 Then Achilles' son
lifted a golden beaker to pour the offering
of wine to his father's ghost and nodded to me
to call for silence.
                "Quiet, Achaeans!" I shouted,   530
"Silence in the ranks!" and instantly a hush
fell upon the army and he began to pray:
"Great ghost of my father Achilles, receive
this offering I pour to charm your spirit up.   535
Rise and drink this gift we give to you,
this virgin's fresh blood. Be gracious to us:
set free our ships and loose our anchor-ropes.
Grant to us all our day of coming home,
grant us all to come home safe from Troy!"   540
So he prayed, and the army with him.
                      Then,
grasping his sword by its golden hilt, he slipped it
from the sheath, and made a sign to the soldiers
to seize her. But she spoke first:
                   "Wait, you Greeks   545
who sacked my city! Of my own free will I die.
Let no man touch me. I offer my throat
willingly to the sword. I will not flinch.
But let me be free for now. Let me die free.   550
I am of royal blood, and I scorn to die
the death of a slave."
              "Free her!" the army roared,
and Agamemnon ordered his men to let her go.
The instant they released their hold, she grasped her
   robes
at the shoulder and ripped them open down the sides   555
as far as the waist, exposing her naked breasts,

bare and lovely like a sculptured goddess.   560
Then she sank, kneeling on the ground, and spoke
her most heroic words:
                          "Strike, captain.
Here is my breast. Will you stab me there?
Or in the neck? Here is my throat, bared   565
for your blow."
                   Torn between pity and duty,
Achilles' son stood hesitating, and then
slashed her throat with the edge of his sword. The blood
gushed out, and she fell, dying, to the ground,
but even as she dropped, managed to fall somehow
with grace, modestly hiding what should be hidden   570
from men's eyes.
                   The execution finished,
the soldiers set to work. Some scattered leaves
upon her corpse, while others brought branches
of pine and heaped her pyre. Those who shirked   575
found themselves abused by the rest.
                                       "You loafers,"
they shouted, "how can you stand there empty-handed,
doing nothing? Where's your present for the girl?
When did you ever see greater courage
than that?"
           And now you know it all.
                             For my part,   580
having seen your daughter die, I count you
of all women the one most blessed in her children
and also the unhappiest.

Coryphaeus

                          Blow after blow
disaster drops from heaven; suffering shakes
my city and the house of Priam.

Hecuba

                          O my child,
how shall I deal with this thronging crowd of blows,   585

these terrors, each with its petition, clamoring
for attention? If I try to cope with one,
another shoulders in, and then a third
comes on, distracting, each fresh wave
breeding new successors as it breaks.

But now,
with this last blow I cannot cope at all,
cannot forget your death, cannot stop   590
crying—
          And yet a kind of comfort comes
in knowing how well you died.
                              But how strange it seems.
Even worthless ground, given a gentle push
from heaven, will harvest well, while fertile soil,
starved of what it needs, bears badly.   595
But human nature never seems to change;
evil stays itself, evil to the end,
and goodness good, its nature uncorrupted
by any shock or blow, always the same,
enduring excellence.
                    Is it in our blood
or something we acquire? But goodness can be taught,   600
and any man who knows what goodness is
knows evil too, because he judges
from the good.
              But all this is the rambling nothing
of despair.
          Talthybius, go to the Greeks
and tell them this from me: not a hand
is to be laid on my child; make them keep   605
the crowd away.
                For in armies the size of this,
men are prone to violence, sailors undisciplined,
the mob gets out of hand, runs wild, worse
than raging fire, while the man who stands apart
is called a coward.

(*Exit Talthybius. Hecuba turns to a Handmaid.*)

—Take your pitcher, old woman,
fill it with water from the sea and then return.   610
I must give my daughter's body its last bath
before her burial, this wedding which is death.
For she marries Hades, and I must bathe the bride
and lay her out as she deserves.

> But how?
I have nothing of my own, nothing precious left.
What then?

> I'll borrow from my women in the tents   615
those few poor trinkets they managed to pilfer
from their own homes.

(Exit Handmaid.)

> Where is greatness gone?
Where is it now, that stately house, home
where I was happy once? King Priam,
blessed with children once, in your pride of wealth?   620
And what am I of all I used to be,
mother of sons, mother of princes?

> Gone,
all gone, and nothing left.

> And yet
we boast, are proud, we plume our confidence—
the rich man in his insolence of wealth,
the public man's conceit of office or success—   625
and we are nothing; our ambition, greatness, pride,
all vanity.

> That man is happiest
who lives from day to day and asks no more,
garnering the simple goodness of a life.

(Hecuba enters the tent.)

Chorus

> That morning was my fate,
that hour doom was done,   630
when Paris felled the tree
that grew on Ida's height

117

and made a ship for sea
and sailed to Helen's bed—
loveliest of women   635
the golden sun has seen.
Grief, and worse than grief,
necessity surrounds us.
One man's folly made
a universal curse,   640
ruin over Simois.
Paris sat as judge
upon three goddesses.   645
His verdict was war.

War, slaughter, and the ruin of my house,
while in her house the Spartan woman mourns,
grieving by the wide Eurotas,   650
and mothers mourn for their sons,
and tear out their snowy hair
and dredge their cheeks with bloody nails.   655

(*The Handmaid rushes in.*)

Handmaid
  Where is the queen, women?
                          Where is Hecuba
  whose sufferings outstrip all rival runners?
  No one shall take that crown away.   660

Coryphaeus
                          Speak.
  What new sorrow do you bring her? Will this news
  of anguish never sleep?

(*Enter other women, carrying on a bier the
            shrouded corpse of Polydorus.*)

Handmaid
                          This is the grief
  I bring to Hecuba. Gentle words are hard
  to find: the burden I bring is disaster.

(Enter Hecuba from the tent.)

Coryphaeus

Look: here she comes now. 665

Handmaid

O my queen,
more wretched, more miserable than I can say.
Now you live no more, the light is gone!

Hecuba

This is mockery, not news. I know it all. 670
But why have you brought Polyxena's body here?
I heard the Greeks were helping with her funeral.

Handmaid

Poor woman, she thinks it is Polyxena.
She does not know the worst. 675

Hecuba

O gods, *no!*
Not my poor mad daughter, Cassandra?

Handmaid

Cassandra is alive. Mourn for this dead boy.

(She strips the shroud from the corpse.)

Look at this naked corpse we found,
this unexpected horror. 680

Hecuba

It is my son!
Polydorus, warded by my friend in Thrace!
No!
O gods in heaven, let me die!

O my son, my son,
now the awful dirge begins, 685
the fiend, the fury,
singing, wailing in me now,
shrieking madness!

119

Handmaid
  What fury? Is it the curse of Paris you mean?

Hecuba
  Horror too sudden to be believed,
    unbelievable loss,
    blow after blow!   690
  And this is all my life:
    the mourning endless,
    the anguish unending.

Coryphaeus
  In loss and suffering we live your lives.

Hecuba
  O my son, my child,   695
    how were you killed?
  What fate, what hand
    could take your life?

Handmaid
  I do not know. I found his body lying
    on the shore.

Hecuba
                  Drowned, his body washed on the sand? 700
  Or was he murdered?

Handmaid
                      The surf had washed his body up.

Hecuba
  O gods, my dream!
                    I see it now,
    those black wings beating the dark,   705
    brushing over him, touching him,
    dead already, even in my dreams!

Coryphaeus
  Who murdered him? Did your dream show you that?

Hecuba

    Who but our noble friend in Thrace,   710
    where his father sent him out of harm,
    to be safe with our friend in Thrace?

Coryphaeus

    Murdered? Murdered by a friend? Killed for gold?

Hecuba

        Unspeakable, unimaginable crime,
        unbearable!
               Where is friendship now?   715
        O fiend, monster, so pitiless,
        to mangle him so, to hack
        his sweet flesh with the sword!   720

Coryphaeus

    Unhappy Hecuba, most miserable of women
    on this earth, how heavily god's anger
    falls on you.
          —But look: I see our master,
    Agamemnon, coming here.
                  Quickly, friends,   725
    withdraw.

              (Enter Agamemnon with attendants.)

Agamemnon

        Why this delay of yours, Hecuba,
    in burying your daughter? I received your message
    from Talthybius that none of our men should touch her,
    and I gave strict orders to that effect.
    Hence I found your delay all the more surprising   730
    and came to fetch you myself. In any case,
    I can report that matters there are well in hand
    and proceeding nicely—if a word like "nicely"
    has any meaning in this connection.

              (He sees the corpse of Polydorus.)

                              Here,
what's that Trojan corpse beside the tents?
I can see from his shroud that he's not a Greek.   735

Hecuba (*aside*)
    O gods, what shall I do?
                        Throw myself
    at his knees and beg for mercy or hold my tongue
    and suffer in silence?

Agamemnon
                    Why do you turn away,
    Hecuba? And what's the meaning of these tears?
    What happened here? Who is this man?   740

Hecuba (*aside*)
    But suppose he treats me with contempt, like a slave,
    and pushes me away? I could not bear it.

Agamemnon
    I am not a prophet, Hecuba. Unless you speak,
    you make it quite impossible for me to help you.

Hecuba (*aside*)
    And yet I could be wrong. Am I imagining?   745
    He may mean well.

Agamemnon
                    If you have nothing to say,
    Hecuba, very well. I have no wish to hear.

Hecuba (*aside*)
    But without his help I lose my only chance
    of revenging my children. So why should I hesitate?   750
    Win or lose, he is my only hope.

                    (*She falls at* Agamemnon's *knees.*)

    Agamemnon, I implore you, I beg you
    by your beard, your knees, by this conquering hand,
        help me!

Agamemnon
    What can I do to help you, Hecuba? Your freedom
    is yours for the asking.

Hecuba
                                No, not freedom.   755
    Revenge. Only give me my revenge
    and I'll gladly stay a slave the rest of my life.

gamemnon
    Revenge? Revenge on whom, Hecuba?

Hecuba
                                My lord,
    not the revenge you think, not that at all.
    Do you see this body here, this naked corpse   760
    for which I mourn?

Agamemnon
                                I see him very well,
    though no one yet has told me who he is.

Hecuba
    This was my son. I gave him birth.

Agamemnon
                                Which son,
    poor woman?

Hecuba
                Not one of those who died
    for Troy.

Agamemnon
                You mean you had another son?   765

Hecuba
    Another son to die. This was he.

Agamemnon
    But where was he living when Troy was taken?

Hecuba
His father sent him away to save his life.

Agamemnon
This was the only son he sent away?
Where did he send him?

Hecuba
Here. To this country
where his body was found.

Agamemnon
He sent him to Polymestor, 770
the king of Thrace?

Hecuba
And with his son he also sent
a sum of fatal gold.

Agamemnon
But how did he die? Who killed him?

Hecuba
Who else?
His loving host, our loyal friend in Thrace.

Agamemnon
Then his motive, you think, was the gold? 775

Hecuba
Yes.
The instant he heard that Troy had fallen, he killed.

Agamemnon
But where was the body found? Who brought him here?

Hecuba
This old servant here. She found his body
lying on the beach.

124

Agamemnon
> What was she doing there?
Searching?

Hecuba
> No. She went to fetch water
for Polyxena's burial.

Agamemnon
> He must have killed him first,   780
then thrown his body in the sea.

Hecuba
> Hacked him, tossed him
to the pounding surf.

Agamemnon
> I pity you, Hecuba.
Your suffering has no end.

Hecuba
> I died
long ago. Nothing can touch me now.

Agamemnon
What woman on this earth was ever cursed   785
like this?

Hecuba
> There is none but goddess Suffering
herself.
> But let me tell you why I kneel
at your feet. And if my sufferings seem just,
then I must be content. But if otherwise,
give me my revenge on that treacherous friend   790
who flouted every god in heaven and in hell
to do this brutal murder.
> At our table
he was our frequent guest; was counted first

among our friends, respected, honored by me,
receiving every kindness that a man could meet—   795
and then, in cold deliberation, killed
my son.

       Murder may have its reasons, its motives,
but this—to refuse my son a grave, to throw him
to the sea, unburied!

       I am a slave, I know,
and slaves are weak. But the gods are strong, and over
    them
there stands some absolute, some moral order   800
or principle of law more final still.
Upon this moral law the world depends;
through it the gods exist; by it we live,
defining good and evil.

       Apply that law
to me. For if you flout it now, and those
who murder in cold blood or defy the gods
go unpunished, then human justice withers,   805
corrupted at its source.

       Honor my request,
Agamemnon.

       Punish this murder.

       Pity me.
Be like a painter. Stand back, see me
in perspective,

       see me whole, observe
my wretchedness—

       once a queen, and now
a slave; blessed with children, happy once,   810
now old, childless, utterly alone,
homeless, lost, unhappiest of women
on this earth. . . .

       (Agamemnon turns away.)

    O gods, you turn away—
what can I do? My only hope is lost.

O this helplessness!
        Why, why
do we make so much of knowledge, struggle so hard   815
to get some little skill not worth the effort?
But persuasion, the only art whose power
is absolute, worth any price we pay,
we totally neglect. And so we fail;
we lose our hopes.
        But as for happiness,
who could look at me and any longer   820
dare to hope:
        I have seen my children die,
and bound to shame I walk this homeless earth,
a slave, and see the smoke that leaps up
over Troy.
        It may be futile now
to urge the claims of love, but let me urge them   825
anyway. At your side sleeps my daughter
Cassandra, once the priestess of Apollo.
What will you give, my lord, for those nights of love?
What thanks for all her tenderness in bed
does she receive from you, and I, in turn,   830
from her?
        Look now at this dead boy,
Cassandra's brother. Revenge him. Be kind to her
by being kind to him.
        One word more.   835
If by some magic, some gift of the gods,
I could become all speech—tongues in my arms,
hands that talked, voices speaking, crying
from my hair and feet—then, all together,
as one voice, I would fall and touch your knees,
crying, begging, imploring with a thousand tongues—   840
O master, greatest light of Hellas,
hear me,
        help an old woman,
            avenge her!
She is nothing at all, but hear her, help her

even so. Do your duty as a man of honor:
see justice done. Punish this murder.   845

Coryphaeus

How strange in their reversals are our lives.
Necessities define us all, as now,
joining enemies in common cause
and alienating friends.

Agamemnon

        I pity you deeply,
Hecuba, for the tragic death of this poor boy.   850
And I am touched and stirred by your request.
So far as justice is concerned, god knows,
nothing would please me more than to bring
this murderer to book.
        But my position
here is delicate. If I give you your revenge,
the army is sure to charge that I connived   855
at the death of the king of Thrace because of my love
for Cassandra. This is my dilemma. The army
thinks of Polymestor as its friend,
this boy as its enemy. You love your son,
but what do your affections matter to the Greeks?   860
Put yourself in my position.
        Believe me,
Hecuba, I should like to act on your behalf
and would come instantly to your defense.
But if the army mutters, then I must
be slow.

Hecuba

        Then no man on earth is truly free.
All are slaves of money or necessity.   865
Public opinion or fear of prosecution
forces each one, against his conscience,
to conform.
        But since your fears make you defer

to the mob, let a slave set you free
from what you fear.

Be my confidant,   870
the silent partner of my plot to kill my son's
murderer. Give me your passive support.
Then if violence breaks out or the Greeks
attempt a rescue, obstruct them covertly
without appearing to act for me.

For the rest,   875
have no fear. I shall manage.

Agamemnon

How?
Poison? Or do you think that shaking hand
could lift a sword and kill? Who would help you?
On whom could you count?

Hecuba

Remember: there are women   880
hidden in these tents.

Agamemnon

You mean our prisoners?

Hecuba
They will help me get revenge.

Agamemnon

But *women?*
Women overpower men?

Hecuba

There is power
in numbers, and cunning makes us strong.

Agamemnon

True,
though I admit to being skeptical of women   885
in a matter like this.

129

Hecuba
>Why?
>>Women killed
Aegyptus' sons. Women emptied Lemnos
of its males: we murdered every one. And so
it shall be here.
>>But of that I say no more.
Let this woman have your safe-conduct
through the army.

>>>>*(Agamemnon nods. Hecuba turns to*
>>>>*the Handmaid.)*

>>Go to Polymestor
and give him this message:
>>>"Hecuba, once queen of Troy,   890
summons you on business that concerns you both
and requests you bring your sons. They also share
in what she has to say."

>>>*(Exit Handmaid with several attendants.)*

>>One more favor,
Agamemnon.
>>>Defer my daughter's funeral   895
until my son's body is placed beside her
on the pyre. Let them burn together,
brother and sister joined in a single flame,
their mother's double grief.

Agamemnon
>>>As you wish.
If we could sail, I could not grant this. But now,
until heaven sends us a favoring wind,   900
we must ride at anchor here.
>>>I wish you luck
in your attempt.
>>The common interests
of states and individuals alike demand
that good and evil receive their just rewards.

(Exit Agamemnon, followed by attendants. Hecuba
and her women withdraw into the tent with
the body of Polydorus.)

Chorus

O Ilium! O my country,   905
whose name men speak no more
among unfallen cities!
So dense a cloud of Greeks
came, spear on spear, destroying!
Your crown of towers shorn away,   910
and everywhere the staining fire,
most pitiful. O Ilium,
whose ways I shall not walk again!

At midnight came my doom.
Midnight when the feast is done
and sleep falls sweetly on the eyes.   915
The songs and sacrifice,
the dances, all were done.
My husband lay asleep,
his spear upon the wall,   920
forgetting for a while
the ships drawn up on Ilium's shore.

I was setting my hair
in the soft folds of the net,
gazing at the endless light
deep in the golden mirror,   925
preparing myself for bed,
when tumult broke the air
and shouts and cries
shattered the empty streets:—
Onward, onward, you Greeks!   930
Sack the city of Troy
and see your homes once more!

Dressed only in a gown
like a girl of Sparta,
I left the bed of love

131

and prayed to Artemis.   935
But no answer came.
I saw my husband lying dead,
and they took me over sea.
Backward I looked at Troy,
but the ship sped on
and Ilium slipped away,   940
and I was dumb with grief.

A curse on Helen,
sister of the sons of Zeus,
and my curse on him,
disastrous Paris   945
whose wedding wasted Troy!
O adulterous marriage!
Helen, fury of ruin!   950
Let the wind blow
and never bring her home!
Let there be no landing
for Helen of Troy!

(*Enter Polymestor, followed by his two young sons
and several attendants. Throughout his speech,
Hecuba refuses to recognize him, keeping
her back turned and her eyes
fixed on the ground.*)

Polymestor
Dearest Hecuba, wife of my dear friend,
poor unhappy Priam!
                    How I pity you,
you and your ruined Troy. And now this latest blow,   955
your daughter's death. . . .
                    What can we take on trust
in this uncertain life? Happiness, greatness,
pride—nothing is secure, nothing keeps.
The inconsistent gods make chaos of our lives,
pitching us about with such savagery of change
that we, out of our anguish and uncertainty,

may turn to them.

        —But how does my sorrow help?   960
Your loss remains.

(*A short silence, while Polymestor waits for
Hecuba to recognize him. When she does
not, he continues with mounting
embarrassment.*)

        But perhaps you are angry with me, Hecuba,
for not coming to you earlier. If so, forgive me.
It just so happened that I was inland, in the mountains
of Thrace, at the time when you arrived. In fact,
I was on the point of coming here myself   965
when your servant arrived and gave me your message.
Needless to say, I lost no time.

Hecuba

          Polymestor,
I am so embarrassed by the state in which you see me,
fallen so low since when you saw me last,
I cannot look you in the face.

            Forgive it,   970
and do not think me rude, Polymestor.
In any case, habit and custom excuse me,
forbidding that a woman look directly at a man.   975

Polymestor

I quite understand.

        Now, how can I help you?
You sent for me on some business, I believe?

Hecuba

I have a matter to discuss with you and your sons.
But privately, if possible.

          Could you ask your men   980
to withdraw?

Polymestor

(*To his bodyguard.*)
You may leave. There is no danger here.
This woman is my friend and the army of the Greeks
is well disposed.
Now, Hecuba, to business.
How can I, your prosperous friend, help you   985
in your time of troubles?

Hecuba

One question first.
How is my son Polydorus, your ward?
Is he alive?
Anything else can wait.

Polymestor
Alive and well. In this respect at least,
you may put your mind at rest.

Hecuba

My dearest friend,   990
how like you your kindness is!

Polymestor

What else
would give you comfort?

Hecuba

Does he still remember his mother?

Polymestor
So much that he wanted to run away
and visit you in secret.

Hecuba

And the gold from Troy?
Is it safe?

Polymestor

Quite safe. Locked in my palace   995
under strong guard.

Hecuba

          Guard it well, my friend.
Do not let it tempt you.

Polymestor

          Have no fears.
What I have of my own is quite enough
to last my life.

Hecuba

        Do you know why I sent for you
and your sons?

Polymestor

        Not yet. We are waiting to hear.

Hecuba

You are my friend, a friend for whom I feel   1000
no less love than you have shown to me.
And my business concerns—

Polymestor

         Yes? Yes? Go on.

Hecuba

—the ancient vaults, the gold of Priam's house.

Polymestor

I am to pass this information to your son?

Hecuba

In person. I know you for a man of honor.

Polymestor

But why did you ask that my sons be present?   1005

Hecuba

I thought they should know. Something, for instance,
might happen to you.

Polymestor
                    A prudent precaution.
  I quite agree.

Hecuba
                Do you know where Athene's temple
  once stood in Troy?

Polymestor
                    The gold is there?
  Is there a marker?

Hecuba
                    A black rock jutting up   1010
  above the ground.

Polymestor
                Is that all?

Hecuba
                        No:
  my jewels. I smuggled some jewels away from Troy.
  Could you keep them for me?

Polymestor
                        You have them with you?
  Where are they hidden?

Hecuba
                        There, inside the tent,
  beneath a heap of spoils.

Polymestor
                        Inside the tent?   1015
  Here, in the Greek camp?

Hecuba
                        The women's quarters
  are separate from the main camp.
                        136

Polymestor

                              Is it safe?
Are there men around?

Hecuba

                    No men; only women.
But come inside. We have no time to lose.
Quick.

          The Greek army is waiting and eager   1020
to raise their anchors and sail for home.

                                        .Then,
when our business here is done, you may go
and take your children where you left my son.

          (*Polymestor and his sons, followed by Hecuba,
                              enter the tent.*)

Coryphaeus

    Death is the debt of life. Now your debt falls due:—

Chorus (*individually*)

    —As though you stumbled in the surf   1025
    —hurled from high ambition down
    —trapped, thrashing with terror
      in the swirling tow
    —   and the water
      closing overhead
    —   until
    you drown.

    —   And now you know:
    —Life is held on loan.
    —The price of life is death.
    —Those who take a life—
    —repay it with their own.
    —Justice and the gods   1030
      exact the loan at last.
    —Gleam of gold misled you.
    —You took the final turn
    —where the bitter road veers off
    —and runs downhill

—   to death!
—Hands which never held a sword
—shall wrench your twisted life away!

>   (*Sudden screams and commotion from
>   inside the tent.*)

Polymestor (*from within*)
  Blind! Blind!
>   O light!
>   Light of my eyes!   1035

Coryphaeus
  That scream of anguish! Did you hear that scream?

Polymestor (*from within*)
>   Help!

  Look out, children!
>   Murder!
>   Run! Murder!

Coryphaeus
  New murder, fresh horror in the tent!

>   (*More screams and uproar; then a sudden furious
>   battering on the walls of the tent.*)

Polymestor (*from within*)
  Run, damn you, run!
>   But I'll get you yet!
  I'll batter down this tent with my bare fists!   1040

Chorus (*individually*)
  —Listen to him hammer at the walls!
  —What should we do?
—   Break down the door
  —Hurry!
—   Hecuba needs our help!

>   (*Hecuba emerges from the tent.*)

Hecuba
  Pound away!

138

Go on, batter down the door!
Nothing in this world can ever give you back   1045
the light of your eyes. Nothing.

                         Never again
shall you see your sons, see them alive.
I have killed your sons, and you are blind!

Coryphaeus

Have you done it? Have you done this thing you say?

Hecuba

Be patient a moment, and then see for yourself.
Watch him as he stumbles and staggers out of the
      tent—   1050
stone-blind.

            See the bodies of his sons,
killed by my women and me.

                 His debt is paid
and I have my revenge.

               But hush: here he comes,
raging from the tent. Let me keep out of his reach.
In his fury he will stop at nothing now.   1055

> (*Polymestor, blood pouring from his eyes, emerges
> from the tent on all fours. Wildly and blindly
> he scrambles about like an animal, searching
> for the women with his hands.*)

Polymestor

Where?
      Where shall I run?
Where shall I stop?
              Where?
Like a raging beast I go,
running on all fours
to track my quarry down!
Where?
       Where?
         Here?
           Where?   1060

Where can I pounce
on those murderous hags of Troy?
Where are you, women?
Where are they hiding,
those bitches of Troy?   1065

O god of the sun,
heal these bleeding eyes!
Give me back the light of my eyes!
Shh.
    The sound of footsteps.   1070
But where?
       Where can I leap?
Gods, to gorge their blood,
to rip the living flesh,
feed like a starving beast,
blood for blood!
      No, no.   1075
Where am I running now?
My children abandoned,
left for Furies to claw,
for savage bitches to gorge,
their mangled bodies thrown
to whiten on the hill!
But where?
    Where shall I run?
Where can I stand at bay?   1080
Run, run, run,
gather robes and run!
Let me run for my lair,
run like a ship,
sails furled, for the shore!
I'll run for my lair
and stand at bay
where my children are!

> (*He rushes into the tent and comes out carrying*
> *the bodies of his children. He lays them down*
> *and crouches over them protectively.*)

Coryphaeus

    Tormented man! Tortured past enduring.   1085
    You suffer now as you made others suffer.

Polymestor

    Help me, you men of Thrace!
    Help!
        Soldiers, horsemen,
    help! Come with spears!   1090
    Achaeans, help! Help me,
    sons of Atreus!
        Help!
            Help!
    Hear me, help me, help!
    Where are you?
        Help me.
    Women have killed my sons.   1095
    Murder, dreadful murder!
    Butchery! Horror!
    Help me!
        Help!
            O gods,
    where can I go?
    Where can I run?
    You gods in heaven,
    give me wings to fly!   1100
    Let me leap to heaven
    where the vaulted stars,
    Sirius and Orion,
    flare out their fire,
    or plunge to Hades
    on the blackened flood!   1105

Coryphaeus

    Who could reproach this man for wanting to die?
    Death is what men want when the anguish of living
    is more than they can bear.

        (Enter Agamemnon, attended by soldiers.)

Agamemnon

                       Shouting and screams
of terror brought me here. Ringing Echo,
born of these mountain crags, resounded the cries,   1110
shunting them back and forth throughout the camp,
alarming the men. Unless we knew for a fact
that Troy had fallen to our arms, this uproar
could have caused no little terror or disturbance.

Polymestor

That voice! I know it.
                   —My friend, Agamemnon!
Look, look at me now—

Agamemnon

                 —Oh. Awful sight!   1115
Poor Polymestor! Those blind bleeding eyes,
those dead children. . . . Who did this, Polymestor?
Who killed these boys? Who put out your eyes?
Whoever it was, he must have hated you and your sons
With a savage, ruthless hate.

Polymestor

              Hecuba. She did it,   1120
she and the other women. They destroyed me,
they worse than destroyed me.

Agamemnon

                You, Hecuba?
Do you admit this hideous, inhuman crime?   1125
Is this atrocity your work?

Polymestor

              Hecuba?
Is she here?
         Where? Tell me where she is,
and I'll claw her to pieces with these bare hands!

Agamemnon

(*Forcibly restraining him.*)
What? Have you lost your mind?

Polymestor

For god's sake,
let me go! Let me rip her limb from limb!

Agamemnon
Stop.
No more of this inhuman savagery now.
Each of you will give his version of the case   1130
and I shall try to judge you both impartially.

Polymestor
Then listen, Agamemnon.
Hecuba had a son
called Polydorus, her youngest. His father Priam,
apprehensive that Troy would shortly be taken,   1135
sent the boy to me to be raised in my own house.
I killed him, and I admit it.
My action, however,
was dictated, as you shall see, by a policy
of wise precaution.
My primary motive was fear,
fear that if this boy, your enemy, survived,
he might someday found a second and resurgent Troy.
Further, when the Greeks heard that Priam's son   1140
was still alive, I feared that they would raise
a second expedition against this new Troy,
in which case these fertile plains of Thrace
would once again be ravaged by war; once again
Troy and her troubles would work her neighbors
    harm—
those same hardships, my lord, which we in Thrace
have suffered in this war.
Hecuba, however,   1145
somehow hearing that her son was dead or murdered,

143

lured me here on the pretext of revealing
the secret hiding-place of Priam's gold
in Troy. Then, alleging that we might be overheard,
she led my sons and me, unattended,
into the tent.

        Surrounded by Trojan women
on every side, I took my seat on a couch.   1150
The atmosphere seemed one of friendliness.
The women fingered my robes, then lifted the cloth
to inspect it under the light, exclaiming shrilly
over the quality of our Thracian weaving.
Still others stood there admiring my lance   1155
and before I knew it I was stripped of spear
and shield alike.

        Meanwhile the young mothers
were fussing over my children, jouncing them in their
    arms
with hugs and kisses and passing them from hand to
    hand
until they were out of reach.

        Then, incredibly,
out of that scene of domestic peace,   1160
they suddenly pulled daggers from their robes
and butchered both my sons, while troops of women
rushed to tackle me, seizing my arms and legs
and holding me down. I tried to leap up   1165
but they caught me by the hair and pulled me down.
I fought to free my arms, but they swamped me
and I went down beneath a flood of women,
unable to move a muscle.

        And then—O gods!—
they crowned their hideous work with worse outrage,
the most inhuman brutal crime of all.
They lifted their brooches and stabbed these bleeding
    eyes   1170
through and through! Then they ran for cover,
scattering through the tent. I leaped to my feet,
groping along the wall, stalking them down

144

like a wounded animal hunting a pack of hounds,
staggering blind on all fours, battering   1175
at the wall.

        This is my reward, Agamemnon,
for my efforts in disposing of your enemies.
What I suffer now I suffer for you.
One word more.

        On behalf of all those dead
who learned their hatred of women long ago,
for those who hate them now, for those unborn
who shall live to hate them yet, I now declare   1180
my firm conviction:

        neither earth nor ocean
produces a creature as savage and monstrous
as woman.

        This is my experience.
I know that this is true.

Coryphaeus

        Do not presume,
Polymestor, whatever your provocation,
to include all women in this sweeping curse   1185
without distinction.

Hecuba

        The clear actions of a man,
Agamemnon, should speak louder than any words.
Good words should get their goodness from our lives
and nowhere else; the evil we do should show,
a rottenness that festers in our speech   1190
and what we say, incapable of being glozed
with a film of pretty words.

        There are men, I know,
sophists who make a science of persuasion,
glozing evil with the slick of loveliness;
but in the end a speciousness will show.
The impostors are punished; not one escapes
his death.

So much by way of beginning. 1195
Now for him.
        He claims he killed my son
on your behalf, Agamemnon, to spare
you Greeks the horrors of a second war.

(She turns to Polymestor.)

                You liar!
First, what possible friendship could there be
between civilized Greeks and half-savages 1200
like you?
      Clearly none.
              Then why this zeal
to serve their cause?
             Are you related to them
or bound by marriage?
             What *is* your motive then?
Fear, you say, that they might sail for Troy
and burn your crops or ravage your kingdom in passing.
Who could believe that preposterous lie?
                  No, 1205
if you want the truth, let me tell you why:
it was your greed for gold that killed my son,
sheer greed and nothing more.
             If not,
what explains your conduct then and now?
Answer me this.
           Why, when Troy still flourished,
when the ramparts ran unbroken about the city,
when Priam was alive and Hector had his day— 1210
why, if you were then so friendly to the Greeks,
did you fail to kill my son or take him prisoner
at least, when you had him at your mercy?
                But no.
You waited, biding your time, until our sun
had set, and the smoke announced the sack of Troy. 1215
Then you moved, killing your guest who sat

helpless at your hearth.
                    And what of this,
which shows your crime for what it was?
                                    Why,
if you loved the Greeks as much as you assert,
did you miss your chance to present them with the
        gold—   1220
that gold you claim does not belong to you
but to Agamemnon? But they were desperate then,
long years away from home.
                            But no. Even now
you cannot bear the thought of giving up
the gold, but hoard it for yourself at home.
One point more.
                    If you had done your duty
by my son, raised him and kept him safe,   1225
men would honor and respect you as a noble friend.
For real friendship is shown in times of trouble;
prosperity is full of friends.
                            And then,
if someday you had stood in need of help,
my son would have been your friend and treasury.
But killing him you killed your loyal friend;   1230
your gold is worthless now, your sons are dead,
and you are as you are.

                    (*She turns back to Agamemnon.*)
                    Agamemnon,
if you acquit this man, you prove yourself
unjust.

        This is a man who betrayed his trust,
who killed against the laws of man and god,
faithless, evil, corrupt.
                        Acquit him now   1235
and we shall say the same is true of you.
I say no more.

Coryphaeus

            Well spoken, Hecuba.

Those whose cause is just will never lack
good arguments.

Agamemnon

                   It gives me no pleasure   1240
to sit as judge on the miseries of others.
But I should cut a sorry figure in the world
if I allowed this case to come to court
and then refused or failed to give a verdict.
I have no choice.
                Know then, Polymestor,
I find you guilty of murder as charged.
You murdered your ward, killed him in cold blood,
and not, as you assert, for the Greeks or me,
but out of simple greed, to get his gold.   1245
You then construed the facts to fit your case
in court.
         Perhaps you think it a trifling matter
to kill a guest.
             We Greeks call it murder.
How, therefore, could I acquit you now
without losing face among men?
                    I could not do it.   1250
You committed a brutal crime; therefore accept
the consequences of your act.

Polymestor

                O gods,
condemned! Defeated by a woman, by a slave!

Hecuba

Condemned for what you did. Justly condemned.

Polymestor

  O my children!
             O light, light of my eyes!   1255

Hecuba

It hurts, does it? And what of me? I mourn
my children too.

Polymestor
                    Does it give you pleasure
to mock at me?

Hecuba
                    I rejoice in my revenge.

Polymestor
Enjoy it now. You shall not enjoy it long.
Hear my prediction.
                    I foretell that you—

Hecuba
Shall be carried on ship across the sea to Hellas?   1260

Polymestor
*—shall drown at sea. You shall climb to the masthead
and fall—*

Hecuba
                    Pushed by force?

Polymestor
                                    *You shall climb the mast
of your own free will—*

Hecuba
                    Climb the mast? With wings?

Polymestor
—changed to a dog, a bitch with blazing eyes.   1265

Hecuba
How could you know of this transformation?

Polymestor
Because our Thracian prophet, Dionysus,
told me so.

Hecuba
                    He neglected, I see, to foretell
your own fate.

149

Polymestor
> Had he told my future then,
> I never would have stumbled in your trap.

Hecuba
Shall I live or die?

Polymestor
> *Die. And when you die*   1270
> *your tomb shall be called—*

Hecuba
> In memory of my change?

Polymestor
—*Cynossema, the bitch's grave, a landmark*
to sailors.

Hecuba
> What do I care how I die?
> I have my revenge.

Polymestor
> *And your daughter Cassandra*   1275
> *must also die—*

Hecuba
> I spit your prophecies back.
> Use them on yourself.

Polymestor

> (*Pointing to Agamemnon.*)

> —*killed by this man's wife,*
> *cut down by the bitter keeper of his house.*

Hecuba
Clytemnestra? She would never do it.

150

Polymestor
  Then she shall lift the dripping axe once more
  and kill her husband too.

Agamemnon
                              Are you out of your head?
  Are you asking for more trouble?

Polymestor
                              Kill me,   1280
  but a bath of blood waits for you in Argos.

Agamemnon
  Slaves, carry him off! Drag him away!

                          (*Servants seize Polymestor.*)
Polymestor
  Have I touched you now?

Agamemnon
                          Stop him. Gag his mouth.

Polymestor
  Gag me. I have spoken.

Agamemnon
                          Take him away
  this instant.
                          Then throw him on some desert island   1285
  since his tongue cannot stop its impudence.

                      (*Attendants leave with Polymestor.*)

  As for you, Hecuba, go now and bury
  your two dead children.
                          The rest of you women,
  go and report at once to your masters' tents.
  For now the sudden wind sits freshly in our sails.   1290
  May heaven grant that our ordeal is done
  at last!
                  May all be well at home in Argos!

*(Exit Agamemnon with remaining attendants.
Hecuba and her women go slowly to the tent,
leaving the stage empty except for the abandoned bodies of Polymestor's sons.
The Chorus files slowly out.)*

Chorus

    Files to the tents,
    file to the harbor.
    There we embark
    on life as slaves.
    Necessity is harsh.   1295
    Fate has no reprieve.

ANDROMACHE

Translated and with an Introduction by

JOHN FREDERICK NIMS

INTRODUCTION TO
ANDROMACHE

Euripides' *Andromache* was written in the first years of the Peloponnesian War, probably between 430 and 424 B.C.; if inspired by a particular Spartan atrocity, the most likely would have been the massacre of the Plataean prisoners in 427. The scholiast reports that the play was not presented at Athens; it may have been performed at Argos (if at all) as part of an Athenian propaganda campaign, or at Epirus, where the young king, educated in Athens, was of the Molossian line acclaimed in the epilogue.

The discontinuity of the plot because of Andromache's disappearance in mid-play has troubled critics; not all have been as candid as D. W. Lucas, for whom the play "falls feebly and mysteriously to pieces. . . . there must be missing clues which would show the play less inept than it seems." (Professor Lucas comes up with a deadpan diagnosis worthy of Euripides himself: the poet, in these difficult days of plague and Spartan incursions, was temporarily out of his head.)

Verrall probably stands alone in defending the plot as such; he assumes (it seems wrongly) that the play is a sequel about a Machiavellian scheme concocted by Menelaus and Orestes. His theory "explains" the apparent breakdown of Menelaus in the presence of Peleus and does away with the time lapse during the chorus (ll. 1009-46), but it depends on effects that only an audience of well-briefed Verrallians could be expected to catch and relate. The breakdown of Menelaus needs no theory to explain it: Euripides' Spartan is a blusterer cowed by any show of vigor. The time lapse (of perhaps a week) is one of several in the extant tragedies; little is gained by pretending it is not there. In the excitement of the performance, who in the audience would be thinking in terms of mileages and time schedules? Who would even notice that the Chorus had been rather casual in informing Peleus of the intended murder of his grandson?

Some have suggested that Euripides, fascinated by character, is indifferent to plot. Once Andromache is out of danger, Euripides dismisses her to concentrate on her lively rival, much as Shakespeare scuttles the Turkish fleet when he has no further need for it.

Still others have found the unity of the play in *dianoia*. In antiquity it was already felt that Euripides often wrote what the poet and not what the plot demanded: Lucan said that "quite without dramatic necessity [Euripides] freely expressed his own opinions." In the words of a twentieth-century observer he "inserts passages suggested as much by the contemporary as by the dramatic situation." For *Andromache*, several key ideas have been proposed: it is about the house of Peleus—unsophisticated northerners undone by a southern alliance; or about the dangers to family life inherent in the practice of slaveholding; or it warns against incautious marriages; or it gives the *aition* of the tomb-worship of Peleus and Thetis; or it records a burning detestation of Sparta and Spartan ways.

Probably a more meaningful approach is that suggested independently by L. H. G. Greenwood and Gunther Zuntz. Euripides, says Greenwood, "is fond of presenting the arguments for or against this or that proposition concerning matters that were the subject of active interest and controversy. . . . he presents these arguments so impartially, and refrains so completely from pronouncing judgement . . . that we really cannot tell what he himself thinks." Zuntz reminds us of the problem of the Euripidean age: How is man to live in a godless world? "Different individuals had different answers, and Euripides gives them all."

It is helpful to keep in mind the philosophical background of the period: the irreconcilable systems of the pre-Socratics had led to the skepticism of the Sophists; if no one way of interpreting reality could be established as the right way, then any way was probably as good as any other. We cannot read long in Euripides before becoming aware of the doctrinal atomism of the age—an age whose values, says Jaeger, were rotten with individualism.

The conviction that standards were what the individual chose to make them was intensified by the war itself. Thucydides (iii. 10) gives a disturbing analysis of how even "words had to change their ordinary meaning and take that which was now given them." This in addition to the moral chaos of the plague of 430 B.C. (cf. ii. 7) which Euripides had lived through not long before he wrote *Andromache*.

It was an age that reminds us in many ways of the similarly disturbed world of the Jacobeans, filled, as Eliot says, with broken fragments of systems. "We have seene the best of our time," Gloucester desponds. "Machinations, hollownesse, treacherie, and all ruinous disorders follow us disquietly to our Graves." Perhaps John Webster has described it most poignantly, with his characters "in a miste" as they face the moment of truth, torn between the religious values of the past and the new self-interest for which Machiavelli was made the lurid figurehead.

In that environment, a restless and passionate temperament might well have been contemptuous of the Aristotelian dramatic formulas—if it could have anticipated them a century in advance. An imitation of an action, without obstreperous episodes or irrational gaps—this, Euripides might have felt, would be no imitation of life as *he* knew it. For the complexities of his vision, an asymmetrical form was just and proper, an objective correlative for the tormented psyche's baroque ado. Euripides (unlike Sophocles) has no *querencia*; his is a restless point of view; and if we, with our more classical habits, stay in one spot to look where he is pointing, we are likely to be left mumbling about the "riddle" of this or that play.

Modern readers may find an enlightening parallel in the work of Picasso, whom they may suspect to be the product of an analogous period: an artist who does not stare flat-footed at his subject and by whom the same face may be painted from quite different coigns of vantage. One celebrated painting shows a lady "nude, dressed, and X-rayed" all at once; it doubles the already multiple image by putting her in front of a mirror. It was with something like this simultaneous point of view that Euripides regarded his subjects; no wonder his portraits too are constructed around an ambiguous axis.

The method is used more brilliantly in the greater plays: in the *Bacchae*, for example, or *Hippolytus*. In *Andromache* the composition is twisted too violently toward propaganda; it has the stridency of caricature. The tone, it has often been observed, is not tragic at all. The events of the play may arouse pity, but they do much to counteract it by arousing the emotion that Aristotle found directly opposed: indignation. Critiques of the play bristle with such phrases as "the glaring colors of melodrama," "the air of a political pamphlet," "the whole tone unheroic," "complete absence of poetic color," "a painful experience" (for admirers of Sophoclean drama). In antiquity it was criticized as a conglomeration of comic ingredients. And yet for the theatergoer there must have been not one dull or undramatic scene in this "hard and brilliant" play.

The author of *On the Sublime* finds Euripides nearly always among those writers who use current colloquial diction. In *Andromache*, with its strongly *ad hoc* bias, colloquial usage seems even more pronounced than elsewhere; lexicographers find here boldly popular and even vulgar expressions. In reading what Norwood calls the "utterly unheroic and unpoetical, but vigorous, terse, and idiomatic" dialogue, we are far from the Olympian resonances of Aeschylus or the nobility of Sophocles, far, in fact, from what the common reader thinks of as "Greek tragedy."

The text translated here is that of Murray's Oxford edition, with his line-numbering (which corresponds to the Greek text, not to the English). I have omitted the bracketed line 7 (probably interpolated by actors), have disregarded Murray's suggested punctuation for line 1030, and have preferred Musgrave's emendation of line 1190.

CHARACTERS

Andromache, widow of Hector, allotted at the fall of
Troy to Neoptolemus, son of Achilles
Slave woman
Chorus of Phthian women
Hermione, daughter of Menelaus and Helen,
wife of Neoptolemus
Menelaus, king of Sparta
Young son of Andromache and Neoptolemus
Peleus, father of Achilles and grandfather of Neoptolemus
Nurse of Hermione
Orestes, son of Agamemnon and Clytemnestra,
formerly betrothed to Hermione
Messenger
The Goddess Thetis
Servants, attendants

ANDROMACHE

SCENE: *The Thessalian plains in Achilles' district of Phthia,
near the city of Pharsalus. Andromache is at the shrine
of the goddess Thetis, placed not far from the dwelling
of Neoptolemus.*

Andromache
Thebé my city, Asia's pride, remember
The glory and the gold of that procession
When I arrived at Priam's royal home?
As Hector's wife, soon mother of Hector's son—
Andromache, in the old days oh so lucky,   5
But sunk in misery now, if anyone is.
To have seen with my own eyes Hector my husband
Dead at Achilles' hand! To have seen our son,
Hector's and mine, Astyanax, hurled headlong   10
Down from the highest tower when Troy was taken!
And I—free as I pleased in homes of leisure
Till then—was clapped in servitude, shipped to Greece
As booty for Neoptolemus, wild islander,
His tidbit from the total spoil of Troy.   15
Phthia is my home now, these fields surrounding
The city of Pharsalia. Sea-born Thetis
Lived here with Peleus once in deep seclusion,
Apart from men. The people of Thessaly
Call it the Altar of Thetis for that reason.   20
That roof you see belongs to Achilles' son,
By whose permission Peleus rules Pharsalia:
The young defers to the older while he lives.

Within that house I've given birth to a boy,
Bred to that same Achilles' son, my master.   25
A hard life even at best, but up to now
Hope led me on—the hope this little child
Might prove my strength and shelter against trouble.
Except for her—Hermione from Sparta!   30
Since my lord married her and snubbed a slave-wife,
I'm persecuted cruelly. She's behind it,
Charging I've made her unable to conceive
With secret drugs and dosings, made him hate her.
Charging I want this house all to myself
And mean to crowd her out of it, bed and all—   35
A bed that from the first I never wanted
And now reject for good. The gods are witness
That was a bed I never crept in gladly.
No talking, though, to her. She's out for blood.
And Menelaus her father's working with her.   40
He's in the house this moment, hot from Sparta,
Bent on this very thing. Suspecting the worst,
I've run next door here to the Altar of Thetis
And here I huddle in the hope she'll save me.
For Peleus and his sons are all devotion   45
Toward this memorial of the ocean marriage.
My one and only son, though!—alarmed for his life
I've smuggled him secretly to others' keeping.
The one who served to beget him serves for nothing
In the hour of need—no help at all to his baby.   50
He's off at Delphi making amends to Apollo
For his mad behavior when, the time before,
He clamored the god should pay for killing his father!
He hopes now to plead free of old offenses
And reconcile Apollo for the future.   55

(*Enter Slave woman.*)

Slave woman
My lady—for I'm faithful to that title—
I never used or thought to use another
In your own palace when we lived in Troy.

You always had my love—your husband too
To the very day he died. Well, now there's news   60
I bring in fear and trembling of our masters,
And in sympathy for you. They've black designs,
Menelaus and his daughter. Oh be careful!

Andromache

Dearest of sister-slaves (for that's our story)
To one your mistress once, though sadly fallen—   65
They're planning what? Up to what further mischief?
What's left to endure but death? Is that their purpose?

Slave woman

They're aiming at your son, my poor, poor lady;
The little boy you hid away: his death.

Andromache

She can't have learned my darling's gone? She can't have!   70
How could she learn? My heart stopped as you spoke.

Slave woman

I couldn't tell you how. I heard it first
From them. But Menelaus is out prowling.

Andromache

My very heart stopped beating! Poor little baby,
A pair of buzzards claw at you for carrion.   75
And his—can I say *father*?—off at Delphi!

Slave woman

You'd never find yourself in this predicament,
To my mind, with him present. Now there's no one.

Andromache

And no report that Peleus means to come?

Slave woman

Suppose he came, what then? Feeble old man!   80

Andromache

I've sent for him and sent for him and sent for him.

161

Slave woman
  Sent whom for him? No friend of yours, be sure.

Andromache
  Ah, so I see! But you—you'd take a message?

Slave woman
  What could I say, being gone from home so long?

Andromache
  Don't tell me you've no bag of tricks. A woman!   85

Slave woman
  She's wary as a watchdog, that Hermione.

Andromache
  Then you—my fine fair-weather friend—refuse?

Slave woman
  That's far from true. You've no need for reproaches.
  I'll do it. What's my life, that I should care
  What happens now? A slave's life, and a woman's.   90

Andromache
  Hurry then; hurry.

                              (*Exit Slave woman*)

                    These same lamentations,
  Sobbings and tears to which my days are given
  I'll now storm heaven with. For nature tempers
  The souls of women so they find a pleasure
  In voicing their afflictions as they come.   95
  I've a wide range of sorrows, not one only:
  My native land destroyed and Hector dead,
  The rigorous fate that shut on me like shackles
  When I awoke—indignity!—to bondage.
  It's vain to say that any man alive   100
  Is in the true sense happy. Wait and ponder
  The manner of his exit from this stage.

(She keens softly.)

Paris brought home no bride, no bride but folly and ruin
   To Ilium high on its hill—welcoming Helen to bed.
She was the cause, O Troy, the Greeks' quick-moving
    battalions   105
   Out of a thousand ships, took you with fire and sword.
She was the cause my man, wretched Andromache's
   Hector,
   Was draggled by Thetis' son from a chariot round
   about Troy.
The cause I was driven away from my quiet nook to the
   seashore,
   There invited to wear slavery's odious yoke.   110
What a torrent of tears on my cheek the day that I left
   forever
   City and roofs I knew, husband dead in the dust.
Doomed Andromache now! why longer look upon
   heaven?—
   Only a slave, *her* slave—one who oppresses me so
That here to the goddess' shrine I come, a suppliant
   clutching,
                           115
   Melting away, all tears, like water welling on rock.

(Enter Chorus of Phthian women.)

Chorus

STROPHE

Lady who, crouched on the ground so long by the chapel
   of Thetis
   Linger and will not away,
Now, though a Phthian indeed I come to you, woman of
   Asia,
   To see if I may   120
     Offer a balm for grievances so deep
Embittering you and Hermione too in a spite-ridden,
   surly,
   Hateful display:
     Over two in a post for one: 125
     The arms of Achilles' son.

ANTISTROPHE

Recognize what you've become and assent to a dismal
   position:
   Though only a Trojan, you sow
Seeds of unrest with your betters—with nobles from
   Sparta!
   Far better go
      Away from the Nereid's place of hecatomb.   130
What good to lie quivering here and sadly bedabble your
   features?
   Their wish is law.
      Necessity's hot on your trail.
      Why struggle to no avail?

STROPHE

Come now, hurry and leave the glorious temple of
   Thetis.   135
   Consider: only a slave
   Here in a foreign state,
   With no apparent friend.
   Least of all, fate—
      Girl of the gamut of woe.   140
A sight for compassionate eyes—my heart said—woman
   of Troy, you
   Entered my master's home.
   Fear keeps me dumb,
   And yet I'm all sorrow.
   But what if Hermione come   145
      And find me in sympathy so?

(*Enter Hermione.*)

Hermione
   Wearing tiaras, notice, of pure gold,
   Draped in garments brilliant and luxurious—
   Neither presented to me, I hasten to add,
   From the homes of Achilles or Peleus—here I am.   150
   These wedding gifts are straight from my own Sparta.
   Menelaus gave me these—my father you know—

With other gifts galore. I'm bound to no one
And free to speak my mind. As I do now.
You! you common slave! you soldiers' winnings!   155
You plan to usurp this house, evicting me!
Your drugs have made me unlovely to my husband;
Withered my womb and left it good for nothing.
This is the sort of thing you Asian women
Have tricky wits for. But you've met your match.   160
This sea-girl's home won't help you save your skin
For all its shrines and altars. Now you've finished!
Or if any god or mortal interfere
In your behalf—well, learn to change your tune,
Eat humble pie and grovel at my knee,   165
Sweep out the house, *my* house, your fingers sprinkling
Brook-water from the pails of beaten gold.
Just where do you think you are? Is Hector here?
Is Priam with his moneybags? You're in Greece now.
You! you were even so rotten with desire   170
You had the gall to cuddle up to the son
Of the very man who killed your husband, breeding
A butcher's children. Well, that's foreigners for you.
Father and daughter intimate, mother and son,
Sister and brother—murder clears the way   175
In family squabbles. Anything goes. No law.
Don't try those methods here. And it's not decent
Either for one man teaming up two wives.
Clean-living husbands love and honor one,
Gluing affectionate eyes only on her.   180

Chorus

There's a touch of jealousy in the female psyche.
It's inclined to be rather tart where polygamy enters.

Andromache

A sort of disease, youth is. Aggravated
When the young soul's addicted to injustice.   185
I suppose my condition of servitude should daunt me
By censoring free discussion, right as I am.

If I got the better, you'd see I suffered for it.
You high and mighty people can look daggers
Hearing from your inferiors the god's truth.   190
However, I'm one for sticking to my principles.
Speak, pretty miss: for what legitimate reason
Would I keep you from your legitimate marriage?
Troy lords it over Sparta, I suppose,
Or would with a bit of luck? I fancy I'm free?   195
Or trusting in a girl's full-breasted beauty,
A city's strength, a multitude of backers,
I'm planning to dispossess you of your home?
Or so I may have sons instead of you,
Slaves every one, like millstones dragging after me?   200
Or else so someone will exalt my boys
To the very throne itself, if you've no children?
I suppose for Hector's sake the Greeks adore me?
Or thinking I was a nobody in Troy?
It wasn't drugs that made your husband shun you;   205
The plain fact is, you're hardly fit to live with.
There's your witchcraft. It's not beauty but
Fine qualities, my girl, that keep a husband.
When something annoys you, it's always Sparta this
And Sparta that. His Skyros?—never heard of it!   210
You flaunter among paupers! They mention your
        father?—
He dwarfs Achilles! No wonder your husband flushes.
A woman, even when married to a cad,
Ought to be deferential, not a squabbler.
Suppose you married a king in wintry Thrace   215
Where the custom is one husband in rotation
Take to his bed god knows how many women.
You'd knife them all? And be in a pretty fix
Screaming, "You hussy!" at every wife in sight.
Disgraceful! Well, we women are infected   220
With a worse disease than men, but try to conceal it.
O dearest Hector, for your sake I even
Welcomed your loves, when Cypris sent you fumbling.
I was wet nurse to your bastards many a time
166

Only to make your life a little easier.   225
And for such conduct he approved and loved me.
But you!—you hardly dare to let your husband
Out in the rain. He might get wet! Your mother
Helen was fond of her man—now wasn't she, dear?
Don't try to outdo her. Sensible children   230
Really ought to avoid the family vices.

Chorus
My lady, as much as you reasonably can,
Come to an understanding with this woman.

Hermione
On your high horse and picking quarrels, eh? Bragging
As if you had a monopoly on virtue?   235

Andromache
You've none at least, one gathers from your talk.

Hermione
We'll never see eye to eye—or so I hope.

Andromache
Young as you are, there's smut enough on your tongue.

Hermione
And on your conscience. Doing your best against me!

Andromache
Still caterwauling your unlucky love!   240

Hermione
I'll not be gagged. Love's all in all to women.

Andromache
And should be: *virtuous* love. The other's foul.

Hermione
Here we don't live by your outlandish standards.

167

Andromache
Shameful is shameful everywhere, Greece or not Greece.

Hermione
We've a deep thinker here! Not long to live, though.   245

Andromache
You see this statue of Thetis, eyeing you?

Hermione
Despising your country, you mean, for Achilles' murder.

Andromache
All Helen's doing, not ours. Your mother you know.

Hermione
You strike at me where it's tenderest, more and more.

Andromache
I've said my say. You'll get no more out of me.   250

Hermione
One thing. There's still the matter that brought me
     here.

Andromache
I only say your mind's a twisted thing.

Hermione
Will you or won't you leave this shrine of Thetis?

Andromache
If you guarantee my life. Otherwise never.

Hermione
I'll guarantee this: your death. And before my husband
     comes.   255

Andromache
Until he come, I'll not surrender. Never!

Hermione
I could light a fire, and let you take your chances—

Andromache

    Light up your fire. Don't think the gods are blind,
      though.

Hermione

    Or tools that tear the flesh—I've ways to get them.

Andromache

    Make all her shrine a shambles. She'll remember.   260

Hermione

    Half-savage creature, all a wild defiance!
    You'd brazen out even death! I'll make you move
    Out of there spryly enough and glad to go.
    I've got the lure for you. Though what it is
    I'll let the event itself disclose, and promptly.   265
    Sit snug and cozy now. But if melted lead
    Had soldered you there, I'd pry you out before
    The son of Achilles comes, your one hope now.

                                    (Exit Hermione.)

Andromache

    My one hope now! Some god found antidotes
    Against all poisonous snakes, but—wonder of
      wonders!—   270
    Against a menace worse than fire or vipers
    No vaccine yet: I mean these vicious women.
    Who knows the trouble we cause the human race!

Chorus

STROPHE

    That was the breeding of bitter affliction, when Hermes,
      Son of Zeus, Maia's son,   275
      Came to Ida, to the glade
      Conducting heaven's lovely team
      Of three divine fillies made
    All accounted for passionate war over who was supreme.
        These came to the farmyard   280
      And sought the boyish shepherd fond of solitude—

A hearthfire
Where but few souls intrude.

ANTISTROPHE

These, when they reached the luxuriant vale, in a
    mountain pool
    Cooled by springs, shone and bathed—   285
    What a reveling of light!
    And then approaching Priam's son
    With glowing words born of spite
They disputed their suit. Aphrodite prevailed—witching
    words
    Most sweet to the young judge,   290
  But deadly too, a lewd confusion to destroy
    And throw low
    All the towers of high Troy.

STROPHE

Oh but if only his mother had broken the
    Sorry creature's skull at once
    Before he
    Settled there on Ida's side—
When the marvelous laurel implored, when shrill   295
    Cassandra wild-eyed clamored "Kill
  The spreading pollution of Troy, our land!"
And frenzied everywhere to needle, wheedle, warn
    Prominent men
  With: "Destroy the newborn!"   300

ANTISTROPHE

    Then on the women of Troy would have fallen no
        Yoke of slavery; lady, you'd
        Have free hand,
      Mistress of a noble home;
    Greece would never have shouldered the ten-years'
    woe
      Or seen the tall young spearmen go   305
    To the stagger of war and the ruck round Troy;

Those beds would never lie by absent love undone,
    Parents be made
  Ancient waifs with no son.

(Enter Menelaus with the young son of Andromache.)

Menelaus
  I've fastened on the child you hid away
  In another house behind my daughter's back.   310
  So you thought the goddess' statue would save you
  And his receivers him? But it turned out
  You weren't as cunning as Menelaus here.
  Now either remove yourself and clear the premises
  Or the boy dies for you—a fair exchange.   315
  So think it over. The option's yours: to die
  Yourself or to see the child die for the wicked
  Wrongs you committed against my daughter and me.

Andromache
  Repute! repute! repute! how you've ballooned
  Thousands of good-for-nothings to celebrity!   320
  Men whose glory is come by honestly
  Have all my admiration. But impostors
  Deserve none: luck and humbug's all they are.
  So you're the commander-in-chief of the Greek elite
  That wrested Troy from Priam—you, you piddler!   325
  You, for the mewlings of your darling daughter
  Come snorting so importantly, up in arms
  Against a woman already down, in bondage.
  Troy's story had no role for the likes of you!
  People that seem so glorious are all show;   330
  Underneath they're like anybody else.
  Unless they have money, of course. Oh money's
    something!
  Well, Menelaus, suppose we thresh this out.
  Assume I lie here dead, thanks to your daughter.
  The curse of bloodshed's heavy on her head.   335
  A guilt that you share too, at least in the court
  Of public opinion. You're involved, no question.

Or assume that I manage somehow to stay alive.
You'll kill my little child? You think the father,
His baby butchered, will stand idly by?   340
At Troy he wasn't commonly thought a coward.
He'll do the right thing now—worthy of Peleus
And of Achilles his father, as you'll find out—
He'll send your daughter packing. With what story
Do you think you'd find her another man? You'd claim   345
Her virtue was simply appalled by such a brute?
Word gets around. Who'd marry her? You'd board her
Single at home till she's a grey-haired witch?
What griefs you'd have if you kept her there, poor man!
Wouldn't you rather she'd time and again be cheated   350
In marital affairs than suffer that way?
There's no use making catastrophes of trifles.
And just because we women are prone to evil,
What's to be gained perverting man to match?
If indeed I've plied your daughter with those potions   355
And made her womb a bungler, as she charges,
I'm ready and willing to submit to trial
(Without invoking sanctuary as now)
Before your assembled kindred, in whose eyes
I'm as guilty as in yours if I made her barren.   360
There—now you know my heart. I'm worried, though,
About your famous weakness. Brawling over
A woman led you to devastate poor Troy.

Chorus

That's quite enough from a female dealing with men.
I'd say your righteousness had gone the limit.   365

Menelaus

Woman, these are admittedly minor matters;
As you say, unworthy of my regime and Greece.
But never forget: whatever one sets his heart on
Gets to be more important than taking Troy.
Being cheated out of marriage now, that matters;   370
That's why my help's enlisted for my daughter.

All other woes a woman bears are minor
But lose her husband!—might as well be dead.
It's right my son-in-law order my slaves about;
Right his be ordered about by any of us.   375
Friends—and I mean real friends—reserve nothing:
The property of one belongs to the other.
Just sitting around and waiting till men came back,
I'd be simple-minded indeed to neglect my interests.
So on your feet; get away from the goddess' shrine.   380
If you decide to die, the boy survives.
If you put your own skin first, he dies instead.
It's one of the two. No other way about it.

Andromache

Oh, here's a gloomy lottery of life,
A gloomy choosing. If I win, I lose;   385
And losing, losing—oh, I'm lost forever!
You there who make such mountains out of molehills,
Listen to reason. You're killing me—why? For whom?
What city did I betray? What child of yours kill?
Whose home set fire to? I was strong-armed into   390
A bully's bed. And it's me you kill, not him
Who caused it all? Oh, you've got everything backwards,
Punishing the effect, and not the cause.
All these troubles! O my wretched land,
What horrors I endure! Why must I bear   395
A child just to redouble throe on throe?
I who saw Hector mangled underwheel,
Who saw our Ilium blindingly afire!   400
I who came shackled to the Grecian fleet,
Haled by the hair! And, once I came to Phthia,
Knew a mock marriage with that murderous brood.
How's living sweet for me? Where should I look—
Toward yesterday's affliction or today's?   405
I had this one son left, light of my life,
And he's to be murdered by such judges now.
Murdered? Oh not to save my scraps of life.
The child has possibilities, if he lives;

173

And if I let him die, shame come to me.   410
So look, I'm leaving the shrine. I'm in your hands
To mangle, murder, bind, hang by the neck.
O child, the one that bore you moves toward death
And all for you. If you escape that doom
Think of your mother, what a fate she suffered!   415
And covering your father's face with kisses,
Melted in tears, crushing your arms around him,
Describe my ending. All men know their children
Mean more than life. If childless people sneer—
Well, they've less sorrow. But what lonesome luck!   420

Chorus

Her speech rouses my pity. Calamities,
Even a stranger's, call for tears in all.
Menelaus, you ought to arrange some peace between
Your daughter and this woman, instead of crushing her.

Menelaus

Now seize her, men! Lock your arms tight around her.   425
She won't take kindly what I've got to say.
Remember how I bobbled the boy's life
Before your face, to pry you off the shrine
And coax you into my clutches here to die?
You know the facts of the matter—in your case.   430
As for the boy, however—suppose we let
My daughter give the word to kill or not.
And now, get in that house. I'll teach you, slave,
To attempt assault and battery on your betters.

Andromache

Made a fool of! Duped and caught by treachery,
        treachery!   435

Menelaus

Go tell the world—who cares? I'm not denying it.

Andromache

This passes for high policy back in Sparta?

174

Menelaus
  Also in Troy: being struck at to strike back.

Andromache
  And there's no heaven above to punish you?

Menelaus
  Heaven I'll handle later. First things first.   440

Andromache
  You'll kill this little baby, snatched from my lap?

Menelaus
  It's out of my hands. His future's up to my daughter.

Andromache
  Then I might as well lament you now, poor darling.

Menelaus
  His prospects, it appears, are none too rosy.

Andromache
  Where's there a man that doesn't find you odious,   445
  You citizens of Sparta, devious schemers,
  Masters of falsehood, specialists in evil,
  Your minds all warped and putrid, serpentine?
  How iniquitous your prosperity in Greece!
  Name any foulness and it's yours: assassins;   450
  Your palms a tetter of itchiness; your tongues
  Off scavenging one way and your minds another.
  Damn your Spartan souls! Death's not so much
  For me as you seem to feel. I died before
  When my poor town in Phrygia was stricken,   455
  My glorious husband too, who many a time
  Whipped you, a whimpering skipper, back to your ships.
  Fine figure of a hero now, you threaten
  Death to a woman. Strike! But not before
  You and your daughter feel the edge of my tongue.   460
  So you think you're really something now in Sparta?

175

Well, so was I in Troy. If I'm destroyed
You've little cause to gloat. For your time's coming.

(Exeunt Andromache and child; Menelaus.)

Chorus

STROPHE

Oh, I'll never approve a double love for any man,   465
    Or children born to juggled wives;
They confuse the home, bringing heavy heartaches.
    I say one man should love and honor one:
        A bride-bed
Theirs alone till life's done.   470

ANTISTROPHE

Nor in states is it right to see a pair of princes rule:
    One tyrant's better far than two
Who indeed breed woe crowding woe and town strife.   475
    Or when two souls compose a single song,
        The muse fans
Livid wrath before long.

STROPHE

Or when the hurricane is scudding ship and all,
    In a huddle of colloquy over the wheel, two heads   480
Are worse than one, and a panel of philosophers
    Worse than a petty but positive mind.
    Only one in command: that's the way in the home
    And the way in the state when it must find
Measures best for mankind.   485

ANTISTROPHE

We've sad example here: the Spartan, daughter of
    Menelaus the general, is running amuck, breathes fire
Against her fellow-wife; her spite destroys the poor
    Trojan. And also her baby I fear.   490
    Ungodly, unlawful, unsanctified crime!
    But alas! O my queen, there's a day near
    When you'll pay and pay dear.

And indeed I see
The close-huddled pair stumble out of the house   495
Under sentence of death.
O lady so stricken, O woebegone boy
Who die on account of your parent's affairs,
Though never involved,
   Nor to blame in the eyes of the rulers!   500

(*Enter Andromache and her son, hands lashed
        together; Menelaus.*)

Andromache

STROPHE

My hands are helpless; roped so tight,
See, there's blood where the fibers bite.
   Only the grave before me.

Son

Mother, O mother, I'm here too
   Close to your side, to die with you.   505

Andromache

Hardly lucky this sacrifice,
Phthian counselors.

Son

       Father, do
Hurry and help if you love us.

Andromache

You'll be snuggled, my little lad,   510
Forever close to your mother's breast,
Dust with dust in the underworld—

Son

Mother, what's to become of me?
   What's for us but misery?

Menelaus

On your way to the grave! You're an enemy brood   515
From an enemy nest. You two are condemned

177

By a separate vote. You, woman, my voice
Has sentenced to death. And this boy of yours
By my daughter's doomed. For it's mad indeed
To let slip through your fingers inveterate foes   520
When by wiping them out
   You can free your home from its nightmare.

Andromache

ANTISTROPHE

Husband, husband, if you could stand
Here in front of us, spear in hand,
   Son of Priam, to help us.   525

Son

   Dark day! Where's there a song to sing
   Likely to charm away this thing?

Andromache

   Plead with him, kneel at his knees and pray,
   Son, for sympathy.

Son

          Dearest lord,   530
   Don't destroy me! Oh let me go!

Andromache

   Only look at my tear-stained face.
   How I weep, like a marble-cupped
   Flowing spring in a sunless place!

Son

   Poor me! Where is an opening now   535
      Out of trouble? Oh tell me how!

Menelaus

   Why snivel to me? I'm hard as a rock.
   You might as well make your appeal to the sea.
   I've a helping hand for kith and kin,
   But I'm wasting no favors, boy, on you.   540
   When I think of the years of life I lost

To capture Troy and that mother of yours—!
She made your fate;
   You can pay for it six feet under.

Chorus

But look at this: old Peleus approaching   **545**
As hurriedly as ancient limbs can bring him.

         (*Enter Peleus, assisted by a servant.*)

Peleus

I'd like to know, from you above all, head-butcher,
What's going on here? What's this? And why's the
    house
Become a chaos, through your lawless dealing?
Menelaus, stop. Enough felonious haste.   **550**
(Get me there quicker, fellow. Now's no time
For hanging back, it appears. Rejuvenation,
It's now I could do with a touch of you—now or never.)
First I'd like to put a bit of wind
In this poor woman's sails. By what right   **555**
Have these men strapped your hands and pushed you off,
You and the boy? Poor sheep, poor little lamb
Bound for the slaughter. All of us away!

Andromache

These, old father, are dragging me and the baby
To our grave, as you can see. What's there to tell?   **560**
I sent for you, though, begging desperately
Not only once but time and time again.
Surely you must have heard of the ill-feeling
His daughter roused in the house—that murderous
    woman!
And now from the Altar of Thetis, mother of   **565**
Your noble son, your own soul's adoration,
They've torn me away by force, without a trial;
Condemned me without waiting for those absent.
For knowing the baby and I were here alone
(Poor blameless innocent) they planned our murder.   **570**
Now I beg of you, father, crumpled here

Before your knees—for I can't get a finger free
To touch your beloved cheek in supplication—
For god's sake extricate me. Else I die—   575
Not only to my pain but your discredit.

Peleus

Loosen these knots or someone smarts for it!
Free the poor woman's cramped-together hands.

Menelaus

I've as much to say as you—in fact I've more
As far as she's concerned—and I forbid it.   580

Peleus

And by what right? You're master in my house,
Not content with lording it over Spartans?

Menelaus

She was my catch. I brought her back from Troy.

Peleus

Full rights to her passed over to my grandson.

Menelaus

Hasn't he a right to my things? I to his?   585

Peleus

To care for, not to abuse. And not to slaughter.

Menelaus

This woman, at any rate, I'll not return.

Peleus

Suppose I break your head in with this scepter?

Menelaus

Just touch me and you'll see! Only come near me!

Peleus

You call yourself a man, foul-blooded creature?   590
May I ask where you're worthy of that name?

You, who lost your own wife to a Phrygian
For leaving the house unlocked and unattended,
As if you had a decent wife indeed
Instead of the world's worst. No Spartan girl   595
Could ever live clean even if she wanted.
They're always out on the street in scanty outfits,
Making a great display of naked limbs.
In those they race and wrestle with the boys too—
Abominable's the word. It's little wonder   600
Sparta is hardly famous for chaste women.
Ask Helen—she should know. She went gallivanting
Out of her house, pooh-poohing family ties
And skipped the country with a lusty buck.
For such a slut you raised the Greek divisions   605
And led those many thousands against Troy?
You shouldn't have lifted a spear. Just sat and spat once
In her direction, when you knew her nature,
And let her stay away; paid to keep her there!
Not you, though. Such a thought never crossed your
          mind.   610
Instead, you squandered thousands of sweet souls,
Left poor old women childless in their houses,
Left grey-haired fathers weeping their strong sons.
I'm one of those bereaved ones. Bloody murderer!
I hold you accountable for Achilles' death!   615
Oh, you returned from Troy without a mark on,
All your pretty armor and regalia
Immaculate as on the day you left!
I warned my grandson, when he courted, never
To marry kin of yours, nor share his home with   620
A filthy woman's litter. They're contagious
With blotches of the mother. (Oh, be careful,
Suitors, to marry a good woman's child!)
Not to speak of your shameless conduct with your
          brother,
Bidding the fat-head butcher his poor girl!—   625
You, in a panic for your ladylove!
And capturing Troy—I'm on your traces, eh?—

You laid your hands on the woman and didn't kill her.
But casting sheep's eyes on her bosom, you
Unbuckled your sword and puckered up for kisses,   630
Petting that traitorous bitch, you toady of lust!
Then, coming to my grandson's in his absence
You loot his home, commit attempted murder
Atrociously on a poor mother and son
Who'll make you and your daughter rue this day,   635
Born bastard though he is. For don't forget
That poor land often outproduces rich,
And bastards get the upper hand of blue bloods.
Now get your daughter out of here. It's better
To make a poor but honest match than land a   640
No-good wealthy father-in-law. Like you.

Chorus

Out of some little thing, too free a tongue
Can make an outrageous wrangle. Really politic
Men are careful not to embroil their friends.

Menelaus

Well! hearing this, why say the old have sense,   645
Or those the Greeks regarded once as sages?
When you, the famous Peleus, so well born,
And kin to us by marriage, rave away
And blacken us, all for an alien woman.
One that you ought to whip beyond the Nile   650
And beyond the Phasis, crying on me to do so,
Seeing she comes from Asia, where so many
Of the valiant men from Hellas fell and moldered.
Your own son's blood, as well as others', on her.
For Paris, the one that killed your boy Achilles,   655
Was brother to Hector, and she's Hector's wife.
Yet you can bear to enter the same doorway,
Can bring yourself to eat at the same table;
Even let her beget her venomous offspring.
I, looking out for you as well as me,   660

Planned her removal, and you snatch her from me.
Listen (a bit of logic's not amiss):
Suppose my daughter barren, her a spawner,
You'd make her children rulers of this country,
This sacred Phthia? Men of foreign blood   665
Would order Greeks about? You think I'm foolish
Because I hold right's right? And you're the shrewd one?
Another thing: Let's just suppose your daughter
Married some citizen and got such treatment,
You'd sit back mum? I doubt it. Yet for a foreigner   670
You're yelping at your relatives by marriage?
When cheated, wife or husband feels the same.
She doesn't like it. He doesn't like it either,
Finding a frivolous woman in the house.
Yet he can mend things with his good right arm;   675
She has to count on friends' or parents' aid.
What's wrong then in my helping out my own?
You're in your doting days! My generalship,
Which you bring up, is evidence in my favor.
Poor Helen had a time of it, not choosing   680
But chosen by the gods to exalt her country.
For innocent before of arms and battles
Greece grew to manhood then. Experience, travel—
These are an education in themselves.
If coming in the presence of my wife   685
I steeled myself and spared her, I was wise.
(I always deplored, by the way, your killing your
      brother.)
Well, there's my speech, wise, moderate, not irascible.
If you fly off the handle, a sore throat's
The most you'll get. I find discretion pays.   690

Chorus

Both of you stop these mad recriminations.
It's the only thing. Before you go too far.

Peleus

Too bad the custom here is topsy-turvy.

When the public sets a war memorial up
Do those who really sweated get the credit?   695
Oh no! Some general wangles the prestige!—
Who, brandishing his one spear among thousands,
Did one man's work, but gets a world of praise.
Those self-important fathers of their country
Think they're above the people. Why they're nothing!   700
The citizen is infinitely wiser,
Gifted with nerve and purpose, anyway.
You were strutters at Troy, you and your brother,
Basking lazily in your high command
And sleek and fat on many another's anguish.   705
I'll show you, though, that Paris, Ida's Paris,
Was a less furious enemy than I am,
Unless you leave this house—my curse upon you!—
You and your childless daughter, that my grandson,
If he's of my blood indeed, will haul by the hair.   710
So the barren creature won't let other women
Have any children until she herself does!
Just because she's a useless reproducer
She means to keep the rest of us from families?
Get back from that woman, slaves. I'd like to see   715
If anyone interferes while I untie her.
Come, straighten up. Although I'm all atremble
I'll unloosen these tightly tangled cords.
You blackguard, look at her mutilated hands!
What did you think you were roping? Bulls? Or lions?   720
You were frightened she'd draw some weapon out and
        rout you?
Come over here, little boy; scoot under my arms;
Help work your mother loose. I'll bring you up
In Phthia to be a nightmare to these Spartans.
They're touted for cold steel and the hour of battle,   725
We're told. For the rest, a thoroughly inferior breed!

Chorus
    Oftener than not the old are uncontrollable;
    Their tempers make them difficult to deal with.

Menelaus

It's clear your inclination is toward slander.
However, I'll not resort to force in Phthia.   730
That vulgar sort of thing is quite beneath me.
For now, though—I've just remembered I'm pressed for
    time—
I must be leaving. There's a—there's a town
Near Sparta, in fact—it used to be quite friendly,
But now makes threatening moves. I'll take steps,   735
And with a little campaigning tranquilize it.
That matter settled to my satisfaction,
I'm coming back. With my son-in-law, man to man,
I'll have a friendly little confabulation.
If he keeps this woman in check, and from now on   740
Behaves as he should, he'll get as good from us.
If he's looking for trouble, trouble's what he'll get.
My meaning's clear: he'll reap just as he sows.
For all your blather I don't care a hoot.
Shrill as you are, you're a feeble shadow in front of me.   745
All you can ever do is talk, talk, talk.

(Exit Menelaus.)

Peleus

Go ahead, little boy, here shivering under my arms.
And you, poor woman. You've had a bad voyage, both.
But now at last you've found a quiet haven.

Andromache

O reverence, god be good to you and yours   750
For saving the baby and me in our affliction.
Be careful, though, that on some lonely road
They don't waylay us all and kidnap me,
Seeing you not so young as once, me helpless,
The boy so very little. Be on guard   755
Or, slipping free for now, we'll be seized later.

Peleus

Let's have no womanish tremors any more.
Proceed. Who dares to bother you? He'll be sorry

185

If he does. For under the gods (and not without
A numerous horse and foot) I'm lord of Phthia.   760
I'm still on my toes and not so old as you think.
If I so much as look hard at that fellow
He'll turn and bolt, along in years as I am.
Stout-hearted oldsters can handle the young all right.
What good are showy muscles to a coward?   765

(*Exeunt Andromache and son; Peleus.*)

Chorus

STROPHE

Best never born, if not of an affluent house,
Of fathers known to fame, with resources to match,
   Then if some appalling disaster befalls, there's   770
    Always a way for the rich.
  For those who are known to be born aristocrats,
Praise and reverence: time can never obscure the estate
   Good men bequeath: their glory (a torch on the tomb)   775
    Has no terminal date.

ANTISTROPHE

Far better not bring home a disgraceful success
Than knock awry all law with a mischievous thrust.   780
   Today's victory flatters the palate of mortals—
    Yes, but tomorrow it must
  Sour, sicken, and turn to an old deep-grown reproach.
This I always have held, to this manner of life I aspire: 785
   May no unjust sway flourish in family affairs
    Or in seat of empire.

EPODE

  White-headed Peleus, I
  Credit that tale: how at the Lapithae wedding   790
    You with the tough centaurs fought
A spectacular fight! Then on the good ship Argo rounded
    the grim cape
  Far beyond those Rolling Rocks few craft escape—
    What voyage more storied than yours?   795
   Next you adventured with Heracles to Troy,

Where he, of the true stock of Zeus, hung garlands of
carnage.

> Your fame fast bound to Heracles',   800
> You returned to the Greek seas.

(Enter Nurse.)

Nurse

O my dear women, what a day we've had!
Sorrow crowding on sorrow is our portion.
The queen in the house there, poor Hermione
Left in the lurch by her father, and knowing now   805
What a heinous thing it was to attempt the murder
Of Andromache and the youngster, wants to die—
Afraid of her husband, afraid she'll be ordered out
Of the house for what she did (think of the scandal!)
Or killed for threatening lives not hers to take.   810
Her bodyguard barely managed to restrain her
From knotting the rope on her neck, then barely
managed
To wrestle the sword from her hand in the nick of time.
It's clear to her now she acted badly, badly;
She's all remorse. And I—I'm quite exhausted   815
Keeping the queen from hanging herself, ladies.
Won't all of you please go into the palace now
And plead with her not to destroy herself? New faces
Have more authority than accustomed ones.

Chorus

Indeed the clamor of servants in the house   820
Substantiates your story. It's unlikely,
Poor thing, she'd keep from seizures of remorse,
Having done the things she did. Look, wild for death,
She's broken from her home and her attendants.

(Enter Hermione.)

Hermione

STROPHE

I'll tear out my hair by the roots; these nails   825
Will furrow my skin!

Nurse

What are you seeking, child? Your beauty's ruin?

Hermione

ANTISTROPHE

Torn from my curls, away, lace veil!   830
Where the wind blows, go!

Nurse

Cover your breast, my darling; pin your garments.

Hermione

STROPHE

If I am bare,
What difference here?
Uncovered, exposed, oh terribly clear
What I plotted against my husband.   835

Nurse

The attempt to kill the other woman rankles?

Hermione

ANTISTROPHE

Now I weep
What I ventured then.
Abominable
In the eyes of men!

Nurse

It's true you went too far. But he'll forgive you.   840

Hermione

Why did you pry the
Sword from my fingers?
Give it back, dear friend. My final hope
Is to strike true once. And why hide the rope?

Nurse

What if I let you die in such distraction?   845

Hermione

    Alas my fate!
    No flames around?
    No rock I can scale
    To plunge in the sea? Or on forest ground?
    Let the gods of the dead receive me.   850

Nurse

  Why carry on so? Divine visitations
  Come to all of us, all of us, late or soon.

Hermione

    Father, you left me derelict here
    Alone by the surf; and no ship near.   855
    It kills me; it kills me: I'll not come
    Ever again to the bridal room!
    Should I supplicate? What shrine's for me?
    Should I fall like a slave at a slave's knee?   860
  What I'd like to be
  Is a black wing leaving the Phthian shore
  Or that skiff of fir
  The earliest oar
    Drove to the end of the ocean.   865

Nurse

  Darling, I disapproved of your excesses
  When you were in the wrong against the Trojan,
  And I disapprove of this irrational panic.
  Your husband won't repudiate your marriage
  Like this, on the mere complaint of a foreigner.   870
  It wasn't you he picked up as a prize
  In Troy—a good man's your father, you had dowry
  In plenty, and your city's influential
  Far more than most. Your father's not forsaken you
  As you seem to fear; he'll see you're not rejected.   875
  Now please go in; don't make a scene in front
  Of the house. It only hurts your reputation
  If people see you here outside the palace.

Chorus

    Look! Look at this man with the foreign air
    Making so hastily in our direction!   880

                                (*Enter Orestes.*)

Orestes

    Dear ladies, strangers: is this indeed the home
    Of Achilles' son? the royal home and palace?

Chorus

    It is. If you care to favor us with your name—?

Orestes

    I'm the son of Agamemnon and Clytemnestra;
    My name's Orestes. And I'm on my way   885
    To the oracle at Dodona. Since I'm here
    In Phthia, I thought I'd inquire about my cousin,
    If she's alive and well, enjoying prosperity—
    Hermione from Sparta. For although
    She's living far away, she's in our thoughts.   890

Hermione

    A port in a storm indeed to this sad sailor,
    O Agamemnon's son! Here at your feet
    I beg of you, pity the object of your care,
    Doing anything but well. My arms, as urgent
    As any garlands are, circle your knees.   895

Orestes

    Well!
    What's this? Am I seeing things, or do I really
    Behold Menelaus' child, who should be queen here?

Hermione

    Menelaus' child. The only one that Helen
    Bore to my father there. Why shouldn't you know?

Orestes

    Savior Apollo, from all this deliver us!   900
    Whatever's the matter? Who's back of this, god or
        mortal?

Hermione

    It's partly my fault. Partly too my husband's.
    Partly some god's. But chaos everywhere.

Orestes

    You have no children—so no trouble that way.
    What else goes wrong for a woman—except her marriage?   905

Hermione

    What else indeed? You've put your finger on it.

Orestes

    You mean your husband loves another woman?

Hermione

    He's sleeping with Hector's wife, that battle trophy.

Orestes

    One man; two loves. No good ever comes of that.

Hermione

    That's how it was. I acted in self-defense.   910

Orestes

    Scheming against your rival, as women do?

Hermione

    I wanted to see her dead. Her and her bastard!

Orestes

    Did you see it through? Or did something interfere?

Hermione

    Yes—Peleus, with his reverence for riffraff.

Orestes

    This deed of blood—was anyone in it with you?   915

Hermione

    My father. He came all the way from Sparta.

Orestes
    And got the worst of it from the old man?

Hermione
    Let's say he respected age. At least, he's left me.

Orestes
    I see. And you've good cause to fear your husband.

Hermione
    Naturally. He's within his rights to kill me.   920
    What's there to say? So I beg, by the God of Kindred,
    Take me out of this land, as far as possible
    Or at least to my father's home. The very walls here
    Seem to be howling at me: go! go! go!
    All Phthia hates me. If my husband comes   925
    Home from Apollo's oracle while I'm here
    He'll kill me on foul charges. Or I'll be a slave
    In the bastard-blooming chambers I was queen of.
    "How did you fall so low?" someone may marvel.
    Visits of poisonous women were my downfall.   930
    They made me lose my head by talk like this:
    "So you let that wretched captive, a slave in the house,
    Have rights to your husband, share and share alike?
    If she, in my home, meddled with my marriage
    I swear by Hera that act would be her last!"   935
    And I, attentive to the siren music
    Of these sly, these lewd, these babbling know-it-alls,
    Swelled up like a great fool. Oh why, oh why
    Did I spy on my husband, having all I wanted?
    Money more than enough. Control of the household.   940
    The children I'd have had fully legitimate,
    Hers illegitimate, half slaves to mine.
    Oh, never, never—I can't say this too often—
    Should a man with any sense, having taken a wife,
    Let other women come and buzz around her.   945
    What are they all but teachers of delinquency?
    For one can make a profit by corrupting her;
    Another has fallen and likes company;

Many love to make trouble—this is why
Our homes are a sink of evil. Against this
Double-lock your doors and bolt them too.   950
For not one wholesome thing has ever come
From gadabout female callers—only grief.

Chorus

Your tongue's a little free with your own sex.
It's understandable now. But women should   955
Paint womanly vices in more flattering colors.

Orestes

A piece of wise advice (whoever gave it):
In disputations, listen to both sides.
I was fully aware of the uproar in this house,
The struggle between you and Hector's widow,   960
And watched and waited to see if you thought it best
To remain here still, or if the attempted killing
Of the slave had terrified you into fleeing.
I came, though you didn't appeal to me by letter,
On the chance of talking together, as we do,   965
Then seeing you safely away. Though mine by right,
You're living with this man—your father's mischief!
He gave your hand to me before invading
Troy, and then peddled you to your present lord
On condition he be of use in destroying the city.   970
When the son of Achilles returned home
(For I overlooked your father's part) I begged him
To give this marriage up, pleading my fortunes
And the evil genius over me—and considering
It wouldn't be easy to marry outside the family   975
When one had reasons for exile such as I had.
He was highly insulting about my mother's death
And hooted over the scarlet-clotted goblins.
Abject, in view of that family situation,
I was in agony, agony, but I bore it   980
And went away halfheartedly without you.
But now, however, since your luck is changing,

Since you're at this impasse, without resources,
I'll take you away and restore you to your father.
Blood's thicker than water, and when one's in trouble   985
Best to seek out a relative's open arms.

Hermione

About my marriage it's not for me to decide.
The whole affair is in my father's hands.
But help me away from here as quickly as possible.
My husband might come sooner than we think   990
And murder me, or old Peleus might get wind of
My escape and order the horsemen after me.

Orestes

The old man's no threat; forget him. And never fear
Achilles' son again—seeing how he scorned me.
It happens there's a death-trap set for him,   995
A noose I can't imagine a way out of,
And all of my contriving. I've said enough now—
But when it springs, the Delphian rock will know.
So he called me mother-killer? Well, I'll teach him,
If my allies at Delphi keep their word,   1000
To take in marriage women mine by right!
Black hour for him when he asked Apollo to pay
For killing his father! No last-minute repentance
Will keep the god from exacting punishment.
At Apollo's hand (my imputations helping)   1005
He'll die—I wouldn't say nicely. And taste my hate!
Let reprobates expect nothing but havoc
From heaven above: god stamps on arrogance.

(*Exeunt Orestes, Hermione, Nurse.*)

Chorus

STROPHE

Apollo, who made Ilium's hill and its strong walls
     heaven-high,
Poseidon, with stallions of rain-grey flashing by   1010
     Over the moors of the sea,
     Out of fury you doomed that town—why?

Child of your art as it was—for 1015
Ares to wreck, who delights in the spear-hand.
   Ruined! Oh, ruined! You
Ruined your betrayed land?

ANTISTROPHE

How many war-cars marshalled on the sand-packed
   riverside,
Proud horses before them! And oh how many men 1020
    Penned in inglorious strife!
And the monarchs of Troy elate then
With their fathers are tombed in dark earth.
Nor on the altars of Troy any fire cries
   "Praise to the bright gods!" and no 1025
Stirring clouds of myrrh rise.

STROPHE

And Agamemnon's dead by the stroke of his wife;
She too, in the grim-faced round of a death for a death
   At her children's own hand.
The god, the god shaped her name with fatal breath, 1030
Dreaming futurity: her son from Argos marched home,
Agamemnon's in blood, and strode to the inner recess—
   Killed his own dear mother there. 1035
   O Phoebus, divine one, how credit this?

ANTISTROPHE

And mothers, scores on scores, in the markets of Greece
Made stones re-echo shrill with lament for a son,
   Wives were torn from old homes
To serve a strange husband. Not on you alone 1040
Nor on friends of yours came such distressing heartache.
But all Hellas was sick to death, and a horror of blood
   Over Troy's gay-fruited fields 1045
Rolled like a storm pouring hell's bitter flood.

(Enter Peleus.)

Peleus

Women of Phthia, there's something I must know.

Tell me the truth. I've heard a vague report
That Menelaus' girl has left this house
And gone off who knows where. I've come in haste   1050
To learn the facts. For when our friends are absent
The ones at home should keep an eye on things.

Chorus

You've heard correctly, Peleus. It's not fitting
For me to hide reverses that I know of.
The queen's gone from the palace. She's in flight.   1055

Peleus

Afraid of what? Out with it, the whole story.

Chorus

Afraid of her husband and her possible exile.

Peleus

On account of her cutthroat tactics toward the boy?

Chorus

Exactly. And in terror too of the slave woman.

Peleus

She left here with her father? Or someone else?   1060

Chorus

Agamemnon's son escorted her away.

Peleus

With what design in mind? Meaning to marry her?

Chorus

Meaning that and worse than that: to kill your grandson.

Peleus

By treachery? Or in fair fight, man to man?

Chorus

At Apollo's holy shrine, with a pack of Delphians.   1065

Peleus

> There's danger in that, no question. Will someone go
> Quick as he can to the holy hall of Delphi
> And tell our good friends there what plot's afoot
> Before his enemies get to Achilles' son?

(Enter Messenger.)

Messenger

> Oh gloomy news!   1070
> I'm under a curse to bring the news I do
> To you, old father, and my master's friends.

Peleus

> Ah, my clairvoyant heart's all apprehension!

Messenger

> You have no grandson, Peleus—hear the worst.
> Swords cut him down, so many and so sharp,   1075
> In the hands of Delphians and that Mycenaean.

Chorus

> What's happening to you there, old man? Don't fall.
> Hold yourself up.

Peleus

>   My strength is gone. All's over.
> My voice is lost. My knees are weak as water.

Messenger

> If you meditate revenge for those you loved,
> Don't let yourself collapse. But hear what happened.   1080

Peleus

> O destiny, at the extreme verge of life
> You've brought to bay a pitiful old man!
> But tell me how he perished, the one son
> Of my one son. I'll hear what no man should.

Messenger

> When we arrived in Apollo's famous territory   1085

197

We spent three entire days, from dawn to dark,
Filling our eyes with all there was to see.
This aroused suspicion, apparently. For the citizens
Gathered in twos and threes, in little huddles.
The son of Agamemnon covered the town   1090
Breathing his slander into every ear:
"Notice that fellow there, who's spying on
Apollo's nooks of bullion, rich donations?
He's back again with the very thing in mind
He had before: to rifle the sanctuary."   1095
This was behind the angry rumor bruited
About the town. The directors and advisers
And other security officers, on their own,
Posted patrols among the colonnades.
But we, however, innocent of this,   1100
With sheep raised on the pastures of Parnassus
Took our places there before the altar,
Attended by our sponsors and the celebrants.
A spokesman put the question: "Now, young man,
What should we ask the god for? What's your mission?"   1105
And he: "I stand here ready to do penance
For my earlier sins against Apollo, charging
He should make payment for my father's death."
It was obvious then Orestes' word prevailed,
Branding my master a liar who really came   1110
Upon some foul design. Reaching the sanctuary
So he could pray to Apollo at the oracle,
We inspected, first, the omens of the fire.
It seems, though, that a heavily armed squad
Lay in ambush in the laurel—Clytemnestra's   1115
Son alone the brains behind this plot.
So my master faced the god and began to implore him,
When they, armed to the teeth, steel sharpened
       specially,
Lunged at him from behind—he wore no corselet.
But he wheeled around, not seriously hit,   1120
Whipped out his sword, snatched from beside the door
Some votive armor hanging on the pegs there,

Took a stance by the altar every inch a warrior!
In a ringing voice he challenged the Delphians:
"Why murder one who comes as a good pilgrim? 1125
And what's the accusation I should die for?"
Not one among so many spoke a word,
Only their hands moved, pelting him with rocks.
Battered on all sides by a hail so blinding,
He heaved with rigid arm his covering shield 1130
Here, there, and everywhere, to intercept them.
No use. For many weapons came at once:
Arrows and javelins and unfastened spits,
Meat-cleavers to kill bulls clanged at his feet.
Then you'd have seen a ghastly jig, as the boy 1135
Tried to outtwist them. Men were edging around him,
Pinning him there, not giving him time to breathe,
When he suddenly rushed from the sacrificial stone,
Leaping the leap that Troy knew to its cost,
And burst upon them. They, like little pigeons 1140
Spying a falcon near, convulsed and panicked.
Many fell in the tumult, some of wounds,
Some trampled by their fellows in jammed exits,
While in the holy place unholy shrieking
Thrilled against stone. A moment of respite then— 1145
He stood spectacular in steely splendor,
Till from some deep recess a voice arose
—So weird our very flesh crept—galvanizing
The rout to a show of valor. Achilles' son
Was toppled then, a sharp sword in his ribs 1150
Thrust by a Delphian, who may claim his death
Though abetted by plenty of others. As he slumped,
Who didn't run with cold steel or a boulder
To bruise or mutilate? His handsome body
All desecrated by the berserk blows! 1155
But he lay dead almost touching the altar, so
They dragged him from the frankincense and myrrh.
We hurried the corpse away quick as we could
And now convey him here for you to weep
And wail, poor, poor old man. And so inter. 1160

All this was done by one hailed as a prophet,
Mind you, distinguisher of right and wrong—
And done to a penitent, poor Achilles' boy.
The prophet brooded, like a spiteful man,
Over wrongs done long ago. That's "wisdom" for you?   1165

(*Exit Messenger.*)

Chorus

Oh, but look! the prince, on a litter there,
Brought slowly home from the Delphian land!
Poor stricken youth! And poor old man
Who must welcome the son of Achilles home
Not as you would if you had your wish.   1170
But you've stumbled yourself on a desperate hour,
One fate swamping the two of you.

(*The body of Neoptolemus is carried in by
his attendants.*)

Peleus

STROPHE

Misery! Oh what a horror to gaze upon!
Horror to gather it into my doorway!
This is the end for us, city of Thessaly,   1175
Finished and done for. Never a child again,
Never in this house.
How I'm destroyed by calamities lashing me!
Where's there a friend I can turn to for comforting?   1180
Fingers I loved so! These cheeks! And these lips!
Oh, if only your days had been numbered in Ilium
By the Simois, that far shore.

Chorus

He would have earned appropriate laurels then
In death, old man, and you been far, far luckier.   1185

Peleus

ANTISTROPHE

Marriage, O marriage, you ruined this house of mine!
All of this town you doomed to confusion!

My son, my son,
Oh, but if only that plague of your marriage, that
Home-wrecking, child-wrecking brood of Hermione   1190
Never had noosed you
Tight for the death-blow, child of my child—
Thunder and lightning ought to have blasted her!
Nor, for the archery death to your father, should
Charges of blood have been flung at Apollo,   1195
   Divine one, by a mere man.

Chorus

STROPHE

With a cry of despair I mourn for my lost lord!
   With those rites
   Due the dead I sing this.

Peleus

With a cry of despair I take my disconsolate turn,   1200
   An old man
   Weighted down, I weep, weep.

Chorus

God wanted this; god brought this thing about.

Peleus

   Dearest, you've
   Left all the house a great vacancy.   1205
You've left me alone, desolate and
Without a son, so late in life.

Chorus

Better you died, old man, before your children.

Peleus

   Why not wrench away my hair?
   Why not batter head and all   1210
With savage hands? O city, see!
   Of both my boys
   This Apollo robbed me!

201

Chorus

ANTISTROPHE

Luckless old man who saw and felt so much!
    From now on
What existence for you?   1215

Peleus

Not a child, not a friend—through unabating pain
    I'll somehow
Fumble toward my death-day.

Chorus

In marriage the gods loved you—all for this?

Peleus

    Flown away;
    Gone for good. Oh, how far
From those heavenly prospects they offered.   1220

Chorus

An empty haunter of an empty house.

Peleus

    City oh no longer mine!
    Scepter, shatter on the ground!
    And you, my Nereid, girl of purple grottoes,
        How utterly
    You behold my ruin.   1225

Chorus

    Look!
What's stirring around? What prodigy's here
I somehow sense? Look! Look over there!
A divinity, girls, on the shimmering air!
And floating this way over paddock and field
    Of Phthia, nearer and nearer.   1230

                    (Enter Thetis.)

Thetis

Because of our marriage, Peleus, long ago,

I journey here from Nereus' home—your Thetis.
First I urge you, in these present troubles,
Not to give way to any inordinate grief.
Even I, who never should have wept for children,   1235
Saw the one son I bore you, dear Achilles,
So fleet of foot—the pride of Greece!—lie dead.
Hark and approve while I reveal my mission:
First for the son of Achilles, cold in death here:
Take him to Delphi; where he fell inter him;
Let the Delphians read his stone and blush recalling   1240
The brutal death he met at Orestes' hand.
Next for the woman won in war, Andromache:
Fate designates, old man, her future in
Molossia, and a marriage there with Helenus.   1245
Her son goes too, the one survivor now
Of your father's line; it's destined his descendants,
King after king, at the summit of prosperity,
Will rule Molossia. Your race and mine
Is not to become extinct as now appears,   1250
Old man; no, neither is Troy's. For the gods keep
An eye on Troy, though passionate Pallas crushed it.
That you may laud our marriage to the skies,
I, a goddess born, a god my father,
Mean to release you from this human dolor   1255
And make you a divinity forever.
There in the house of Nereus, arm in arm,
Goddess with god, we'll live the future out.
And moving dry-shod over the foaming ocean
You'll see your son and mine, dearest Achilles,   1260
Lording it in his island home, on the shore
Of remote Leuké past the Hellespont.
Be off now to the sacred town of Delphi,
Escorting the corpse, and once he's under earth
Come to that grotto in the ancient reef   1265
Cuttlefish love; there take your ease until
I soar from the sea with Nereus' fifty daughters
To choir you home. What fate determines, now
Yours to effect. Great Zeus has spoken so.

And no more lamentation for the fallen.   1270
For every mother's son the gods have posted
A great assessment only death can pay.

Peleus

O royalest of companions, O my queen,
Most welcome, girl of Nereus! All these matters
You've disposed both to your glory and the children's.   1275
Farewell to sorrow at your bidding, goddess.
I'll bury this boy and hurry to Pelion's gorges
Where first I pressed your beauty in these arms.
Did I not say one ought to marry true-hearts   1280
And into honest homes, if one's for virtue?
And never yearn for dishonorable matches
Though there's a world of dowry for the having?
That way the gods are at your side forever.

(*Exit Peleus.*)

Chorus

Past our telling, the ways of heaven.
The gods accomplish the unforeseen.   1285
What all awaited, fails of achievement;
God arranges what none could dream.
   So in the course of our story.

THE TROJAN WOMEN

Translated and with an Introduction by

RICHMOND LATTIMORE

INTRODUCTION TO
THE TROJAN WOMEN

In Aelian's *Varia historica* (ii. 8), written about the begin-
ning of the third century A.D., we find the following notice:
"In [the first year of] the ninety-first Olympiad [415 B.C.]
. . . Xenocles and Euripides competed against each other.
Xenocles, whoever he may have been, won the first prize with
Oedipus, Lycaon, Bacchae, and *Athamas* (a satyr-play). Eu-
ripides was second with *Alexander, Palamedes, The Trojan
Women,* and *Sisyphus* (a satyr-play)."

Athens was nominally at peace when Euripides composed
this set of tragedies, of which only *The Trojan Women* is extant; but Athens had only a few years earlier emerged from an
indecisive ten years' war with Sparta and her allies and was in
the spring of 415 weeks away from launching the great Sicilian
Expedition, which touched off the next war or, more accu-
rately, the next phase of the same war. This was to end in
404 B.C. with the capitulation of Athens.

During the earlier years of the war Euripides wrote a number of "patriotic" plays and may have believed or tried to
force himself to believe in the rightness of the Periclean cause
and the wickedness of the enemy. By 415 he had reason to
conclude that, at least in the treatment of captives, neither
side was better than the other. A group of Thebans, working
with Plataean traitors, tried to seize Plataea, failed, surrendered in the belief that their lives would be spared, and
were executed (Thuc. ii. 1-6). Four years later, when Plataea
surrendered to the Lacedaemonians and Thebans, the entire

garrison was put to death, the women were sold as slaves, and the city itself systematically destroyed (Thuc. iii. 68). About the same time the Athenians suppressed a revolt by the people of Mytilene and other cities of Lesbos. They voted to kill all grown men and enslave the women and children but then thought better of it, rescinded the order just in time, and ended by putting to death *only* rather more than a thousand men (Thuc. iii. 50). In 421 the Athenians recaptured Scione, which had revolted, put all grown men to death, and enslaved the women and children (Thuc. v. 32). In 417 the Lacedaemonians seized a small town called Hysiae and killed all free persons whom they caught (Thuc. v. 83). The neutral island city of Melos was invited, in peacetime, to join the Athenian alliance, refused, was besieged in force, and capitulated. The Athenians put all grown males to death and enslaved the women and children (Thuc. v. 116). This was in the winter of 416-415, a few months before *The Trojan Women* was presented. That same winter, the Athenians decided to conquer Sicily (Thuc. vi. 1). This expedition was, like that against Melos, unprovoked; unlike the Melian aggression, it was foolhardy, at least obviously very dangerous. It ended in disaster, and Athens never completely recovered.

The Sicilian venture had been voted and was in preparation when Euripides presented his trilogy, which, in the manner of Aeschylus, dealt with three successive episodes in the story of Troy, complemented with a burlesque of satyrs on a kindred theme. The first play is the story of Paris (Alexander), how it was foretold at his birth that he must destroy his own city, how the baby was left to die in the mountains, miraculously rescued (as such babies invariably are), and at last recognized and restored. The hero of the second story is Palamedes, the wisest and most inventive of the Achaeans at Troy, more truly wise than Odysseus, who therefore hated him and treacherously contrived his condemnation and death. While the third tragedy, our play, ends with the destruction of Troy, the prologue looks into the future, beyond the end of the action, where the conquerors are to be wrecked on the home voyage because they have abused their conquest and turned the gods against them.[1] The plot of *Sisyphus* is not known, but the Athenian poets were partial to the scandalous story that Sisyphus, a notorious liar and cheat, seduced Anticlea and was therefore the true father of Odysseus. This story is post-Homeric, as is most of the matter of the whole trilogy (Homer does not mention Palamedes, shows no knowledge of the exposure of Paris, makes Poseidon the enemy not the protector of Troy, etc.); it would go well with the fact that Odysseus, here seen as the unscrupulous politician, is the open villain of *Palamedes* and the villain-behind-the-scenes of *The Trojan Women*.

The effect of current events and policies on *The Trojan Women* is, I think, so obvious that it scarcely needs further elaboration, but I do not believe in the view that the play, loose as it is, is nothing but an outburst, a denunciation of aggressive war and imperialism. The general shapelessness is perhaps permitted partly because the play was one member of a trilogy; no piece which stood by itself could pass with so little dramatic action and such a nihilistic conclusion. The play-long presence of Hecuba on the stage necessitates padding, which is supplied by elaborate rhetorical debates between Hecuba and Cassandra, and Hecuba and Andromache. Out-of-character generalizations bespeak the inspirations of Euripides rather than of his dramatis personae. The trial scene of Helen is a bitter little comedy-within-tragedy, but its juridical refinements defeat themselves and turn preposterous, halting for a time the emotional force of the play. In candor, one can hardly call *The Trojan Women* a good piece of work, but it seems nevertheless to be a great tragedy.

1. Not only is the parallel of Troy with Melos painfully close, but, with an armada about to set forth, nothing could have been worse-omened than this dramatic prediction of a great fleet wrecked at sea. Aelian seems outraged that Euripides came second to Xenocles; I can hardly understand how the Athenians let him present this play at all.

CHARACTERS

Poseidon
Athene
Hecuba
Talthybius
Cassandra
Andromache
Astyanax
Menelaus
Helen
Chorus of Trojan women

THE TROJAN WOMEN

SCENE: *The action takes place shortly after the capture of Troy. All Trojan men have been killed, or have fled; all women and children are captives. The scene is an open space before the city, which is visible in the background, partly demolished and smoldering. Against the walls are tents, or huts, which temporarily house the captive women. The entrance of the Chorus is made, in two separate groups which subsequently unite, from these buildings, as are those of Cassandra and Helen. The entrances of Talthybius, Andromache, and Menelaus are made from the wings. It is imaginable that the gods are made to appear high up, above the level of the other actors, as if near their own temples on the Citadel. As the play opens, Hecuba is prostrate on the ground (it is understood that she hears nothing of what the gods say).*

(*Enter Poseidon.*)

Poseidon

I am Poseidon. I come from the Aegean depths
of the sea beneath whose waters Nereid choirs evolve
the intricate bright circle of their dancing feet.
For since that day when Phoebus Apollo and I laid down
on Trojan soil the close of these stone walls, drawn true   5
and straight, there has always been affection in my heart
unfading, for these Phrygians and for their city;
which smolders now, fallen before the Argive spears,
ruined, sacked, gutted. Such is Athene's work, and his,

the Parnassian, Epeius of Phocis, architect   10
and builder of the horse that swarmed with inward steel,
that fatal bulk which passed within the battlements,
whose fame hereafter shall be loud among men unborn,
the Wooden Horse, which hid the secret spears within.
Now the gods' groves are desolate, their thrones of power   15
blood-spattered where beside the lift of the altar steps
of Zeus Defender, Priam was cut down and died.
The ships of the Achaeans load with spoils of Troy
now, the piled gold of Phrygia. And the men of Greece
who made this expedition and took the city, stay   20
only for the favoring stern-wind now to greet their wives
and children after ten years' harvest wasted here.

The will of Argive Hera and Athene won
its way against my will. Between them they broke Troy.
So I must leave my altars and great Ilium,   25
since once a city sinks into sad desolation
the gods' state sickens also, and their worship fades.
Scamander's valley echoes to the wail of slaves,
the captive women given to their masters now,
some to Arcadia or the men of Thessaly   30
assigned, or to the lords of Athens, Theseus' strain;
while all the women of Troy yet unassigned are here
beneath the shelter of these walls, chosen to wait
the will of princes, and among them Tyndareus' child
Helen of Sparta, named—with right—a captive slave.   35

Nearby, beside the gates, for any to look upon
who has the heart, she lies face upward, Hecuba
weeping for multitudes her multitude of tears.
Polyxena, one daughter, even now was killed
in secrecy and pain beside Achilles' tomb.   40
Priam is gone, their children dead; one girl is left,
Cassandra, reeling crazed at King Apollo's stroke,
whom Agamemnon, in despite of the gods' will
and all religion, will lead by force to his secret bed.

O city, long ago a happy place, good-bye;   45
good-bye, hewn bastions. Pallas, child of Zeus, did this.
But for her hatred, you might stand strong-founded still.

(*Athene enters.*)

Athene

August among the gods, O vast divinity,
closest in kinship to the father of all, may one
who quarreled with you in the past make peace, and
    speak?   50

Poseidon

You may, lady Athene; for the strands of kinship
close drawn work no weak magic to enchant the mind.

Athene

I thank you for your gentleness, and bring you now
questions whose issue touches you and me, my lord.

Poseidon

Is this the annunciation of some new word spoken   55
by Zeus, or any other of the divinities?

Athene

No; but for Troy's sake, on whose ground we stand, I
    come
to win the favor of your power, and an ally.

Poseidon

You hated Troy once; did you throw your hate away
and change to pity now its walls are black with fire?   60

Athene

Come back to the question. Will you take counsel with **me**
and help me gladly in all that I would bring to pass?

Poseidon

I will indeed; but tell me what you wish to do.
Are you here for the Achaeans' or the Phrygians' sake?

Athene
> For the Trojans, whom I hated this short time since,   65
> to make the Achaeans' homecoming a thing of sorrow.

Poseidon
> This is a springing change of sympathy. Why must
> you hate too hard, and love too hard, your loves and
>   hates?

Athene
> Did you not know they outraged my temple, and
>   shamed me?

Poseidon
> I know that Ajax dragged Cassandra there by force.   70

Athene
> And the Achaeans did nothing. They did not even speak.

Poseidon
> Yet Ilium was taken by your strength alone.

Athene
> True; therefore help me. I would do some evil to them.

Poseidon
> I am ready for anything you ask. What will you do?

Athene
> Make the home voyage a most unhappy coming home.   75

Poseidon
> While they stay here ashore, or out on the deep sea?

Athene
> When they take ship from Ilium and set sail for home
> Zeus will shower down his rainstorms and the weariless
>   beat
> of hail, to make black the bright air with roaring winds.
> He has promised my hand the gift of the blazing
>   thunderbolt   80

214

to dash and overwhelm with fire the Achaean ships.
Yours is your own domain, the Aegaean crossing. Make
the sea thunder to the tripled wave and spinning surf,
cram thick the hollow Euboean fold with floating dead;
so after this Greeks may learn how to use with fear   85
my sacred places, and respect all gods beside.

Poseidon

This shall be done, and joyfully. It needs no long
discourse to tell you. I will shake the Aegaean Sea.
Myconos' nesses and the swine-back reefs of Delos,
the Capherean promontories, Scyros, Lemnos   90
shall take the washed up bodies of men drowned at sea.
Back to Olympus now, gather the thunderbolts
from your father's hands, then take your watcher's post,
    to wait
the chance, when the Achaean fleet puts out to sea.

That mortal who sacks fallen cities is a fool,   95
who gives the temples and the tombs, the hallowed places
of the dead to desolation. His own turn must come.

> (*The gods leave the stage. Hecuba seems to
> waken, and gets slowly to her
> feet as she speaks.*)

Hecuba

Rise, stricken head, from the dust;
lift up the throat. This is Troy, but Troy
and we, Troy's kings, are perished.   100
Stoop to the changing fortune.
Steer for the crossing and the death-god,
hold not life's prow on the course against
wave beat and accident.
Ah me,   105
what need I further for tears' occasion,
state perished, my sons, and my husband?
O massive pride that my fathers heaped
to magnificence, you meant nothing.
Must I be hushed? Were it better thus?   110

Should I cry a lament?
Unhappy, accursed,
limbs cramped, I lie
backed on earth's stiff bed.
O head, O temples   115
and sides; sweet, to shift,
let the tired spine rest
weight eased by the sides alternate,
against the strain of the tears' song
where the stricken people find music yet   120
in the song undanced of their wretchedness.

You ships' prows, that the fugitive
oars swept back to blessed Ilium
over the sea's blue water
by the placid harbors of Hellas   125
to the flute's grim beat
and the swing of the shrill boat whistles;
you made the crossing, made fast ashore
the Egyptians' skill, the sea cables,
alas, by the coasts of Troy;   130
it was you, ships, that carried the fatal bride
of Menelaus, Castor her brother's shame,
the stain on the Eurotas.
Now she has killed
the sire of the fifty sons,   135
Priam; me, unhappy Hecuba,
she drove on this reef of ruin.

Such state I keep
to sit by the tents of Agamemnon.
I am led captive   140
from my house, an old, unhappy woman,
like my city ruined and pitiful.
Come then, sad wives of the Trojans
whose spears were bronze,
their daughters, brides of disaster,
let us mourn the smoke of Ilium.   145

And I, as among winged birds
the mother, lead out
the clashing cry, the song; not that song
wherein once long ago,
when I held the scepter of Priam,   150
my feet were queens of the choir and led
the proud dance to the gods of Phrygia.

(*The First Half-chorus comes out of the shelter
at the back.*)

First Half-chorus
Hecuba, what are these cries?
What news now? For through the walls
I heard your pitiful weeping.   155
and fear shivered in the breasts
of the Trojan women, who within
sob out the day of their slavery.

Hecuba
My children, the ships of the Argives
will move today. The hand is at the oar.   160

First Half-chorus
They will? Why? Must I take ship
so soon from the land of my fathers?

Hecuba
I know nothing. I look for disaster.

First Half-chorus
Alas!
Poor women of Troy, torn from your homes,   165
bent to forced hard work.
The Argives push for home.

Hecuba
Oh,
let her not come forth,
not now, my child
Cassandra, driven delirious   170

217

to shame us before the Argives;
not the mad one, to bring fresh pain to my pain.
Ah no.
Troy, ill-starred Troy, this is the end;
your last sad people leave you now,   175
still alive, and broken.

*(The Second Half-chorus comes out of the shelter
at the back.)*

Second Half-chorus
Ah me. Shivering, I left the tents
of Agamemnon to listen.
Tell us, our queen. Did the Argive council
decree our death?
Or are the seamen manning the ships now,   180
oars ready for action?

Hecuba
My child, do not fear so. Lighten your heart.
But I go stunned with terror.

Second Half-chorus
Has a herald come from the Danaans yet?
Whose wretched slave shall I be ordained?   185

Hecuba
You are near the lot now.

Second Half-chorus
Alas!
Who will lead me away? An Argive?
To an island home? To Phthiotis?
Unhappy, surely, and far from Troy.

Hecuba
And I,   190
whose wretched slave
shall I be? Where, in my gray age,
a faint drone,

poor image of a corpse,
weak shining among dead men? Shall
I stand and keep guard at their doors,
shall I nurse their children, I who in Troy   195
held state as a princess?

(*The two half-choruses now unite to form a*
single Chorus.)

Chorus

So pitiful, so pitiful
your shame and your lamentation.
No longer shall I move the shifting pace
of the shuttle at the looms of Ida.   200
I shall look no more on the bodies of my sons.
No more. Shall I be a drudge besides
or be forced to the bed of Greek masters?
Night is a queen, but I curse her.
Must I draw the water of Pirene,   205
a servant at sacred springs?
Might I only be taken to Athens, domain
of Theseus, the bright, the blessed!
Never to the whirl of Eurotas, not Sparta   210
detested, who gave us Helen,
not look with slave's eyes on the scourge
of Troy, Menelaus.

I have heard the rumor
of the hallowed ground by Peneus,   215
bright doorstone of Olympus,
deep burdened in beauty of flower and harvest.
There would I be next after the blessed,
the sacrosanct hold of Theseus.
And they say that the land of Aetna,   220
the Fire God's keep against Punic men,
mother of Sicilian mountains, sounds
in the herald's cry for games' garlands;
and the land washed
by the streaming Ionian Sea,   225

that land watered by the loveliest
of rivers, Crathis, with the red-gold tresses
who draws from the depths of enchanted wells
blessings on a strong people.

See now, from the host of the Danaans   230
the herald, charged with new orders, takes
the speed of his way toward us.
What message? What command? Since we count as
   slaves
even now in the Dorian kingdom.

               (Talthybius enters, followed by a detail of
                               armed soldiers.)

Talthybius
   Hecuba, incessantly my ways have led me to Troy   235
   as the messenger of all the Achaean armament.
   You know me from the old days, my lady; I am sent,
   Talthybius, with new messages for you to hear.

Hecuba
   It comes, beloved daughters of Troy; the thing I feared.

Talthybius
   You are all given your masters now. Was this your dread?   240

Hecuba
   Ah, yes. Is it Phthia, then? A city of Thessaly?
   Tell me. The land of Cadmus?

Talthybius
   All are allotted separately, each to a man.

Hecuba
   Who is given to whom? Oh, is there any hope
   left for the women of Troy?   245

Talthybius
   I understand. Yet ask not for all, but for each apart.

Hecuba

Who was given my child? Tell me, who shall be lord
of my poor abused Cassandra?

Talthybius

King Agamemnon chose her. She was given to him.

Hecuba

Slave woman to that Lacedaemonian wife?
My unhappy child!   250

Talthybius

No. Rather to be joined with him in the dark bed of
  love.

Hecuba

She, Apollo's virgin, blessed in the privilege
the gold-haired god gave her, a life forever unwed?

Talthybius

Love's archery and the prophetic maiden struck him
  hard.   255

Hecuba

Dash down, my daughter,
the keys of your consecration,
break the god's garlands to your throat gathered.

Talthybius

Is it not high favor to be brought to a king's bed?

Hecuba

My poor youngest, why did you take her away from me?   260

Talthybius

You spoke now of Polyxena. Is it not so?

Hecuba

To whose arms did the lot force her?

Talthybius
She is given a guardianship, to keep Achilles' tomb.

Hecuba
To watch, my child? Over a tomb?   265
Tell me, is this their way,
some law, friend, established among the Greeks?

Talthybius
Speak of your child in words of blessing. She feels no
    pain.

Hecuba
What did that mean? Does she live in the sunlight still?

Talthybius
She lives her destiny, and her cares are over now.   270

Hecuba
The wife of bronze-embattled Hector: tell me of her,
Andromache the forlorn. What shall she suffer now?

Talthybius
The son of Achilles chose her. She was given to him.

Hecuba
And I, my aged strength crutched for support on staves,   275
whom shall I serve?

Talthybius
You shall be slave to Odysseus, lord of Ithaca.

Hecuba
Oh no, no!
Tear the shorn head,
rip nails through the folded cheeks.   280
Must I?
To be given as slave to serve that vile, that slippery man,
right's enemy, brute, murderous beast,
that mouth of lies and treachery, that makes void   285

faith in things promised
and that which was beloved turns to hate. Oh, mourn,
daughters of Ilium, weep as one for me.
I am gone, doomed, undone,
O wretched, given   290
the worst lot of all.

Chorus

I know your destiny now, Queen Hecuba. But mine?
What Hellene, what Achaean is my master now?

Talthybius

Men-at-arms, do your duty. Bring Cassandra forth
without delay. Our orders are to deliver her   295
to the general at once. And afterwards we can bring
to the rest of the princes their allotted captive women.
But see! What is that burst of a torch flame inside?
What can it mean? Are the Trojan women setting fire
to their chambers, at point of being torn from their land   300
to sail for Argos? Have they set themselves aflame
in longing for death? I know it is the way of freedom
in times like these to stiffen the neck against disaster.
Open, there, open; let not the fate desired by these,
dreaded by the Achaeans, hurl their wrath on me.   305

Hecuba

You are wrong, there is no fire there. It is my Cassandra
Whirled out on running feet in the passion of her frenzy.

(*Cassandra, carrying a flaming torch, bursts
from the shelter.*)

Cassandra

Lift up, heave up; carry the flame; I bring fire of wor-
    ship,
torches to the temple.
Io, Hymen, my lord. Hymenaeus.   310
Blessed the bridegroom.
Blessed am I indeed to lie at a king's side,

223

blessed the bride of Argos.
Hymen, my lord, Hymenaeus.
Yours were the tears, my mother, 315
yours was the lamentation for my father fallen,
for your city so dear beloved,
but mine this marriage, my marriage,
and I shake out the torch-flare, 320
brightness, dazzle,
light for you, Hymenaeus,
Hecate, light for you,
for the bed of virginity as man's custom ordains.

Let your feet dance, rippling the air; let go the chorus, 325
as when my father's
fate went in blessedness.
O sacred circle of dance.
Lead now, Phoebos Apollo; I wear your laurel,
I tend your temple, 330
Hymen, O Hymenaeus.
Dance, Mother, dance, laugh; lead; let your feet
wind in the shifting pattern and follow mine,
keep the sweet step with me,
cry out the name Hymenaeus 335
and the bride's name in the shrill
and the blessed incantation.
O you daughters of Phrygia robed in splendor,
dance for my wedding,
for the lord fate appointed to lie beside me. 340

Chorus

Can you not, Queen Hecuba, stop this bacchanal before
her light feet whirl her away into the Argive camp?

Hecuba

Fire God, in mortal marriages you lift up your torch,
but here you throw a melancholy light, not seen
through my hopes that went so high in days gone past.
O child, 345

there was a time I dreamed you would not wed like this,
not at the spear's edge, not under force of Argive arms.
Let me take the light; crazed, passionate, you cannot
    carry
it straight enough, poor child. Your fate is intemperate
as you are, always. There is no relief for you.   350

(*Attendants come from the shelter. Hecuba gently
takes the torch from Cassandra and gives
it to them to carry away.*)

You Trojan women, take the torch inside, and change
to songs of tears this poor girl's marriage melodies.

Cassandra

O Mother, star my hair with flowers of victory.
I know you would not have it happen thus; and yet
this is a king I marry; then be glad; escort   355
the bride. Oh, thrust her strongly on. If Loxias
is Loxias still, the Achaeans' pride, great Agamemnon
has won a wife more fatal than ever Helen was.
Since I will kill him; and avenge my brothers' blood
and my father's in the desolation of his house.   360
But I leave this in silence and sing not now the ax
to drop against my throat and other throats than mine,
the agony of the mother murdered, brought to pass
from our marriage rites, and Atreus' house made desolate.
I am ridden by God's curse still, yet I will step so far   365
out of my frenzy as to show this city's fate
is blessed beside the Achaeans'. For one woman's sake,
one act of love, these hunted Helen down and threw
thousands of lives away. Their general—clever man—
in the name of a vile woman cut his darling down,   370
gave up for a brother the sweetness of children in his
    house,
all to bring back that brother's wife, a woman who went
of her free will, not caught in constraint of violence.
The Achaeans came beside Scamander's banks, and died

225

day after day, though none sought to wrench their land
    from them   375
nor their own towering cities. Those the War God caught
never saw their sons again, nor were they laid to rest
decently in winding sheets by their wives' hands, but lie
buried in alien ground; while all went wrong at home
as the widows perished, and barren couples raised and
    nursed   380
the children of others, no survivor left to tend
the tombs, and what is left there, with blood sacrificed.
For such success as this congratulate the Greeks.
No, but the shame is better left in silence, for fear
my singing voice becomes the voice of wretchedness.   385
The Trojans have that glory which is loveliest:
they died for their own country. So the bodies of all
who took the spears were carried home in loving hands,
brought, in the land of their fathers, to the embrace of
    earth
and buried becomingly as the rite fell due. The rest,   390
those Phrygians who escaped death in battle, day by day
came home to happiness the Achaeans could not know;
their wives, their children. Then was Hector's fate so
    sad?
You think so. Listen to the truth. He is dead and gone
surely, but with reputation, as a valiant man.   395
How could this be, except for the Achaeans' coming?
Had they held back, none might have known how great
    he was.
The bride of Paris was the daughter of Zeus. Had he
not married her, fame in our house would sleep in silence
    still.
Though surely the wise man will forever shrink from
    war,   400
yet if war come, the hero's death will lay a wreath
not lustreless on the city. The coward alone brings
    shame.
Let no more tears fall, Mother, for our land, nor for

this marriage I make; it is by marriage that I bring
to destruction those whom you and I have hated most.   405

Chorus

You smile on your disasters. Can it be that you
some day will illuminate the darkness of this song?

Talthybius

Were it not Apollo who has driven wild your wits
I would make you sorry for sending the princes of our
    host
on their way home in augury of foul speech like this.   410
Now pride of majesty and wisdom's outward show
have fallen to stature less than what was nothing worth
since he, almighty prince of the assembled Hellenes,
Atreus' son beloved, has stooped—by his own will—
to find his love in a crazed girl. I, a plain man,   415
would not marry this woman or keep her as my slave.
You then, with your wits unhinged by idiocy,
your scolding of Argos and your Trojans glorified
I throw to the winds to scatter them. Come now with me
to the ships, a bride—and such a bride—for Agamem-
    non.   420

Hecuba, when Laertes' son calls you, be sure
you follow; if what all say who came to Ilium
is true, at the worst you will be a good woman's slave.

Cassandra

That servant is a vile thing. Oh, how can heralds keep
their name of honor? Lackeys for despots be they, or   425
lackeys to the people, all men must despite them still.
You tell me that my mother must be slave in the house
of Odysseus? Where are all Apollo's promises
uttered to me, to my own ears, that Hecuba
should die in Troy? Odysseus I will curse no more,   430
poor wretch, who little dreams of what he must go
    through

227

when he will think Troy's pain and mine were golden
    grace
beside his own luck. Ten years he spent here, and ten
more years will follow before he at last comes home, for-
    lorn
after the terror of the rock and the thin strait,   435
Charybdis; and the mountain striding Cyclops, who eats
men's flesh; the Ligyan witch who changes men to swine,
Circe; the wreck of all his ships on the salt sea,
the lotus passion, the sacred oxen of the Sun
slaughtered, and dead flesh moaning into speech, to
    make   440
Odysseus listening shiver. Cut the story short:
he will go down to the water of death, and return alive
to reach home and the thousand sorrows waiting there.

Why must I transfix each of Odysseus' labors one by
    one?
Lead the way quick to the house of death where I shall
    take my mate.   445
Lord of all the sons of Danaus, haughty in your mind of
    pride,
not by day, but evil in the evil night you shall find your
    grave
when I lie corpse-cold and naked next my husband's sep-
    ulcher,
piled in the ditch for animals to rip and feed on, beaten
    by
streaming storms of winter, I who wore Apollo's sacra-
    ments.   450
Garlands of the god I loved so well, the spirit's dress of
    pride,
leave me, as I leave those festivals where once I was so
    gay.
See, I tear your adornments from my skin not yet defiled
    by touch,
throw them to the running winds to scatter, O lord of
    prophecy,

Where is this general's ship, then? Lead me where I
    must set my feet on board.   455
Wait the wind of favor in the sails; yet when the ship
    goes out
from this shore, she carries one of the three Furies in my
    shape.
Land of my ancestors, good-bye; O Mother, weep no
    more for me.
You beneath the ground, my brothers, Priam, father of
    us all,
I will be with you soon and come triumphant to the
    dead below,   460
leaving, behind me, wrecked, the house of Atreus, which
    destroyed our house.

(*Cassandra is taken away by Talthybius and his
soldiers. Hecuba collapses.*)

Chorus

Handmaids of aged Hecuba, can you not see
how your mistress, powerless to cry out, lies prone? Oh,
    take
her hand and help her to her feet, you wretched maids.
Will you let an aged helpless woman lie so long?   465

Hecuba

No. Let me lie where I have fallen. Kind acts, my maids,
must be unkind, unwanted. All that I endure
and have endured and shall, deserves to strike me down.
O gods! What wretched things to call on—gods!—for
    help
although the decorous action is to invoke their aid   470
when all our hands lay hold on is unhappiness.
No. It is my pleasure first to tell good fortune's tale,
to cast its count more sadly against disasters now.
I was a princess, who was once a prince's bride,
mother by him of sons pre-eminent, beyond   475
the mere numbers of them, lords of the Phrygian
    domain,

such sons for pride to point to as no woman of Troy,
no Hellene, none in the outlander's wide world might
    match.
And then I saw them fall before the spears of Greece,
and cut this hair for them, and laid it on their graves.   480
I mourned their father, Priam. None told me the tale
of his death. I saw it, with these eyes. I stood to watch
his throat cut, next the altar of the protecting god.
I saw my city taken. And the girls I nursed,
choice flowers to wear the pride of any husband's eyes,   485
matured to be dragged by hands of strangers from my
    arms.
There is no hope left that they will ever see me more,
no hope that I shall ever look on them again.
There is one more stone to key this arch of wretched-
    ness:
I must be carried away to Hellas now, an old   490
slave woman, where all those tasks that wrack old age
    shall be
given me by my masters. I must work the bolt
that bars their doorway, I whose son was Hector once;
or bake their bread; lay down these withered limbs to
    sleep
on the bare ground, whose bed was royal once; abuse   495
this skin once delicate the slattern's way, exposed
through robes whose rags will mock my luxury of long
    since.
Unhappy, O unhappy. And all this came to pass
and shall be, for the way one woman chose a man.
Cassandra, O Daughter, whose excitements were the
    god's,   500
you have paid for your consecration now; at what a
    price!
And you, my poor Polyxena, where are you now?
Not here, nor any boy or girl of mine, who were
so many once, is near me in my unhappiness.
And you would lift me from the ground? What hope?
    What use?   505

Guide these feet long ago so delicate in Troy,
a slave's feet now, to the straw sacks laid on the ground
and the piled stones; let me lay down my head and die
in an exhaustion of tears. Of all who walk in bliss
call not one happy yet, until the man is dead.   510

(Hecuba, after being led to the back of the stage,
        flings herself to the ground once more.)

Chorus
    Voices of singing, stay
    with me now, for Ilium's sake;
    take up the burden of tears,
    the song of sorrow;
    the dirge for Troy's death   515
    must be chanted;
    the tale of my captivity
    by the wheeled stride of the four-foot beast of the
        Argives,
    the horse they left in the gates,
    thin gold at its brows,   520
    inward, the spears' high thunder.
    Our people thronging
    the rock of Troy let go the great cry:
    "The war is over! Go down,
    bring back the idol's enchanted wood   525
    to the Maiden of Ilium, Zeus' daughter."
    Who stayed then? Not one girl, not one
    old man, in their houses,
    but singing for happiness
    let the lurking death in.   530

    And the generation of Troy
    swept solid to the gates
    to give the goddess
    her pleasure: the colt immortal, unbroken,
    the nest of Argive spears,
    death for the children of Dardanus   535
    sealed in the sleek hill pine chamber.

In the sling of the flax twist shipwise
they berthed the black hull
in the house of Pallas Athene   540
stone paved, washed now in the blood of our people.
Strong, gay work
deep into black night
to the stroke of the Libyan lute
and all Troy singing, and girls'   545
light feet pulsing the air
in the kind dance measures;
indoors, lights everywhere,
torchflares on black
to forbid sleep's onset.   550

I was there also: in the great room
I danced the maiden of the mountains,
Artemis, Zeus' daughter.
When the cry went up, sudden,   555
bloodshot, up and down the city, to stun
the keep of the citadel. Children
reached shivering hands to clutch
at the mother's dress.
War stalked from his hiding place.   560
Pallas did this.
Beside their altars the Trojans
died in their blood. Desolate now,
men murdered, our sleeping rooms gave up
their brides' beauty   565
to breed sons for Greek men,
sorrow for our own country.

> *(A wagon comes on the stage. It is heaped with a
> number of spoils of war, in the midst of which
> sits Andromache holding Astyanax. While
> the chorus continues speaking, Hecuba
> rises once more.)*

Hecuba look, I see her, rapt
to the alien wagon, Andromache,

close to whose beating breast clings   570
the boy Astyanax, Hector's sweet child.
O carried away—to what land?—unhappy woman,
on the wagon floor, with the brazen arms
of Hector, of Troy
captive and heaped beside you,
torn now from Troy, for Achilles' son   575
to hang in the shrines of Phthia.

Andromache
I am in the hands of Greek masters.

Hecuba
  Alas!

Andromache
      Must the incantation

Hecuba
  (ah me!)

Andromache
       of my own grief win tears from you?

Hecuba
  It must—O Zeus!

Andromache
        My own distress?   580

Hecuba
  O my children

Andromache
       once. No longer.

Hecuba
  Lost, lost, Troy our dominion

Andromache
  unhappy

233

Hecuba
> and my lordly children.

Andromache
Gone, alas!

Hecuba
> They were mine.

Andromache
Sorrows only.

Hecuba
> Sad destiny   585

Andromache
of our city

Hecuba
> a wreck, and burning.

Andromache
Come back, O my husband.

Hecuba
Poor child, you invoke
a dead man: my son once

Andromache
my defender.   590

Hecuba
And you, whose death shamed the Achaeans,

Andromache
lord of us all once,
O patriarch, Priam,

Hecuba
take me to my death now.

Andromache
  Longing for death drives deep;

Hecuba

                            O sorrowful, such is our
      fortune;   595

Andromache
  lost our city

Hecuba

            and our pain lies deep under pain piled over.

Andromache
  We are the hated of God, since once your youngest
      escaping
  death, brought down Troy's towers in the arms of a
      worthless woman,
  piling at the feet of Pallas the bleeding bodies of our
      young men
  sprawled, kites' food, while Troy take up the yoke of
      captivity.   600

Hecuba
  O my city, my city forlorn

Andromache

                        abandoned, I weep this

Hecuba
  miserable last hour

Andromache

                        of the house where I bore my chil-
      dren.

Hecuba
  O my sons, this city and your mother are desolate of
      you.
  Sound of lamentation and sorrow,

tears on tears shed. Home, farewell, since the dead have
    forgotten   605
all sorrows, and weep no longer.

Chorus
    They who are sad find somehow sweetness in tears, the
        song
    of lamentation and the melancholy Muse.

Andromache
    Hecuba, mother of the man whose spear was death   610
    to the Argives, Hector: do you see what they have done
        to us?

Hecuba
    I see the work of gods who pile tower-high the pride
    of those who were nothing, and dash present grandeur
        down.

Andromache
    We are carried away, sad spoils, my boy and I; our life
    transformed, as the aristocrat becomes the serf.   615

Hecuba
    Such is the terror of necessity. I lost
    Cassandra, roughly torn from my arms before you came.

Andromache
    Another Ajax to haunt your daughter? Some such thing
    it must be. Yet you have lost still more than you yet
        know.

Hecuba
    There is no numbering my losses. Infinitely   620
    misfortune comes to outrace misfortune known before.

Andromache
    Polyxena is dead. They cut your daughter's throat
    to pleasure dead Achilles' corpse, above his grave.

Hecuba

O wretched. This was what Talthybius meant, that speech

cryptic, incomprehensible, yet now so clear. 625

Andromache

I saw her die, and left this wagon seat to lay

a robe upon her body and sing the threnody.

Hecuba

Poor child, poor wretched, wretched darling, sacrificed,

but without pity, and in pain, to a dead man.

Andromache

She is dead, and this was death indeed; and yet to die 630

as she did was better than to live as I live now.

Hecuba

Child, no. No life, no light is any kind of death,

since death is nothing, and in life the hopes live still.

Andromache

O Mother, our mother, hear me while I reason through

this matter fairly—might it even hush your grief? 635

Death, I am sure, is like never being born, but death

is better thus by far than to live a life of pain,

since the dead with no perception of evil feel no grief,

while he who was happy once, and then unfortunate,

finds his heart driven far from the old lost happiness. 640

She died; it is as if she never saw the light

of day, for she knows nothing now of what she suffered.

But I, who aimed the arrows of ambition high

at honor, and made them good, see now how far I fall,

I, who in Hector's house worked out all custom that

brings 645

discretion's name to women. Blame them or blame them

not,

there is one act that swings the scandalous speech their

way

beyond all else: to leave the house and walk abroad.

I longed to do it, but put the longing aside, and stayed
always within the inclosure of my own house and court.   650
The witty speech some women cultivate I would
not practice, but kept my honest inward thought, and
    made
my mind my only and sufficient teacher. I gave
my lord's presence the tribute of hushed lips, and eyes
quietly downcast. I knew when my will must have its way   655
over his, knew also how to give way to him in turn.
Men learned of this; I was talked of in the Achaean
    camp,
and reputation has destroyed me now. At the choice
of women, Achilles' son picked me from the rest, to be
his wife: a lordly house, yet I shall be a slave.   660
If I dash back the beloved memory of Hector
and open wide my heart to my new lord, I shall be
a traitor to the dead love, and know it; if I cling
faithful to the past, I win my master's hatred. Yet
they say one night of love suffices to dissolve   665
a woman's aversion to share the bed of any man.
I hate and loathe that woman who casts away the once
beloved, and takes another in her arms of love.
Even the young mare torn from her running mate and
    teamed
with another will not easily wear the yoke. And yet   670
this is a brute and speechless beast of burden, not
like us intelligent, lower far in nature's scale.
Dear Hector, when I had you I had a husband, great
in understanding, rank, wealth, courage: all my wish.
I was a virgin when you took me from the house   675
of my father; I gave you all my maiden love, my first,
and now you are dead, and I must cross the sea, to serve,
prisoner of war, the slave's yoke on my neck, in Greece.
No, Hecuba; can you not see my fate is worse
than hers you grieve, Polyxena's? That one thing left   680
always while life lasts, hope, is not for me. I keep
no secret deception in my heart—sweet though it be
to dream—that I shall ever be happy any more.

Chorus

> You stand where I do in misfortune, and while you
>   mourn
> your own life, tell me what I, too, am suffering.   685

Hecuba

> I have never been inside the hull of a ship, but know
> what I know only by hearsay and from painted scenes,
> yet think that seamen, while the gale blows moderately,
> take pains to spare unnecessary work, and send
> one man to the steering oar, another aloft, and crews   690
> to pump the bilge from the hold. But when the tempest
>   comes,
> and seas wash over the decks they lose their nerve, and
>   let
> her go by the run at the waves' will, leaving all to
>   chance.
> So I, in this succession of disasters, swamped,
> battered by this storm immortally inspired, have lost   695
> my lips' control and let them go, say anything
> they will. Yet still, beloved child, you must forget
> what happened with Hector. Tears will never save you
>   now.
> Give your obedience to the new master; let your ways
> entice his heart to make him love you. If you do   700
> it will be better for all who are close to you. This boy,
> my own son's child, might grow to manhood and bring
>   back—
> he alone could do it—something of our city's strength.
> On some far day the children of your children might
> come home, and build. There still may be another Troy.   705
>
> But *we* say this, and others will speak also. See,
> here is some runner of the Achaeans come again.
> Who is he? What news? What counsel have they taken
>   now?

(Talthybius enters again with his escort.)

Talthybius
O wife of Hector, once the bravest man in Troy,
do not hate me. This is the will of the Danaans and   710
the kings. I wish I did not have to give this message.

Andromache
What can this mean, this hint of hateful things to come?

Talthybius
The council has decreed for your son—how can I say
this?

Andromache
That he shall serve some other master than I serve?

Talthybius
No man of Achaea shall ever make this boy his slave.   715

Andromache
Must he be left behind in Phrygia, all alone?

Talthybius
Worse; horrible. There is no easy way to tell it.

Andromache
I thank your courtesy—unless your news be really good.

Talthybius
They will kill your son. It is monstrous. Now you know
the truth.

Andromache
Oh, this is worse than anything I heard before.   720

Talthybius
Odysseus. He urged it before the Greeks, and got his
way.

Andromache
This is too much grief, and more than anyone could
bear.

Talthybius
He said a hero's son could not be allowed to live.

Andromache
Even thus may his own sons some day find no mercy.

Talthybius
He must be hurled from the battlements of Troy.

> (*He goes toward Andromache, who clings fast
> to her child, as if to resist.*)

No,
wait!   725
Let it happen this way. It will be wiser in the end.
Do not fight it. Take your grief as you were born to take
    it,
give up the struggle where your strength is feebleness
with no force anywhere to help. Listen to me!
Your city is gone, your husband. You are in our power.   730
How can one woman hope to struggle against the arms
of Greece? Think, then. Give up the passionate contest.
    This
will bring no shame. No man can laugh at your sub-
    mission.
And please—I request you—hurl no curse at the
    Achaeans
for fear the army, savage over some reckless word,   735
forbid the child his burial and the dirge of honor.
Be brave, be silent; out of such patience you can hope
the child you leave behind will not lie unburied here,
and that to you the Achaeans will be less unkind.

Andromache
O darling child I loved too well for happiness,   740
your enemies will kill you and leave your mother forlorn.
Your own father's nobility, where others found
protection, means your murder now. The memory
of his valor comes ill-timed for you. O bridal bed,

O marriage rites that brought me home to Hector's
     house   745
a bride, you were unhappy in the end. I lived
never thinking the baby I had was born for butchery
by Greeks, but for lordship over all Asia's pride of earth.
Poor child, are you crying too? Do you know what they
will do to you? Your fingers clutch my dress. What use,   750
to nestle like a young bird under the mother's wing?
Hector cannot come back, not burst from underground
to save you, that spear of glory caught in the quick hand,
nor Hector's kin, nor any strength of Phrygian arms.
Yours the sick leap head downward from the height, the
     fall   755
where none have pity, and the spirit smashed out in
     death.
O last and loveliest embrace of all, O child's
sweet fragrant body. Vanity in the end. I nursed
for nothing the swaddled baby at this mother's breast;
in vain the wrack of the labor pains and the long sick-
     ness.   760
Now once again, and never after this, come close
to your mother, lean against my breast and wind your
     arms
around my neck, and put your lips against my lips.

(*She kisses Astyanax and relinquishes him.*)

Greeks! Your Greek cleverness is simple barbarity.
Why kill this child, who never did you any harm?   765
O flowering of the house of Tyndareus! Not his,
not God's daughter, never that, but child of many
     fathers
I say; the daughter of Vindictiveness, of Hate,
of Blood, Death; of all wickedness that swarms on earth.
I cry it aloud: Zeus never was your father, but you   770
were born a pestilence to all Greeks and the world be-
     side.
Accursed; who from those lovely and accursed eyes

brought down to shame and ruin the bright plains of
    Troy.
Oh, seize him, take him, dash him to death if it must be
    done;
feed on his flesh if it is your will. These are the gods   775
who damn us to this death, and I have no strength to
    save
my boy from execution. Cover this wretched face
and throw me into the ship and that sweet bridal bed
I walk to now across the death of my own child.

> (*Talthybius gently lifts the child out of the
> wagon, which leaves the stage,
> carrying Andromache away.*)

Chorus

Unhappy Troy! For the sweetness in one woman's arms'   780
embrace, unspeakable, you lost these thousands slain.

Talthybius

Come, boy, taken from the embrace beloved
of your mourning mother. Climb the high circle
of the walls your fathers built. There
end life. This was the order.   785
Take him.

> (*He hands Astyanax to the guards,
> who lead him out.*)

        I am not the man
to do this. Some other
without pity, not as I ashamed,
should be herald of messages like this.

> (*He goes out.*)

Hecuba

O child of my own unhappy child,   790
shall your life be torn from your mother
and from me? Wicked. Can I help,
dear child, not only suffer? What help?

243

Tear face, beat bosom. This is all
my power now. O city,   795
O child, what have we left to suffer?
Are we not hurled
down the whole length of disaster?

Chorus
  Telamon, O king in the land where the bees swarm,
  Salamis the surf-pounded isle where you founded your
        city   800
  to front that hallowed coast where Athene broke
  forth the primeval pale branch of olive,
  wreath of the bright air and a glory on Athens the
        shining:
  O Telamon, you came in your pride of arms
  with Alcmena's archer   805
  to Ilium, our city, to sack and destroy it
  on that age-old venture.
  This was the first flower of Hellenic strength Heracles
        brought in anger
  for the horses promised; and by Simois' calm waters   810
  checked the surf-wandering oars and made fast the ships'
        stern cables.
  From which vessels came out the deadly bow hand,
  death to Laomedon, as the scarlet wind of the flames
        swept over
  masonry straight-hewn by the hands of Apollo.   815
  This was a desolation of Troy
  twice taken; twice in the welter of blood the walls Dar-
        danian
  went down before the red spear.

  In vain, then, Laomedon's child,   820
  you walk in delicate pride
  by the golden pitchers
  in loveliest servitude
  to fill Zeus' wine cups;
  while Troy your mother is given to the flame to eat,   825

and the lonely beaches
mourn, as sad birds sing
for the young lost,   830
for the sword hand and the children
and the aged women.
Gone now the shining pools where you bathed,
the fields where you ran
all desolate. And you,
Ganymede, go in grace by the thrones of God   835
with your young, calm smile even now
as Priam's kingdom
falls to the Greek spear.   840

O Love, Love, it was you
in the high halls of Dardanus,
the sky-daughters of melody beside you,
who piled the huge strength of Troy
in towers, the gods' own hands   845
concerned. I speak no more
against Zeus' name.
But the light men love, who shines
through the pale wings of morning,
balestar on this earth now,   850
watched the collapse of tall towers:
Dawn. Her lord was of this land;
she bore his children,
Tithonus, caught away by the golden car
and the starry horses,   855
who made our hopes so high.
For the gods loved Troy once.
Now they have forgotten.

(*Menelaus comes on the stage, attended by
a detail of armed soldiers.*)

Menelaus

O splendor of sunburst breaking forth this day, whereon   860
I lay my hands once more on Helen, my wife. And yet
it is not, so much as men think, for the woman's sake

245

I came to Troy, but against that guest proved treach-
    erous,   865
who like a robber carried the woman from my house.
Since the gods have seen to it that *he* paid the penalty,
fallen before the Hellenic spear, his kingdom wrecked,
I come for *her* now, the wife once my own, whose name
I can no longer speak with any happiness,   870
to take her away. In this house of captivity
she is numbered among the other women of Troy, a
    slave.
And those men whose work with the spear has won her
    back
gave her to me, to kill, or not to kill, but lead
away to the land of Argos, if such be my pleasure.   875
And such it is; the death of Helen in Troy I will let
pass, have the oars take her by sea ways back to Greek
soil, and there give her over to execution;
blood penalty for friends who are dead in Ilium here.
Go to the house, my followers, and take her out;   880
no, drag her out; lay hands upon that hair so stained
with men's destruction. When the winds blow fair astern
we will take ship again and bring her back to Hellas.

Hecuba

O power, who mount the world, wheel where the world
    rides,
O mystery of man's knowledge, whosoever you be,   885
Zeus named, nature's necessity or mortal mind,
I call upon you; for you walk the path none hears
yet bring all human action back to right at last.

Menelaus

What can this mean? How strange a way to call on gods.

Hecuba

Kill your wife, Menelaus, and I will bless your name.   890
But keep your eyes away from her. Desire will win.
She looks enchantment, and where she looks homes are
    set fire;

she captures cities as she captures the eyes of men.
We have had experience, you and I. We know the truth.

(*Men at arms bring Helen roughly out of the
shelter. She makes no resistance.*)

Helen

Menelaus, your first acts are argument of terror   895
to come. Your lackeys put their hands on me. I am
      dragged
out of my chambers by brute force. I know you hate
me; I am almost sure. And still there is one question
I would ask you, if I may. What have the Greeks decided
to do with me? Or shall I be allowed to live?   900

Menelaus

You are not strictly condemned, but all the army gave
you into my hands, to kill you for the wrong you did.

Helen

Is it permitted that I argue this, and prove
that my death, if I am put to death, will be unjust?

Menelaus

I did not come to talk with you. I came to kill.   905

Hecuba

No, Menelaus, listen to her. She should not die
unheard. But give me leave to take the opposite case;
the prosecution. There are things that happened in Troy
which you know nothing of, and the long-drawn argu-
      ment
will mean her death. She never can escape us now.   910

Menelaus

This is a gift of leisure. If she wishes to speak
she may. But it is for your sake, understand, that I give
this privilege I never would have given to her.

Helen

Perhaps it will make no difference if I speak well
or badly, and your hate will not let you answer me.   915

247

All I can do is to foresee the arguments
you will use in accusation of me, and set against
the force of your charges, charges of my own.

First, then!
She mothered the beginning of all this wickedness.
For Paris was her child. And next to her the old king,   920
who would not destroy the infant Alexander, that dream
of the firebrand's agony, has ruined Troy, and me.
This is not all; listen to the rest I have to say.
Alexander was the judge of the goddess trinity.
Pallas Athene would have given him power, to lead   925
the Phrygian arms on Hellas and make it desolate.
All Asia was Hera's promise, and the uttermost zones
of Europe for his lordship, if her way prevailed.
But Aphrodite, picturing my loveliness,
promised it to him, if he would say her beauty surpassed   930
all others. Think what this means, and all the conse-
    quence.
Cypris prevailed, and I was won in marriage: all
for Greek advantage. Asia is not your lord; you serve
no tyrant now, nor take the spear in his defense.
Yet Hellas' fortune was my own misfortune. I,   935
sold once for my body's beauty stand accused, who
    should
for what has been done wear garlands on my head.

I know

You will say all this is nothing to the immediate charge:
I did run away; I did go secretly from your house.
But when he came to me—call him any name you will: 940
Paris? or Alexander? or the spirit of blood
to haunt this woman?—he came with a goddess at his
    side;
no weak one. And you—it was criminal—took ship for
    Crete
and left me there in Sparta in the house, alone.

You see?

I wonder—and I ask this of myself, not you— 945
why *did* I do it? What made me run away from home
with the stranger, and betray my country and my
    hearth?
Challenge the goddess then, show your greater strength
    than Zeus'
who has the other gods in his power, and still is slave
to Aphrodite alone. Shall I not be forgiven? 950
Still you might have some show of argument against me.
When Paris was gone to the deep places of death, below
ground, and the immortal practice on my love was gone,
I should have come back to the Argive ships, left Troy.
I did try to do it, and I have witnesses, 955
the towers' gatekeepers and the sentinels on the wall,
who caught me again and again as I let down the rope
from the battlements and tried to slip away to the
    ground.
For Deiphobus, my second husband: he took me away
by force and kept me his wife against the Phrygians'
    will. 960

O my husband, can you kill me now and think you kill
in righteousness? I was the bride of force. Before,
I brought their houses to the sorrow of slavery
instead of conquest. Would you be stronger than the
    gods?
Try, then. But even such ambition is absurd. 965

Chorus

O Queen of Troy, stand by your children and your
    country!
Break down the beguilement of this woman, since she
    speaks
well, and has done wickedly. This is dangerous.

Hecuba

First, to defend the honor of the gods, and show
that the woman is a scandalous liar. I will not 970

believe it! Hera and the virgin Pallas Athene
could never be so silly and empty-headed
that Hera would sell Argos to the barbarians,
or Pallas let Athenians be the slaves of Troy.
They went to Ida in girlish emulation, vain   975
of their own loveliness? Why? Tell me the reason Hera
should fall so much in love with the idea of beauty.
To win some other lord more powerful than Zeus?
Or has Athene marked some god to be her mate,
she, whose virginity is a privilege won from Zeus,   980
who abjures marriage? Do not trick out your own sins
by calling the gods stupid. No wise man will believe you.
You claim, and I must smile to hear it, that Aphrodite
came at my son's side to the house of Menelaus;
who could have caught up you and your city of Amyclae   985
and set you in Ilium, moving not from the quiet of
    heaven.
Nonsense. My son was handsome beyond all other men.
You looked at him, and sense went Cyprian at the sight,
since Aphrodite is nothing but the human lust,
named rightly, since the word of lust begins the god's
    name.   990
You saw him in the barbaric splendor of his robes,
gorgeous with gold. It made your senses itch. You
    thought,
being queen only in Argos, in little luxury,
that once you got rid of Sparta for the Phrygian city
where gold streamed everywhere, you could let extrava-
    gance   995
run wild. No longer were Menelaus and his house
sufficient to your spoiled luxurious appetites.
So much for that. You say my son took you away
by force. What Spartan heard you cry for help? You did
cry out? Or did you? Castor, your brother, was there, a
    young   1000
man, and his twin not yet caught up among the stars.
Then when you had reached Troy, and the Argives at
    your heels

came, and the agony of the murderous spears began,
when the reports came in that Menelaus' side
was winning, you would praise him, simply to make my
    son   1005
unhappy at the strength of his love's challenger,
forgetting your husband when the luck went back to
    Troy.
You worked hard: not to make yourself a better
    woman,
but to make sure always to be on the winning side.
You claim you tried to slip away with ropes let down   1010
from the ramparts, and this proves you stayed against
    your will?
Perhaps. But when were you ever caught in the stran-
    gling noose,
caught sharpening a dagger? Which any noble wife
would do, desperate with longing for her lord's return.
Yet over and over again I gave you good advice: 1015
"Make your escape, my daughter; there are other girls
for my sons to marry. I will help you get away
to the ships of the Achaeans. Let the Greeks, and us,
stop fighting." So I argued, but you were not pleased.
Spoiled in the luxury of Alexander's house   1020
you liked foreigners to kiss the ground before your feet.
All that impressed you.
                 And now you dare to come out-
    side,
figure fastidiously arranged, to look upon
the same air as your husband, O abominable
heart, who should walk submissively in rags of robes,   1025
shivering with anxiety, head Scythian-cropped,
your old impudence gone and modesty gained at last
by reason of your sinful life.
              O Menelaus,
mark this, the end of my argument. Be true to your
high reputation and to Hellas. Grace both, and kill   1030
Helen. Thus make it the custom toward all womankind
hereafter, that the price of adultery is death.

Chorus
> Menelaus, keep the ancestral honor of your house.
> Punish your wife, and purge away from Greece the
> stigma
> on women. You shall seem great even to your enemies.　1035

Menelaus
> All you have said falls into line with my own thought.
> This woman left my household for a stranger's bed
> of her own free will, and all this talk of Aphrodite
> is for pure show. Away, and face the stones of the mob.
> Atone for the long labors of the Achaeans in　　　　1040
> the brief act of dying, and know your penance for my
> shame.

> *(Helen drops before him and embraces his knees.)*

Helen
> No, by your knees! I am not guilty of the mind's
> infection, which the gods sent. Do not kill! Have pity!

Hecuba
> Be true to the memory of all your friends she murdered.
> It is for them and for their children that I plead.　　1045

> *(Menelaus pushes Helen away.)*

Menelaus
> Enough, Hecuba. I am not listening to her now.
> I speak to my servants: see that she is taken away
> to where the ships are beached. She will make the voy-
> age home.

Hecuba
> But let her not be put in the same ship with you.

Menelaus
> What can you mean? That she is heavier than she was?　1050

Hecuba
> A man in love once never is out of love again.

Menelaus

    Sometimes; when the beloved's heart turns false to him.
    Yet it shall be as you wish. She shall not be allowed
    in the same ship I sail in. This was well advised.
    And once in Argos she must die the vile death earned   1055
    by her vile life, and be an example to all women
    to live temperately. This is not the easier way;
    and yet her execution will tincture with fear
    the lust of women even more depraved than she.

        (Helen is led out, Menelaus following.)

Chorus

    Thus, O Zeus, you betrayed all   1060
    to the Achaeans: your temple
    in Ilium, your misted altar,
    the flame of the clotted sacraments,
    the smoke of the skying incense,
    Pergamum the hallowed,   1065
    the ivied ravines of Ida, washed
    by the running snow. The utter
    peaks that surprise the sun bolts,
    shining and primeval place of divinity.   1070

    Gone are your sacrifices, the choirs'
    glad voices singing to the gods
    night long, deep into darkness;
    gone the images, gold on wood
    laid, the twelves of the sacred moons,   1075
    the magic Phrygian number.
    Can it be, can it be, my lord, you have forgotten
    from your throne high in heaven's
    bright air, my city which is ruined
    and the flame storm that broke it?   1080

    O my dear, my husband,
    O wandering ghost
    unwashed, unburied; the sea hull must carry me   1085
    in the flash of its wings' speed
    to Argos, city of horses, where

the stone walls built by giants invade the sky.   1090
The multitudes of our children stand
clinging to the gates and cry through their tears.
And one girl weeps:
"O Mother, the Achaeans take me away
lonely from your eyes
to the black ship
where the oars dip surf   1095
toward Salamis the blessed,
or the peak between two seas
where Pelops' hold
keeps the gates at the Isthmus."

Oh that as Menelaus' ship   1100
makes way through the mid-sea
the bright pronged spear immortal of thunder might
    smash it
far out in the Aegaean,
as in tears, in bondage to Hellas   1105
I am cut from my country;
as she holds the golden mirror
in her hands, girls' grace,
she, God's daughter.
Let him never come home again, to a room in Laconia   1110
and the hearth of his fathers;
never more to Pitana's streets
and the bronze gates of the Maiden;
since he forgave his shame
and the vile marriage, the sorrows   1115
of great Hellas and the land
watered by Simois.

(*Talthybius returns. His men carry, laid on the
        shield of Hector, the body of Astyanax.*)

But see!
Now evils multiply in our land.
Behold, O pitiful wives
of the Trojans. This is Astyanax,   1120

254

dead, dashed without pity from the walls, and borne
by the Danaans, who murdered him.

Talthybius
Hecuba, one last vessel of Achilles' son
remains, manned at the oar sweeps now, to carry back
to the shores of Phthiotis his last spoils of war.   1125
Neoptolemus himself has put to sea. He heard
news of old Peleus in difficulty and the land
invaded by Acastus, son of Pelias.
Such news put speed above all pleasure of delay.
So he is gone, and took with him Andromache,   1130
whose lamentations for her country and farewells
to Hector's tomb as she departed brought these tears
crowding into my eyes. And she implored that you
bury this dead child, your own Hector's son, who died
flung from the battlements of Troy. She asked as well   1135
that the bronze-backed shield, terror of the Achaeans
      once,
when the boy's father slung its defense across his side,
be not taken to the hearth of Peleus, nor the room
where the slain child's Andromache must be a bride
once more, to waken memories by its sight, but used   1140
in place of the cedar coffin and stone-chambered tomb
for the boy's burial. He shall be laid in your arms
to wrap the body about with winding sheets, and
      flowers,
as well as you can, out of that which is left to you.
Since she is gone. Her master's speed prevented her   1145
from giving the rites of burial to her little child.

The rest of us, once the corpse is laid out, and earth
is piled above it, must raise the mast tree, and go.
Do therefore quickly everything that you must do.
There is one labor I myself have spared you. As   1150
we forded on our way here Scamander's running water,
I washed the body and made clean the wounds. I go
now, to break ground and dig the grave for him, that
      my

255

work be made brief, as yours must be, and our tasks end
together, and the ships be put to sea, for home.   1155

Hecuba

Lay down the circled shield of Hector on the ground:
a hateful thing to look at; it means no love to me.

(*Talthybius and his escort leave. Two soldiers wait.*)

Achaeans! All your strength is in your spears, not in
the mind. What were you afraid of, that it made you
    kill
this child so savagely? That Troy, which fell, might be   1160
raised from the ground once more? Your strength
    meant nothing, then.
When Hector's spear was fortunate, and numberless
strong hands were there to help him, we were still de-
    stroyed.
Now when the city is fallen and the Phrygians slain,
this baby terrified you? I despise the fear   1165
which is pure terror in a mind unreasoning.

O darling child, how wretched was this death. You
    might
have fallen fighting for your city, grown to man's
age, and married, and with the king's power like a
    god's,
and died happy, if there is any happiness here.   1170
But no. You grew to where you could see and learn, my
    child,
yet your mind was not old enough to win advantage
of fortune. How wickedly, poor boy, your fathers' walls,
Apollo's handiwork, have crushed your pitiful head
tended and trimmed to ringlets by your mother's hand,   1175
and the face she kissed once, where the brightness now
    is blood
shining through the torn bones—too horrible to say
    more.
O little hands, sweet likenesses of Hector's once,

now you lie broken at the wrists before my feet;
and mouth beloved whose words were once so confident,   1180
you are dead; and all was false, when you would lean
    across
my bed, and say: "Mother, when you die I will cut
my long hair in your memory, and at your grave
bring companies of boys my age, to sing farewell."
It did not happen; now I, a homeless, childless, old   1185
woman must bury your poor corpse, which is so young.
Alas for all the tendernesses, my nursing care,
and all your slumbers gone. What shall the poet say,
what words will he inscribe upon your monument?
Here lies a little child the Argives killed, because   1190
they were afraid of him. That? The epitaph of Greek
    shame.
You will not win your father's heritage, except
for this, which is your coffin now: the brazen shield.

O shield, who guarded the strong shape of Hector's
    arm:
the bravest man of all, who wore you once, is dead.   1195
How sweet the impression of his body on your sling,
and at the true circle of your rim the stain of sweat
where in the grind of his many combats Hector leaned
his chin against you, and the drops fell from his brow!

Take up your work now; bring from what is left some
    robes   1200
to wrap the tragic dead. The gods will not allow us
to do it right. But let him have what we can give.

That mortal is a fool who, prospering, thinks his life
has any strong foundation; since our fortune's course
of action is the reeling way a madman takes,   1205
and no one person is ever happy all the time.

        (*Hecuba's handmaidens bring out from the shelter
        a basket of robes and ornaments. During the*

*scene which follows, the body of Astyanax
is being made ready for burial.)*

Chorus

Here are your women, who bring you from the Trojan
    spoils
such as is left, to deck the corpse for burial.

Hecuba

O child, it is not for victory in riding, won
from boys your age, not archery—in which acts our
    people   1210
take pride, without driving competition to excess—
that your sire's mother lays upon you now these
    treasures
from what was yours before; though now the accursed
    of God,
Helen, has robbed you, she who has destroyed as well
the life in you, and brought to ruin all our house.   1215

Chorus

My heart,
you touched my heart, you who were once
a great lord in my city.

Hecuba

These Phrygian robes' magnificence you should have
    worn
at your marriage to some princess uttermost in pride
in all the East, I lay upon your body now.   1220
And you, once so victorious and mother of
a thousand conquests, Hector's huge beloved shield:
here is a wreath for you, who die not, yet are dead
with this body; since it is better far to honor you
than the armor of Odysseus the wicked and wise.   1225

Chorus

Ah me.
Earth take you, child;
our tears of sorrow.
Cry aloud, our mother.

Hecuba

        Yes.

Chorus

    The dirge of the dead.

Hecuba

              Ah me.   1230

Chorus

    Evils never to be forgotten.

Hecuba

    I will bind up your wounds with bandages, and be
    your healer: a wretched one, in name alone, no use.
    Among the dead your father will take care of you.

Chorus

    Rip, tear your faces with hands   1235
    that beat like oars.
    Alas.

Hecuba

    Dear women. . . .

Chorus

    Hecuba, speak to us. We are yours. What did you cry
        aloud?

Hecuba

    The gods meant nothing except to make life hard for
        me,   1240
    and of all cities they chose Troy to hate. In vain
    we sacrificed. And yet had not the very hand
    of God gripped and crushed this city deep in the
        ground,
    we should have disappeared in darkness, and not given
    a theme for music, and the songs of men to come.   1245
    You may go now, and hide the dead in his poor tomb;

he has those flowers that are the right of the underworld.
I think it makes small difference to the dead, if they
are buried in the tokens of luxury. All this
is an empty glorification left for those who live.   1250

   (*The soldiers take up and carry away the body
           of Astyanax.*)

Chorus

Sad mother, whose hopes were so huge
for your life. They are broken now.
Born to high blessedness
and a lordly line
your death was horror.   1255

But see, see
on the high places of Ilium
the torchflares whirling in the hands
of men. For Troy
some ultimate agony.

   (*Talthybius comes back, with numerous men.*)

Talthybius

I call to the captains who have orders to set fire   1260
to the city of Priam: shield no longer in the hand
the shining flame. Let loose the fire upon it. So
with the citadel of Ilium broken to the ground
we can take leave of Troy, in gladness, and go home.

I speak to you, too, for my orders include this.   1265
Children of Troy, when the lords of the armament
  sound
the high echoing crash of the trumpet call, then go
to the ships of the Achaeans, to be taken away
from this land. And you, unhappiest and aged woman,
go with them. For Odysseus' men are here, to whom   1270
enslaved the lot exiles you from your native land.

Hecuba

Ah, wretched me. So this is the unhappy end

and goal of all the sorrows I have lived. I go
forth from my country and a city lit with flames.
Come, aged feet; make one last weary struggle, that I   1275
may hail my city in its affliction. O Troy, once
so huge over all Asia in the drawn wind of pride,
your very name of glory shall be stripped away.
They are burning you, and us they drag forth from our
    land
enslaved. O gods! Do I call upon those gods for help?   1280
I cried to them before now, and they would not hear.
Come then, hurl ourselves into the pyre. Best now
to die in the flaming ruins of our fathers' house!

Talthybius

    Unhappy creature, ecstatic in your sorrows! Men,
    take her, spare not. She is Odysseus' property.   1285
    You have orders to deliver her into his hands.

Hecuba

    O sorrow.
    Cronion, Zeus, lord of Phrygia,
    prince of our house, have you seen
    the dishonor done to the seed of Dardanus?   1290

Chorus

    He has seen, but the great city
    is a city no more, it is gone. There is no Troy.

Hecuba

    O sorrow.
    Ilium flares.   1295
    The chambers of Pergamum take fire,
    the citadel and the wall's high places.

Chorus

    Our city fallen to the spear
    fades as smoke winged in the sky,
    halls hot in the swept fire   1300
    and the fierce lances.

Hecuba
O soil where my children grew.

Chorus
Alas.

Hecuba
O children, hear me; it is your mother who calls.

Chorus
They are dead you cry to. This is a dirge.

Hecuba
I lean my old body against the earth   1305
and both hands beat the ground.

Chorus
I kneel to the earth, take up
the cry to my own dead,
poor buried husband.

Hecuba
We are taken, dragged away

Chorus
                                        a cry of pain, pain   1310

Hecuba
under the slave's roof

Chorus
                        away from my country.

Hecuba
Priam, my Priam. Dead
graveless, forlorn,
you know not what they have done to me.

Chorus
Now dark, holy death   1315
in the brutal butchery closed his eyes.

Hecuba
O gods' house, city beloved

Chorus
alas

Hecuba
you are given the red flame and the spear's iron.

Chorus
You will collapse to the dear ground and be nameless.

Hecuba
Ash as the skyward smoke wing   1320
piled will blot from my sight the house where I lived
once.

Chorus
Lost shall be the name on the land,
all gone, perished. Troy, city of sorrow,
is there no longer.

Hecuba
Did you see, did you hear?

Chorus
          The crash of the citadel.   1325

Hecuba
The earth shook, riven

Chorus
        riven to engulf the city.

Hecuba
O
shaking, tremulous limbs,
this is the way. Forward:
into the slave's life.   1330

Chorus
Mourn for the ruined city, then go away
to the ships of the Achaeans.

(*Hecuba is led away, and all go out, leaving
the stage empty.*)

ION

Translated and with an Introduction by

RONALD FREDERICK WILLETTS

INTRODUCTION TO *ION*

The *Ion* can be fairly certainly assigned, on stylistic and metrical grounds, to the decade 420-410 B.C. There is no conclusive evidence for a more exact date within this period.

Creusa was the daughter of Erechtheus, the autochthonous king of Athens. While still a girl, she was seduced by Apollo and gave birth to a son whom she exposed from fear of her parents. She naturally supposed that the child had died. But, unknown to her, Apollo sent Hermes to take the child to Delphi and leave him beside the temple. There he was found by the prophetess, who brought him up. He eventually became a steward in the temple. Knowing nothing of the circumstances of his birth, he lives a sheltered life and is happy in the service of the god. In the meantime his mother has married Xuthus. He, though a foreigner, won his bride as a reward for his services to Athens in war. Though long married, they are childless. They have therefore decided to come to Delphi to consult the god about their chances of having children.

Such is the situation at the opening of the play. It arose from an old wrong, the seduction of Creusa by Apollo. It lends itself to development in a number of different ways. The wrong can be righted and Athens glorified by accepting Ion's divine birth as a mark of favor to the Ionian tribes. Or the romantic can be rejected in favor of a more realistic approach. Euripides was sometimes romantic, more often realistic, in his treatment of myths. Here he chose to handle the theme realistically and was preoccupied with the human problem it presented. He weaves the strands of the Ion legend together to form the framework outlined above. He then tears from the story its mythological and supernatural pretensions—at least until Athene appears as *dea ex machina*. Here, at first sight, it seems that the playwright welcomes her with gratitude to supply a ready-made solution for his tangled plot.

The essence of the realist method in this play lies in the double-edged treatment of mythology. Euripides accepts Apollo as the divine lover of Creusa and then invests him with human attributes. In consequence, Apollo emerges in very poor light as a barbarian god whose ethics are shattered by the probings of a civilized and skeptical mind. This exposure is achieved not only by Creusa's intense denunciation of the god in a moment of high climax in the unfolding of the intricate plot. It is more subtly managed through the impact of the whole action upon the boy, Ion. Perhaps the chief merit of this well-designed play is the careful study of Ion's development, the revelation of the changes brought about by the abrupt contact of youthful, cloistered virtue with worldliness. At times we may suspect that the boy grows up too quickly— not so quickly, however, that he becomes a cynic: though he learns with rapidity, he also learns ingenuously. As he becomes more and more disturbed, and therefore more and more disturbing, to his initial charm are added self-confidence and strength of will.

As the plot is presented, Ion is foisted as a son upon Xuthus by the oracle. This leads to the attempt of the mother to kill her son. When this is foiled there follows the further attempt of the son to kill his mother. The rest of the play falls into two parts—the cleverly contrived recognition scene between mother and son and the appearance of Athene as *dea ex machina*.

To accept the resolution of the play at its face value is impossible if we are to believe that there is any serious purpose behind it. Until the end we have no doubts that Euripides is, in fact, dealing with an important theme in earnest. At the end we are likely to feel that our emotions have been cheated; for the explanations of the goddess seem paltry and inconsistent with the dramatic quality and the seriousness of all that has gone before. The contrast is so marked that the play cannot be easily accepted as a tragicomic fairy tale with a well-knit, tense plot and a happy ending, designed to extol the Apolline origin of the Athenian race. The poignant dramatic structure, we feel, must not be reduced to the level of a preface to a pamphlet, even if delivered by an Olympian.

In other words, there is a critical problem to be solved here. Now the "rationalizing" view of the play, associated particularly with A. W. Verrall, had the merit of recognizing that this problem exists. Verrall agreed with the argument that the *Ion* is an attack upon Delphi and must be interpreted in this way; that the oracle delivered to Xuthus, like the recognition scene between Creusa and Ion, is a Delphian fraud, the attribution of Ion to Apollo and Creusa being due to a change of tactics following upon Creusa's confession and denunciation of Apollo.

But this "rationalizing" solution ignores a most important point. Creusa, even when Ion takes her aside in confidence and suggests the possibility, will not admit that her lover was a mortal man. The whole design of the play depends on the assumption that Apollo seduced Creusa. Are the design and the assumption sustained throughout? Let us examine the last two scenes with this query in mind.

As Ion and the crowd advance threateningly toward Creusa, after she has been discovered in refuge at the altar, the Pythian priestess enters from the temple, carrying a cradle bound with fillets of wool resembling those on the altar. She had kept the cradle in which she had found Ion, together with his swaddling clothes and ornaments, and now gives them to him in case he should find a clue to his mother's identity in Athens or elsewhere. Ion examines the cradle with great interest, marveling at the freshness of its fastenings. On the "rationalist" view this would have been part of the fraud perpetrated by the Delphians, since Euripides could not have intended such magical hocus-pocus to be taken seriously: that would have been inconsistent with his "rationalism." But Euripides is consistently irrational in such respects in other plays; though inconsistency is one of his strongest characteristics as a playwright.

When Ion unties the fillets, Creusa recognizes the cradle, is overwhelmed for the moment and then rushes from the altar to embrace him, prepared to risk death, and greets him as her child. He supposes she is playing a trick on him, orders the guards to seize her, and then decides on a better method. He will test her knowledge of the contents of the cradle. But Creusa answers all his questions. Ion is convinced she is his mother. In the joy of her discovery all thought of Xuthus is obliterated. Her son has brought her her personal triumph. As she had tried to murder him as a menace, so now she welcomes him as the savior of her house. The stigma of childlessness is removed together with the memory of Xuthus as the partner of her unhappiness. He has no mention in her triumphant outburst.

Ion puts an end to this rapture by asking for his father to be there to share their happiness. Creusa is again obliged to describe the seduction by Apollo. Ion is guarded in his reception of the story, though his sympathy with his mother as she describes her suffering is spontaneously generous. He can credit the story—with reservations. This is clear when, after making some platitudinous remarks about the workings of providence, intended for the Chorus and others on the stage, he draws his mother aside and puts the question that is uppermost in his mind. Is Apollo being made into a convenient scapegoat?

This is a crucial passage where the "rationalist" explanation breaks down. Ion makes a natural assumption. It demands a truthful answer. There have been enough complications in the plot. Let us suppose that Creusa had agreed with his suggestion. She would presumably have made some confession of an intrigue in her youth. Ion would then have asked the reason for the oracle's deception in giving him to Xuthus as his son. The fraud which the "rationalizers" are anxious to prove would have been most obvious and the play would become more of an open attack upon Delphi than a criticism of Olympian morals. Creusa and Ion might then have agreed, for the sake of convenience, to leave Xuthus in blissful ignorance of the facts, the happy ending would be dramatically justified, the purpose of propaganda achieved, and Athene could have predicted Ion's future without having to make lame excuses for Apollo. The main objection to all this is that, since no one was aware of the birth and exposure of the child except the mother, there was no reason to put any blame upon Apollo. Yet Euripides purposely adopts that version of the story.

Instead, what happens? Creusa vehemently denies any suggestion of deceit. The play proceeds and still gains its effects from the assumption that Apollo was the father. The characters still continue to judge him by human standards. For Ion immediately asks why Apollo should give his own son to Xuthus, with the plain falsehood that he was the father. Creusa, now quite happy in the possession of her son, is content to let moral problems go by the board. Apollo, she says, practiced the deceit out of kindness to Ion. But Ion is not satisfied. He has already received some shocks to his beliefs. His only wish now is to decide finally whether Apollo is a sham:

> But, mother, does Apollo tell the truth,
> Or is the oracle false? With some good reason
> That question troubles me.

Creusa offers the same explanation again, but Ion's question "cannot be so lightly answered." He is about to enter the temple to ask the oracle if Apollo is his father when Athene appears. She begins by saying that Apollo did not care to come, since some criticism of his previous conduct might be expected. This answer to Creusa's earlier challenge is intentionally farcical. Apollo now becomes contemptible. Ion is saved the trouble of consulting the oracle. Athene assures him that Apollo is really his father. The legend is preserved to the end. But Ion's question is ignored. The answer is too obvious.

Athene's final remarks are all the more ironic because redundant. They are an appeal to faith, and Euripides has done his best to destroy the basis of faith. Even now Apollo can go merrily on from one deceit to another. Xuthus is not to know the truth, and Apollo makes Creusa and Ion partners in his falsehood. Only Athene, Hermes, and Creusa seem satisfied that Apollo "has managed all things well." Certainly no reader of the play can be. But Creusa, at least, may be pardoned for grasping her long-awaited reward without too much questioning.

Athene serves a double function. As in other plays of Euripides with a *deus ex machina*, she commemorates the foundation of a hero-cult and prophesies future Athenian history. At the same time, by uttering her divine commonplaces, she adds nothing to our knowledge but fits in with the dramatic purpose of the play. Before her appearance Apollo had still some chance to justify himself. After it, he retains no shred of dignity.

CHARACTERS

Hermes

Ion

Chorus (Creusa's attendants)

Creusa

Xuthus

Old Man

A Servant

Pythian priestess

Athene

ION

SCENE: *Before the temple of Apollo at Delphi, just before sunrise.*

(Enter Hermes.)

Hermes

Atlas, who wears on back of bronze the ancient
Abode of gods in heaven, had a daughter
Whose name was Maia, born of a goddess:
She lay with Zeus and bore me, Hermes, servant
Of the immortals. I have come here to Delphi   5
Where Phoebus sits at earth's mid-center, gives
His prophecies to men, and passes judgment
On what is happening now and what will come.
  For in the famous city of the Greeks
Called after Pallas of the Golden Spear,
Phoebus compelled Erechtheus' daughter Creusa   10
To take him as her lover—in that place
Below Athene's hill whose northern scarp
The Attic lords have named the Long Rocks.
Her father, by the god's own wish, did not
Suspect her, and she carried her child in secret.   15
And when the time had come, her son was born,
Inside the palace. Then she took the child
To the same cave where she had lain with Phoebus,
And in a wicker cradle there exposed
Him to his death. She kept an ancient custom   20
Begun in Athens when Athene placed
By Erichthonius, son of Earth, two snakes
As guardians, when the daughters of Aglaurus

273

Were given charge of him.

                 And so Creusa tied   25
To him whatever girlish ornaments
She had, before she left him to his death.
My brother Phoebus then made this request:
"You know Athene's city well," he said,
"Now will you journey to the earth-born people   30
Of glorious Athens? There, inside a cave
A newborn child is hidden. Take the child,
His cradle, and his swaddling clothes and bring
Them to my oracle at Delphi, where
They must be left before the temple entrance.   35
I will arrange the rest. The child is mine."
    I did as Loxias my brother wished,
Took up the wicker cradle, brought it here,
Setting it on the temple steps before
I opened it, so that someone might see
The child. Now when the sun began to ride   40
In heaven, the prophetess was entering
The holy shrine. Her eyes were drawn toward
The helpless child. Astonished that a girl
Of Delphi should dare to cast her secret child
Before Apollo's temple, she would have taken it   45
Outside the sacred precinct, but her pity
Expelled the cruel impulse—and the god
Designed to keep his son within his house.
And so she took the child and reared him,
Not knowing who his mother was, or that   50
Apollo was his father; while the child
Has never known his parents. His childhood home
Has been about the altars where he played
And wandered. But when he was fully grown,
The Delphians appointed him their steward,   55
The trusted guardian of Apollo's gold.
And he has lived a holy life until
This day, within the shrine.

                 Creusa, whose son
He is, has married Xuthus. This is how

The marriage occurred. A war was surging high
Between Chalcidians of Euboea and Athens,   60
Whose ally, Xuthus, helped to end the strife.
Though he was not a native, but Achaean,
Son of Aeolus, son of Zeus, the prize
He won was marriage to Creusa. But
In all these years no children have been born.   65
Desire for children is now bringing them
To Apollo's shrine. Apollo seems indifferent,
But he controls their fate and guides them here.
When Xuthus comes before the shrine, the god
Will give him his own son, declaring Xuthus   70
The father. Thus the boy shall be received
Into his mother's house, made known to her.
And while Apollo's intrigue is kept secret,
His son may have what is his due. Moreover,
Apollo will bestow on him the name
Of Ion, make that name renowned through Greece   75
As founder of ancient cities.
                              Now, because
I wish to see this young boy's destiny
Complete, I shall conceal myself within
These laurel groves. This is Apollo's son,
Who comes here now, with branches of bay, to make
The portals bright before the temple. And I
Will be the first of all the gods to call   80
Him by his future name of—Ion.

> (*The central doors of the temple open, and Ion
> comes out with a group of Delphian servants. He
> is wearing a brightly colored tunic and cloak,
> and on his head is a wreath of bay leaves. He
> carries a bow and arrow, symbol of his serv-
> ice to Apollo, which is to have a more
> practical purpose later in the scene. The
> two peaks of Parnassus which over-
> look the temple have caught the
> first rays of the dawn, and Ion*

points to them as he begins
to speak.)

Ion

    Look, now the sun's burning chariot comes
    Casting his light on the earth.
    Banned by his flame, the stars flee
    To the awful darkness of space.   85
    The untrodden peaks of Parnassus,
    Kindling to flame, receive for mankind
    The disk of the day.
       The smoke of unwatered myrrh drifts
    To the top of the temple.   90
    The Delphian priestess sits on the
    Sacred tripod chanting to the Greeks
    Echoes of Apollo's voice.
       You Delphians, attendants of Phoebus,
    Go down to Castalia's silvery eddies: 95
    When you have bathed in its holy dews,
    Return to the temple.
    Let your lips utter no words
    Of ill-omen, may your tongues
    Be gracious and gentle to those who   100
    Come to the oracle.
       As for myself, mine is the task
    I have always done since my childhood.
    With these branches of bay and these sacred
    Garlands I will brighten Apollo's
    Portals, cleanse the floor with   105
    Sprinklings of water,
    Put to flight with my arrows the birds
    Who foul the offerings.
    Since I have neither mother nor father,
    I revere the temple of Phoebus   110
    Where I have lived.

    Come, fresh-blooming branch
    Of lovely laurel,

With which I sweep clean
The precinct below the shrine,   115
Sprung from the eternal garden
Where the sacred spring sends
A welling, never failing stream
From the myrtle grove
To water the sacred leaves,   120
Leaves I brush over his fane,
Every day serving with my daily task
When the sun's swift wing appears.

O Healer! O Healer!   125
My blessing! My blessing!
O Leto's son!

Fair, fair is the labor,
O Phoebus, which
I am doing for you,
Honoring the prophetic place.   130
I have a glorious task:
To set my hands to serve
Not a man but the immortals.
I will never weary
Over my pious tasks.   135
I praise him who feeds me, Phoebus
My father—his love deserves the name,
Phoebus, lord of the temple.   140

O Healer! O Healer!
My blessing! My blessing!
O Leto's son!

Now I have finished my sweeping
With my broom of bay,   145
I will pour from golden bowls
Water risen from the earth,
Drawn from the spring
Of Castalia.
Myself holy and chaste, I can

Cast the lustral water. 150
Always thus may I serve Phoebus,
Service without end—
Or an end come with good issue.
  Look! Look!
Here come the birds already,
Leaving their nests on Parnassus. 155
Keep away from the cornices
And the gold-decked abode.
I will strike you again with my arrows,
You herald of Zeus,
Though your beak is strong,
Surpassing the other birds. 160
Here sails another to the temple steps,
A swan.—Take to another place
Your red shining feet.
You may have your music,
But Apollo's lyre will not save you
At all from my bow, 165
Turn your wings,
Speed on to the lake of Delos.
If you do not obey,
You will raise, and in blood,
That clear-toned song.
  Look! Look! 170
What is this other bird here on its way?
Is it going to build in the cornice
A nest of dry twigs for its young?
The twang of my bow will prevent it.
Go, I tell you and rear
Your young in the eddies of Alpheus 175
Or the Isthmian grove,
Without fouling the offerings
And Apollo's shrine.
Yet I scruple to kill you
Who announce to mankind
The will of the gods. 180
But I will bend to the labors

Of my devotion,
Never ceasing to honor him
Who gives me life.

> (*Ion goes out. The Delphian servants enter in
> silence and perform a sacrifice on the altar of the
> temple. After the sacrifice the Chorus, young
> girl servants of Creusa, enter. They pass up
> and down, excitedly admiring the temple
> buildings.*)

Chorus

Not only in holy Athens after all
Are there courts of the gods   185
With fair columns, and homage paid
To Apollo who protects the streets.
Here too on this temple
Of Leto's son shows
The bright-eyed beauty of twin façades.

Look, look at this: Zeus's son   190
Is killing the Lernaean Hydra
With a golden sickle,
Look there, my dear.

Yes—and near him another is raising
On high a flaming torch.   195
Can it be he whose story I hear
As I sit at my weaving,
Iolaus the shield-bearer,
Companion of Heracles,
Whom he helped to endure his labors?   200

And look at this one
On a horse with wings.
He is killing the mighty three-bodied
Fire-breathing monster.

My eyes dart everywhere.   205
See! The battle of the giants
On the marble walls.

Yes we are looking.

Can you see her, brandishing
Her Gorgon shield against Enceladus—?   210
I can see my goddess Pallas Athene.

Oh! The terrible thunderbolt
With fire at each end which Zeus holds
Ready to throw.

Yes I see. Raging Mimas
Is burnt up in the flames.   215

And Bacchus, the boisterous god,
With unwarlike wand of ivy is killing
Another of Earth's giant sons.

(Ion enters through the central doors of the temple.)

Chorus Leader
You there by the temple,
May we with naked feet   220
Pass into this sanctuary?

Ion
You may not, strangers.

Chorus Leader
Perhaps you would tell me—?

Ion
Tell me, what do you want?

Chorus Leader
Is it true that Apollo's temple
Really contains the world's center?

Ion
Yes, wreathed in garlands, flanked by Gorgons.

Chorus Leader
That is the story we have heard.   225

Ion

If you have offered sacrificial food
In front of the temple, and you have a question
For Apollo to answer, come to the altar steps.
But do not pass into the inner shrine
Unless you have slaughtered a sheep.

Chorus Leader

I understand.
We are not for transgressing Apollo's law.   230
The outside charms us enough.

Ion

Look where you please at what is lawful.

Chorus Leader

Our masters have allowed us
To look over this sanctuary of Apollo.

Ion

In whose house do you serve?

Chorus Leader

The dwelling place of Pallas   235
Is the house of our masters.
But the person you ask about is here.

                                                    (*Enter Creusa.*)

Ion

Whoever you may be, you are a noble,
Your looks reveal your character: by looks
Nobility is often to be judged.   240
But?—You surprise me—why, your eyes are closed,
That noble face is wet with tears—and now!
When you have seen Apollo's holy temple.
What reason can there be for your distraction?
Where others are glad to see the sanctuary,   245
Your eyes are filled with tears.

281

Creusa

That you should be surprised about my tears
Is not ill-bred. But when I saw this temple,
I measured an old memory again,   250
My mind elsewhere, though I stand here.
(*aside*) Unhappy women! Where shall we appeal
For justice when the injustice of power
Is our destruction?

Ion

What is the cause of this strange melancholy?   255

Creusa

Nothing. Now I have loosed my shaft I shall
Be silent, and you will not think of it.

Ion

But tell me who you are, your family,
Your country. And what is your name?

Creusa

Creusa is my name, Erechtheus' daughter,   260
And Athens is my native land.

Ion

A famous city and a noble race!
How fortunate you are!

Creusa

Yes, fortunate in that—but nothing else.

Ion

There is a story told—can that be true?   265

Creusa

But tell me what you want to know.

Ion

Your father's ancestor sprang from the earth?

Creusa
Yes, Erichthonius—the glory is no help.

Ion
Athene really took him from the earth?

Creusa
Into her virgin arms, though not her son.   270

Ion
And then she gave him as we see in paintings—

Creusa
To Cecrops' daughters, who were to keep him hidden.

Ion
I have been told they opened the cradle.

Creusa
And died for it. The rocks were stained with blood.

Ion
Oh. (*pauses*)
The other story? Is that true or not?   275

Creusa
Which one is that?—I have time to answer.

Ion
Well, did your father sacrifice your sisters?

Creusa
He had the courage. They were killed for Athens.

Ion
How was it you were saved, the only one?

Creusa
I was a baby in my mother's arms.   280

Ion
And was your father buried in a chasm?

Creusa
The sea-god's trident blows destroyed him.

Ion
There is a place there which is called Long Rocks?

Creusa
Oh, why ask that?—You are reminding me.—

Ion
The lightning-fire of Phoebus honors it.   285

Creusa
Vain honor. I wish I had never seen it.

Ion
Why do you hate a place he dearly loves?

Creusa
No matter.—But I know its secret shame.—

Ion
And what Athenian became your husband?

Creusa
My husband is no citizen of Athens.   290

Ion
Who then? He must have been of noble birth.

Creusa
Xuthus, the son of Aeolus and Zeus.

Ion
A stranger. How then could he marry you?

Creusa
A neighboring land of Athens is Euboea—

Ion
Which has a sea for boundary they say.   295

Creusa

—Which Athens conquered with the help of Xuthus.

Ion

The ally came, and you were his reward?

Creusa

Dowry of war, the prize won with his spear.

Ion

And have you come alone or with your husband?

Creusa

With him. But he stayed at Trophonius' shrine.   300

Ion

To see it or consult the oracle?

Creusa

To ask the same as he will ask of Phoebus.

Ion

Is it about your country's crops—or children?

Creusa

Though married long ago, we have no children.

Ion

No children? You have never had a child?   305

Creusa

Apollo knows my childlessness.

Ion

Ah! That misfortune cancels all your blessings.

Creusa

And who are you? Your mother must be happy!

Ion

I am what I am called, Apollo's slave.

Creusa
A city's votive gift or sold by someone?   310

Ion
I only know that I am called Apollo's.

Creusa
So now it is my turn to pity you!

Ion
Because my parents are unknown to me.

Creusa
You live inside the temple? Or at home?

Ion
Apollo's home is mine, wherever I sleep.   315

Creusa
And did you come here as a child?

Ion
A child, they say who seem to know.

Creusa
What Delphian woman suckled you?

Ion
No breast fed me. But she who reared me.—

Creusa
Yes, who, poor child? (*aside*) A sorrow like my own.   320

Ion
The prophetess, I think of her as mother.

Creusa
But what supported you as you grew up?

Ion
The altars and the visitors who came.

Creusa

And your unhappy mother! Who was she then?

Ion

My birth perhaps marked her betrayal.   325

Creusa

You are not poor? Your robes are fine enough.

Ion

These robes belong to him, the god I serve.

Creusa

But have you never tried to find your parents?

Ion

How can I when I have no clues to guide?

Creusa

Ah yes. (*pause*)
Another suffered as your mother did.   330

Ion

Who was she then? If she would help me in my grief!   331

Creusa

On her behalf I came before my husband.   332

Ion

Why did you come? Tell me and I will help.   333

Creusa

I have a friend—who says—she lay with Phoebus.   338

Ion

Not Phoebus and a mortal woman. No!

Creusa

And had a child unknown to her own father.   340

Ion

She is ashamed to own some man's betrayal.

Creusa
But she says not. Her life has been most wretched.

Ion
Why, if her lover was a god?

Creusa
She put from out the house the child she had.

Ion
Where is the child? Is it alive?   345

Creusa
I have come here to ask, for no one knows.

Ion
If he is dead, how did he die?

Creusa
Killed by wild beasts, she thinks.

Ion
What reason could she have for thinking so?

Creusa
She could not find him when she went again.   350

Ion
But were there drops of blood upon the ground?

Creusa
She says not, though her search was careful.

Ion
And how long is it since the child was killed?

Creusa
He would have been your age by now.

Ion
Apollo is unjust. She has my pity.   355

Creusa

For she has never had another child.

> (*Pause as Ion reflects. He is still unwilling
> to believe Apollo guilty.*)

Ion

Supposing Phoebus reared him in secret?

Creusa

To keep that pleasure for himself is wrong.

Ion (sighs)

Ah! This misfortune echoes my own grief.

Creusa

And some unhappy mother misses you.   360

Ion

Do not revive the grief I had forgotten.

Creusa

No.—Then you will see to my request?

Ion

But do you know where that request is faulty?

Creusa

What is not faulty for that wretched woman?

Ion

Will Phoebus tell the secret he wants to hide?   365

Creusa

If oracles are open to all Greeks.

Ion

Do not press him to reveal his shame.

Creusa

His shame means suffering to her!

Ion

No one will give this oracle to you.
Convicted of evil here inside his own temple,   370
Apollo would justly take vengeance on
His prophet. Think no more of it: avoid
A question which the god himself opposes.
This foolishness we should commit in trying
By any means to force reluctant answers,   375
Whether by slaying sheep before the altar
Or taking omens from the flight of birds.
The benefits we win by force against
Their will are never blessed. We only profit
By what the gods give with their blessing.   380

Chorus Leader

The woes assailing human life are many,
The forms of woe diverse. And happiness
Is rare and rarely comes to light on man.

Creusa

(*Raising her hands toward the temple.*)

Apollo! Then and now unjust to her,
The absent woman whose complaints are here.   385
You did not save the child you should have saved.
A prophet, you have no answer for its mother.
But now that hope must die, because the god   390
Prevents me learning what I wish to know.
But I can see my noble husband, Xuthus,
Arriving from Trophonius' cave. He is
Quite near; I beg you, stranger, tell him nothing
Of what we have been saying. Or I may   395
Be suspect, meddling in these secret matters,
And then this story will not have the end
We have designed. For trouble is very easy
When women deal with men. Since good and bad
Are not distinguished, all of us are hated.
To this misfortune we are born.   400

(Xuthus enters with servants and Delphians.)

Xuthus

My greeting first is to the god, and then
To you my wife.

(He sees she is upset.)

But has my long delay
Caused you alarm?

Creusa

No. Your arrival has prevented that.
What oracle did Trophonius give about
Our hopes of having children?   405

Xuthus

He was unwilling to anticipate
Apollo's answer. But he has told me this,
That neither you nor I shall go from here
Without a child.

Creusa

O holy mother of Apollo, may   410
Our journey here end well, our dealings with
Your son have a happier issue than before!

Xuthus

So it will be! But who speaks here for Phoebus?

Ion

Sir, that is my role outside the temple—
Inside are others, near the shrine, the nobles   415
Of Delphi, chosen by lot.

Xuthus

Ah! Good. I now know all I need to know,
And shall go in. They say the victim, which
Is offered on behalf of strangers, has
Already fallen before the altar. Omens   420
Today are good, and I would like to have

My answer from the oracle. Will you,
Creusa, with laurel branches in your hand,
Go round the altars praying to the gods
That I may bring an oracle with promise
Of children from Apollo's house.

(*Xuthus enters the temple, Creusa watches him go and speaks with her hands raised toward the temple.*)

Creusa

So it will be! So it will be!
               And now   425
If Phoebus at least amends his former wrongs,
Although his love can never be complete,
Because he is a god, I will accept
Whatever he bestows.

                                (*Exit.*)

Ion

Why does this stranger always speak in riddles,
Reproach the god with covert blasphemy?   430
Is it through love of her on whose behalf
She comes before the oracle? Perhaps
She hides a secret which she cannot tell.
But what concern have I with Erechtheus' daughter?
No, that is not my business.—I will pour
The holy water out of golden pitchers   435
Into the lustral bowls. I must confront
Apollo with his wrongs. To force a girl
Against her will and afterward betray!
To leave a child to die which has been born
In secret! No! Do not act thus. But since
You have the power, seek the virtuous path.   440
All evil men are punished by the gods.
How then can it be just for you to stand
Accused of breaking laws you have yourselves
Laid down for men? But if—here I suppose
What could not be—you gave account on earth
For wrongs which you have done to women, you,   445

Apollo and Poseidon and Zeus who rules
In heaven, payment of your penalties
Would see your temples empty, since you are
Unjust to others in pursuing pleasure
Without forethought. And justice now demands
That we should not speak ill of men if they   450
But imitate what the gods approve, but those
Who teach men their examples.

Chorus   (*Exit.*)

STROPHE

O my Athene, born
Without birth pains,
Brought forth from the head of Zeus
By Prometheus, the Titan,
Blessed goddess of Victory,   455
Take flight from the golden halls
Of Olympus, come I entreat you,
Here to the Pythian temple,
Where at earth's center Apollo's shrine   460
Proclaims unfailing prophecy,
At the tripod where they dance and sing.
Come with Artemis, Leto's daughter,
Virgin goddess both,   465
Holy sisters of Phoebus.
Beseech him, O maidens,
That the ancient race of Erechtheus may
At last be sure by a clear response
Of the blessing of children.   470

ANTISTROPHE

Wherever gleams bright the flame
And strength of youth,
A promise to the house of growth,
There a man has a fund
Of joy overflowing;   475
From the fathers the children will gather

293

Hereditary wealth, and in turn
Pass it on to their own.   480
They are a defense in adversity,
In happiness a delight,
And in war their country's shield of safety.
For myself I would choose, rather than wealth   485
Or a palace of kings, to rear
And love my own children:
Shame to him who prefers
A childless life, hateful to me.
May I cling to the life of few possessions,   490
Enriched by children.

EPODE

O haunts of Pan,
The rock flanking
The caves of the Long Cliffs,
Where the daughters of Aglaurus   495
Dance, and their feet tread
The green levels before the shrines
Of Pallas, in time to the changing
Music of the pipes, when you play,   500
O Pan, in your sunless caves,
Where a girl in misery
Bore a child to Phoebus
And exposed it, a prey for birds,
Food for wild beasts to rend, shame
Of a cruel love.   505
Our legends, our tales at the loom,
Never tell of good fortune to children
Born of a god and a mortal.

(*Enter Ion from the central doors of the temple.*)
Ion
  Serving women who are keeping watch here at the steps   510
  Of the house of sacrifice, awaiting your master,
  Tell me, has Xuthus already left the sacred tripod

And the oracle, or does he still remain within,
Seeking answers to his question?

Chorus Leader

He is still inside. He has not passed this threshold yet.
But the noise the door has made shows someone is now
there.
Look, it is my master coming.   515

> (*Xuthus appears from the temple. As soon as he
> sees Ion, he shows great excitement, runs to
> him and tries to embrace him. Ion, much
> surprised by this behavior, resists.*)

Xuthus

Son, my blessing.—It is right to greet you in this way.

Ion

Sir, my thanks. We are both well—if you are not mad.

Xuthus

Let me kiss your hand, embrace you.

Ion

Are you sane? Or can the god have made you mad somehow?   520

Xuthus

Mad, when I have found my own and want to welcome
him?

Ion

Stop.—Or if you touch it, you may break Apollo's
crown.

Xuthus

I will touch you. And I am no robber. You are mine.

Ion

Must I shoot this arrow first, or will you loose me now?

295

Xuthus
Why must you avoid me just when you found your
    nearest?   525

Ion
Mad and boorish strangers are no pleasure to instruct.

Xuthus
Kill me, and then bury me. For you will kill your father.

Ion
You my father! This is fool's talk.—How can that be?
    No!

Xuthus
Yes.—The story which I have to tell will make it clear.

Ion
What have you to say?

Xuthus
            I am your father. You are my son.   530

Ion
Who has told you this?

Xuthus
            Apollo, he who reared my son.

Ion
You are your own witness.

Xuthus
              But I know my oracle too.

Ion
You mistook a riddle.

Xuthus
            Then my hearing must have
    failed.

Ion

And what is Apollo's prophecy?

Xuthus

That him I met—

Ion

Oh! A meeting? Where?

Xuthus

As I came from the temple
here. 535

Ion

Yes, and what would happen to him?

Xuthus

He would be my
son.

Ion

Your own son or just a gift?

Xuthus

A gift and my own son.

Ion

I was then the first you met?

Xuthus

Yes, no one else, my son.

Ion

But how strange this is!

Xuthus

I am just as amazed as you.

Ion

Well?—Who is my mother?

297

Xuthus

That I cannot say.   540

Ion
  And Apollo?

Xuthus

      Happy with this news, I did not ask.

Ion
  Earth then was my mother!

Xuthus

          Children do not spring up
    there.

Ion
  How could I be yours?

Xuthus

        Apollo, not I, has the answer.

Ion (*after a pause*)
  Let us try another tack.

Xuthus

        Yes, that will help us more.

Ion
  Have you had a secret lover?

Xuthus

          Yes, a youthful folly.   545

Ion
  And before you were married?

Xuthus

          Yes, but never afterward.

Ion
  So that could be my origin?

Xuthus

Time at least agrees.

Ion

Then what am I doing here?

Xuthus

I cannot tell you that.

Ion

Here, so far away?

Xuthus

That is my puzzle too.

Ion

Have you been before to Delphi?

Xuthus

To the wine-god's
torch feast.   550

Ion

You stayed with a temple steward?

Xuthus

He—there were girls
of Delphi.   551

Ion

He introduced you to their rites?

Xuthus

Yes, they were
Bacchanals.   552

Ion

You had drunk well?

Xuthus

I was reveling in the wine-god's
feast.   553

299

Ion
  Then that was the time.

Xuthus
                    The girl perhaps exposed her
  child.   555

Ion (*after a pause*)
  I am not a slave then.

Xuthus
                    And you can accept a father.   556

Ion
  Could I wish for better?

Xuthus
                    That you might have seen
  before.   558

Ion
  Than descent from Zeus's son?

Xuthus
                    This is indeed your birth-
  right.   559

Ion
  Shall I touch my father then?

Xuthus
                    Yes, have faith in the god.   560

Ion
  Father—

Xuthus
    How dear is the sound of the name you have
  spoken!

Ion

We should both bless this day.

Xuthus

It has brought me happi-
ness.

(They embrace.)

Ion

My dear mother! Shall I ever see your face as well?
Now, whoever you may be, I long to see you even
More. But she is dead perhaps, and I can have no hope.   565

Chorus Leader

We also share this house's happiness.
Yet I could wish my mistress too might have
The joy of children, and Erechtheus' race.

Xuthus

My son, Apollo rightly prophesied
That I should find you, and united us.   570
You found a father whom you never knew.
Your natural desire I share myself
That you will find your mother, I, in her
The woman who gave me a son. And if
We leave all that to time, perhaps we shall   575
Succeed. But end your waif's life in the temple.
Let me persuade you, come with me to Athens,
For there your father's prosperous power awaits
You, and great wealth. Though now you suffer
In one respect, you shall not have the name
Of bastard and of beggar, but highborn   580
And well endowed with wealth. But why so silent?
Why do you hold your eyes downcast? Now you have
changed
Your father's joy to fear.

Ion

Things have a different face as they appear   585

Before the eyes or far away. I bless
My fortune now that I have found a father.
But, father, listen to what is in my mind:
The earth-born people of glorious Athens are said
To be no alien race. I should intrude   590
There marked by two defects, a stranger's son,
Myself a bastard. And if I remain
Obscure, with this disgrace they will account
Me nothing, nobody's son. If I aspire
To the city's helm, ambitious for a name,   595
I shall be hated by the powerless.
Authority is never without hate.
And those who have ability for power
But wisely keep their silence, are not eager
For public life, will mock my folly, blindly   600
Deserting peace for Athens' crowded fears.
And then if I invade positions which
Are filled, I shall be countered by the moves
Of those with knowledge who control affairs.
For so it always happens, father: men   605
Who hold the cities and their dignities
Above all are opposed to rivalry.
    Then, coming to another's house, a stranger,
To live with one who has no children, who
Before had you to share the sorrow—now,   610
Abandoned to a private grief, she will
Have cause for bitterness and cause enough
To hate me when I take my place as heir:
Without a child herself, she will not kindly
Regard your own. Then you must either turn   615
To her, betraying me, or honor me
And bring confusion to your house: there is
No other way. How many wives have brought
Their men to death with poison or the knife!
Then, childless, growing old, she has my pity.   620
For this affliction does not suit her birth.
    The praise of royalty itself is false—
A fair façade to hide the pain within.

What happiness or blessing has the man
Who looks askance for violence, and fear
Draws out his days? I would prefer to live   625
A happy citizen than be a king,
Compelled to have the evil as his friends,
Who must abhor the good for fear of death.
You might reply that gold outweighs all this,
The joys of wealth—no joy for me to guard   630
A fortune, hear reproaches, suffer its pains.
Let me avoid distress, win moderation.

    But father, hear the good points of my life
In Delphi: leisure first of all, most dear
To any man, the friendly people, no one   635
To thrust me rudely from my path; to yield,
Give elbow room to those beneath us is
Intolerable. Then I was busy with
My prayers to gods or talk with men,
Serving the happy, not the discontented.
I was receiving guests or sending them   640
Away again, a fresh face always smiling
On fresh faces. I had what men should pray,
Even against their will, to have: duty
And inclination both contrived to make
Me righteous to god. When I compare the two,   645
Father, I think I am more happy here.
Let me live here. Delight in splendor is
No more than happiness with little: for both
Have their appeal.

Chorus (*aside*)

Well have you spoken if indeed your words
Mean happiness for her I love.

Xuthus

No more of this! Learn to enjoy success.   650
Let us inaugurate our life together
By holding here, where I have found my son,
A public banquet, and make the sacrifices

Omitted at your birth. I will pretend
To bring you to my house, a guest, and give
A feast for you; and then take you along   655
With me to Athens, not as my son but as
A visitor. I do not want to hurt
My childless wife with my own happiness.
But when I think the time is ripe, I will
Persuade my wife to give consent to your
Assumption of my rule.   660
　　　Your name shall be Ion, a name to fit
Your destiny; you were the first to meet
Me coming from Apollo's shrine. But now
Collect your friends together, say farewell
With feast and sacrifice, before you leave   665
This town of Delphi. And, you women slaves,
I order you, say nothing of our plans.
To tell my wife will mean your death.

Ion

Yes, I will go. But one piece of good luck
Eludes me still: unless I find my mother,
My life is worthless. If I may do so,   670
I pray my mother is Athenian,
So that through her I may have rights of speech.
For when a stranger comes into a city
Of pure blood, though in name a citizen,
His mouth remains a slave: he has no right
Of speech.   675

(*Exeunt.*)

Chorus

STROPHE

I see tears and mourning
Triumphant, a sorrowful entrance,
When the queen hears of the son,
The blessing bestowed on her husband
Alone, still childless herself.   680
O Latona's prophetic son, what reply have you chanted?

304

From where came this child, reared
In your temple, and who is his mother?
This oracle does not please me.
 There may be a fraud.   685
  I fear the issue
  Of this encounter.
For these are strange matters,   690
A strange command on my silence.
Treachery and chance combine
In this boy of an alien blood.
  Who will deny it?

ANTISTROPHE

My friends, shall we clearly   695
Cry out in the ears of my mistress
Blame upon him who alone
Afforded her hope she could share?
Now she is maimed by his joy.
She is falling to gray age, he does not honor his love.   700
 A stranger he came, wretch,
To the house, and betrays the fortune
Bestowed. He wronged her.—Die then!
  And may he not gain
  From god the prayer   705
  He sends with incense
Ablaze on bright altars.
He shall be sure of my feeling,
How much I love the queen.   710
The new father and son are now near
  To their new banquet.

EPODE

O the ridge of the rocks of Parnassus
Which hold in the skies the watchtower   715
Where Bacchus holds the two-flamed
Torch, leaping lightly with his
Nighttime wandering Bacchanals:
  Let the boy never see my city,

Let him die and leave his new life. 720
A city in trouble has reason
To welcome the coming of strangers.
But Erechtheus, our ancient founder,
   United us long ago.

*(Creusa enters with an Old Man, a slave and
trusted servant of the family. They begin
to climb the temple steps, Creusa
supporting him.)*

Creusa

Erechtheus, my father, long before he died 725
Made you the guardian of his children: *(pauses)*
Come up with me to Phoebus' oracle
To share my pleasure if his prophecy
Gives hope of children; since it is a joy
To share success with those we love; and if— 730
I pray that they may not—reverses come,
There is a balm in seeing friendly eyes.
And, though I am your mistress, I love you
As if you were my father, as you did
My own.

Old Man

My daughter, you preserve a noble spirit 735
And equal to your noble ancestors:
You have not shamed your fathers, sons of Earth.
Give me your help, and bring me to the temple.
The shrine is steep, you know. Support my limbs
And heal my weak old age. 740

Creusa

Come then. Be careful how you place your feet.

Old Man *(as he stumbles)*

You see. My mind is nimbler than my feet.

Creusa

Lean with your staff upon the path around.

Old Man
And that is blind now when my eyes are weak.

Creusa
Yes, true. But fight against your weariness. 745

Old Man
I do. But now I have no strength to summon.

(*He turns slowly and with Creusa's help settles
himself on the temple steps, looking toward
the audience. They are now face to face
with the Chorus. Creusa addresses
the Chorus.*)

Creusa
You women, faithful servants of my loom
And shuttle, what hope of children did my husband
Receive before he left? We came for that.
Tell me; and if the news is good you will 750
Not find your mistress faithless or ungrateful.

Chorus
An evil fate!

Old Man
Your prelude is not one that suits good luck.

Chorus
Unhappy lot!

Old Man
But what is wrong about the oracle? 755

Chorus
What can we do when death is set before us?

Creusa
What strain is this? Why should you be afraid?

Chorus
Are we to speak or not? What shall we do?

Creusa
O speak! You know of some misfortune coming.

Chorus Leader
You shall be told then, even if I die 760
Twice over.—You will never have a child
To hold, or take one to your breast.

(*Creusa sinks down to the steps beside the slave.*)

Creusa
I wish I were dead.

Old Man
Daughter—

Creusa
O this blow
Is hard, this pain put upon me,
I cannot endure it, my friends.

Old Man
Hopeless now, my child.

Creusa
Yes, ah! yes. 765
This blow is fatal, a heart-thrust.
The sorrow has pierced within.

Old Man
Mourn no more—

Creusa
I have reason enough.

Old Man
Till we know—

Creusa
Is there anything to know? 770

Old Man
　　—If you alone have this misfortune, or
　　Our master too must share the same.

Chorus Leader
　　To him Apollo gave a son, but this
　　Good luck is his alone, his wife has nothing.　775

Creusa
　　One after the other you have cried out my griefs.
　　　　This is the worst to deplore.

Old Man
　　And did the oracle concern a living son,
　　Or must some woman yet give birth to him?

Chorus Leader
　　Phoebus gave him a son already born,　　　780
　　A full-grown youth; and I myself was witness.

Creusa
　　How can it be true? No! an incredible thing.
　　　　It is surely fantastic.

Old Man
　　Fantastic! Tell me how the oracle　　　785
　　Is carried out, and who the son can be.

Chorus Leader
　　He gave your husband for a son the one
　　He should meet first as he came from the temple.

Creusa
　　Then it is settled.
　　Mine is the childless part,　　　790
　　The solitary life in a desolate house.

Old Man
　　Who then was chosen for Xuthus to meet?
　　And tell me how and where he saw his child.

Chorus Leader

There was a boy who swept the temple here.
You know him? For he is the son.   795

Creusa

Would that I might fly
Through the gentle air far away
From Greek earth to the evening stars.
Such is my anguish, my friends.

Old Man

What was the name his father gave to him?   800
You know it? Or does that remain uncertain?

Chorus Leader

He called him Ion, since he met him first.

Old Man

Who is his mother?

Chorus Leader

That I cannot say.
But Xuthus, to tell you all I know, old man,
Has gone away unknown to her, his wife,
To offer in the consecrated tent   805
A birthday sacrifice, to pledge the bond
Of friendship in a banquet with his son.

Old Man

My lady, we have been betrayed by your
Own husband—for I share your grief; we are
Insulted by design, cast from the house   810
Of Erechtheus: this I say not out of hatred,
But rather since I love you more than him:
The foreigner who married you and came
Into the city and your house, received
Your heritage, and now is proved the father
Of children by another—secretly.   815
How secretly I will explain to you.

Aware that you would have no children,
He scorned to suffer equally with you
In this mischance, and had a secret child
By some slave woman, and sent him away
For someone in Delphi to rear. The boy   820
Was dedicated to Apollo's temple,
And there grew in concealment. While the father,
Now knowing that the boy was grown, pressed you
To travel here because you had no child.
And so Apollo did not lie, but he   825
Who has long reared the child. This is his web
Of deceit: discovered, he would lay the blame
Upon the god; if not, to guard against
The blows of time, his plan was to invest
Him with the city's rule. As time went on,
The new name Ion was invented, suiting   830
This trick of meeting him outside the temple.

Chorus Leader

I hate all evil men who plot injustice,
Then trick it out with subterfuge. I would
Prefer as friend a good man ignorant
Than one more clever who is evil too.   835

Old Man

Worst shame of all that he should bring into
Your house a cipher, motherless, the child
Of some slave woman. For the shame at least
Would have been open, if, with your consent,
Because you could not bear a child yourself,   840
He had an heir by one highborn. If this
Had been too much, he should have been content
To marry an Aeolian.
      And so you must now act a woman's part:
Kill them, your husband and his son, by sword,
By poison or some trick before death comes   845
To you from them. Unless you act your life
Is lost; for when two enemies have met

311

Together in a house, the one must be
Unlucky. Now I will help you kill the son: 850
Visit the place where he prepares the feast,
To pay the debt I owe my masters, thus,
To live or die. A slave bears only this
Disgrace: the name. In every other way   855
An honest slave is equal to the free.

Chorus Leader

I too, dear mistress, want to share your fate,
To die, or live with honor.

Creusa

(After a pause, then coming to the front.)

O my heart, how be silent?
Yet how can I speak of that secret   860
Love, strip myself of all shame?
Is one barrier left still to prevent me?
Whom have I now as my rival in virtue?
Has not my husband become my betrayer?
I am cheated of home, cheated of children,   865
Hopes are gone which I could not achieve,
The hopes of arranging things well
By hiding the facts,
By hiding the birth which brought sorrow.
No! No! But I swear by the starry abode   870
Of Zeus, by the goddess who reigns on our peaks
And by the sacred shore of the lake
Of Tritonis, I will no longer conceal it:
When I have put away the burden,
My heart will be easier.   875
Tears fall from my eyes, and my spirit is sick,
Evilly plotted against by men and by gods;
I will expose them,
Ungrateful betrayers of women.   880

O you who give the seven-toned lyre
A voice which rings out of the lifeless,

Rustic horn the lovely sound
Of the Muses' hymns,
On you, Latona's son, here   885
In daylight I will lay blame.
You came with hair flashing
Gold, as I gathered
Into my cloak flowers ablaze
With their golden light.   890
Clinging to my pale wrists
As I cried for my mother's help
You led me to bed in a cave,
A god and my lover,
With no shame,   895
Submitting to the Cyprian's will.
In misery I bore you
A son, whom in fear of my mother
I placed in that bed
Where you cruelly forced me.   900
Ah! He is lost now,
Snatched as food for birds,
My son and yours; O lost!
   But you play the lyre,
    Chanting your paeans.   905

O hear me, son of Latona,
Who assign your prophecies
From the golden throne
And the temple at earth's center,   910
I will proclaim my words in your ears:
You are an evil lover;
Though you owed no debt
To my husband, you have
Set a son in his house.   915
But my son, yes and yours, hard-hearted,
Is lost, carried away by birds,
The clothes his mother put on him abandoned.
   Delos hates you and the young
    Laurel which grows by the palm   920

313

With its delicate leaves, where Latona
Bore you, a holy child, fruit of Zeus.

(She breaks down, weeping, on the temple steps.
The Chorus gathers round her.)

Chorus Leader

O what a store of miseries is now
Disclosed; who could but weep at hearing them?

Old Man

O child, your face has riveted my gaze,   925
My reason is distracted. For just when
I banished from my heart a wave of trouble,
A second rose at the stern, caused by the words
You spoke about your present woes, before
You trod the evil path of other sorrows.   930
What do you say? What child is this you claim
To bear? Where in the city did you put
This welcome corpse for beasts? Tell me again.

Creusa

I will tell you, although I feel ashamed.

Old Man

Yes, I know how to feel with friends in trouble.   935

Creusa

Then listen. You know the cave which lies above
The north of Cecrops' hill, its name Long Rocks?

Old Man

I know. Pan's altars and his shrine are near.

Creusa

It was there I endured a fearful trial.

Old Man

Yes? My tears spring to meet your words.   940

Creusa

Phoebus became my lover against my will.

Old Man
My child, could that have been the thing I heard?

Creusa
I shall acknowledge truth if you tell me.

Old Man
When you were suffering from a secret illness?

Creusa
That was the sorrow which I now reveal.   945

Old Man
How did you hide this union with Apollo?

Creusa
I had a child.—Please hear my story out.

Old Man
But where, who helped you? Or were you alone?

Creusa
Alone in that cave where I met Apollo.

Old Man
Where is the child? You need not be childless.   950

Creusa
Dead. He was left for beasts to prey upon.

Old Man
Dead? Then Phoebus was false, gave you no help?

Creusa
He did not help. The child grew up in Hades.

Old Man
But who exposed the child? Of course not you?

Creusa
I did: I wrapped him in my robes at night.   955

Old Man
And there was no accomplice in your deed?

Creusa
No, nothing but the silence and my grief.

Old Man
How could you leave your child there, in the cave?

Creusa
How, but with many tender words of pity?—

Old Man
Ah, you were harsh; Apollo harsher still.   960

Creusa
If you had seen the child stretch out his hands!

Old Man
To find your breast, lie in your arms?

Creusa
To find what I was cruelly refusing.

Old Man
But why did you decide to expose your child?

Creusa
Because I hoped the god would save his own.   965

Old Man
A storm embroils the fortunes of your house.

(*A pause.*)

Creusa
Why do you hide your head, old man, why weep?

Old Man
I see your father and yourself so stricken.

Creusa
Such is man's life. All things must change.

316

(A pause, as the Old Man leads Creusa to the
front of the stage.)

Old Man

My child, let us no longer cling to tears.   970

Creusa

What can I do? For pain has no resource.

Old Man

Avenge yourself on him who wronged you first.

Creusa

How can a mortal fight immortal power?

Old Man

Burn down Apollo's sacred oracle.

Creusa

I am afraid.—I have enough of sorrow.   975

Old Man

Then kill your husband. This is in your power.

Creusa

He was once loyal, and I honor that.

Old Man

The son then who has come to menace you.

Creusa

But how? If only I might! I would do that!

Old Man

By putting swords in your attendants' hands.   980

(A pause.)

Creusa

Let us begin. But where can it be done?

Old Man

The sacred tent, where he is feasting friends.

317

Creusa
  Murder is flagrant; slaves are poor support.

Old Man (*despairingly*)
  You play the coward; come, give me your plan now.

>   (*A pause, as she prepares to explain her scheme;
>   she goes near to him, speaking softly and
>   urgently, as if to emphasize her
>   own resolution.*)

Creusa
  Yes, I have something which is sure and subtle.   985

Old Man
  And I can help in both these ways.

Creusa
  Then listen. You know the war fought by Earth's sons?

Old Man
  When giants fought against the gods at Phlegra.

Creusa
  Earth there produced an awful monster, Gorgon.

Old Man
  To harass all the gods and help her children?   990

Creusa
  Yes, but destroyed by Zeus's daughter Pallas.

Old Man
  Is this the tale which I have heard before?

Creusa
  Yes, that she wears its skin upon her breast.   995

Old Man
  Athene's armor which they call her aegis?

Creusa
  So called from how she rushed into the battle.

Old Man
What was the form of this barbaric thing?

Creusa
A breastplate armed with serpent coils.

(*An impatient pause.*)

Old Man
But my child, what harm can this do to your foes?

Creusa
You know Erichthonius?—Of course you must.

Old Man
The founder of your house, the son of Earth.   1000

Creusa
A newborn child, Athene gave to him—

(*She pauses.*)

Old Man
Yes, what is this you hesitate to say?

Creusa (*slowly*)
Two drops of Gorgon's blood.

Old Man
And these have some effect on men?

Creusa
One is poisonous, the other cures disease.   1005

Old Man
But how did she attach them to the child?

Creusa
A golden chain which he gave to my father.

Old Man
And when he died it came to you?

319

Creusa
Yes. I always wear it on my wrist.

Old Man
How is the twofold gift compounded then?   1010

Creusa
The drop extracted from the hollow vein—

Old Man
How is it to be used? What power has it?

Creusa
It fosters life and keeps away disease.

Old Man
What action does the other of them have?

Creusa
It kills—a poison from the Gorgon's snakes.   1015

Old Man
You carry them apart or mixed together?

Creusa
Apart. For good and evil do not mingle.

Old Man
O my dear child, you have all that you want!

Creusa
By this the boy shall die, and you shall kill him.

Old Man
But when and how? Tell me, it shall be done.   1020

Creusa
In Athens when he comes into my house.

                              (*A pause, as the slave considers.*)

Old Man
No, I distrust this plan as you did mine.

320

Creusa
Why?—Can we both have seen the same weak point?

Old Man
They will accuse you, innocent or guilty.

Creusa
Since foster mothers must be jealous.   1025

Old Man
But kill him now and so deny the crime.

Creusa
And in that way I taste my joy the sooner.

Old Man
And turn his own deceit upon your husband.

Creusa
You know then what to do? Here, take
This golden bracelet from my hand, Athene's   1030
Old gift; go where my husband holds his feast
In secret; when they end the meal, begin
To pour the gods' libation, then drop this,
Under cover of your robe, into
The young man's cup—in his alone, no more.   1035
Reserve the drink for him who would assume
The mastery of my home. Once this is drained,
He will be dead, stay here and never see
Our glorious Athens.

Old Man
Now go to our host's house, and I will do
The task appointed for me.   1040

                              (*Pause.*)

Old foot, come now, take on a youthful strength
For work, although the years deny it you.
March with your masters upon the enemy,
And help to kill and cast him from the house.

Right that the fortunate should honor virtue,   1045
But when we wish to harm our enemies
There is no law which can prevent.

(Exeunt.)

Chorus

STROPHE

Demeter's daughter, guarding the roadway, ruling
What wings through the paths of the night
And the daytime, O guide the potion   1050
Of the death-heavy cup
To whom the queen sends it, brew
Of the blood drops from the Gorgon's severed throat,   1055
To him who lifts his presumptuous hand
Against the house of Erechtheus.
   Let no others ever have
   Sway in the city:
   Only the sons of Erechtheus.   1060

ANTISTROPHE

My mistress is planning a death, and if it should fail,
The occasion of action go past,
Now her sole anchor of hope,
She will sharpen a sword
Or fasten a noose to her neck,   1065
Ending sorrow by sorrows, pass down to the realm of
    change.
For she would never endure to see
Foreigners ruling the house,   1070
   Not while living her eyes
   Still have their clarity—
   She, born of a noble line.

STROPHE

O the shame to many-hymned Dionysus, if by the
    springs
Where lovely choruses are danced,   1075
Apollo's bastard son shall behold
Unsleeping, keeping the watch,

The torches burning on the festival night,
When the star-faced heavens join in the dance,   1080
With the moon and the fifty Nereids
Who dance in the depths of the sea,
In perennial river-springs,
Honoring the gold-crowned Maid   1085
And her mother, holy Demeter:
    There, where he hopes
    To rule, usurping
    What others have wrought.

ANTISTROPHE

All you poets who raise your unjust strains   1090
Singing the unsanctioned, unholy loves
Of women, see how much we surpass
In virtue the unrighteous race   1095
Of men. Let a song of different strain
Ring out against men, harshly indicting
Their love. For here is one
Of the offspring of Zeus who shows
His ingratitude, refusing   1100
To bring good luck to the house
With his and Creusa's child:
    But yielding to passion
    For another, has found
    A bastard son.   1105

(*Enter a Servant of Creusa, greatly agitated.*)

Servant

Women, can you tell me where I may find
Erechtheus' noble daughter? I have searched
The city everywhere without success.

Chorus Leader

What is it, friend? Why are you hurrying?
What is the message you have brought?   1110

Servant

They are behind. The Delphian officers are looking
For her to stone to death.

323

Chorus Leader
    What do you mean? Have they discovered then
    The secret plot we made to kill the boy?

Servant
    Correct—and you will not be the last to suffer.   1115

Chorus Leader
    How was this scheme, unknown to them, discovered?

Servant
    The god refused to be defiled, and so
    Found means of combating the victory
    Of justice over the unjust.

Chorus Leader
    But how? I beg you tell me that: for if
    I have to die, I shall die more content   1120
    Because I know my fate.

        (*The women press nearer to the Servant.*)

Servant
    Creusa's husband came out from the shrine
    Of Phoebus, and then took his new-found son
    Away to join the feast and sacrifice
    He was preparing for the gods. Xuthus
    Himself was going to the place where   1125
    The sacred Bacchanalian fires leap,
    To sprinkle the twin crags of Dionysus
    With victim's blood for having seen his son.
    "My son," he said, "will you stay here and see
    That workmen build a tent inclosed on all
    Its sides. And if I should be long away,
    While sacrificing to the gods of birth,   1130
    Begin the banquet with such friends as come."
    He took the victims then and went away.
    Ion had the framework built in ritual form
    On upright poles without a wall, and paid
    Attention to the sun, so that he might   1135

Avoid its midday and its dying rays
Of flame, and measuring a square, its sides
A hundred feet, so that he could invite
All Delphians to the feast. To shade the tent   1140
He took from store some sacred tapestries,
A wonder to behold. And first he cast
Above the roof a wing of cloth, spoil from
The Amazons, which Heracles, the son
Of Zeus, had dedicated to the god.   1145
And there were figures woven in design:
For Uranus was mustering the stars
In heaven's circle; and Helios drove his horses
Toward his dying flame and trailed the star
Which shines bright in the West. While black-robed
   Night,   1150
Drawn by a pair, urged on her chariot,
Beside the stars kept pace with her. The Pleiades
And Orion, his sword in hand, moved through
The sky's mid-path; and then, above, the Bear
Who turned his golden tail within the vault.
The round full moon threw up her rays, dividing   1155
The month; the Hyades, the guide most sure
For sailors; then light's herald, Dawn, routing
The stars. The side he draped with tapestries
Also, but of barbarian design.
There were fine ships which fought with Greeks, and
   creatures,   1160
Half-man, half-beast, and horsemen chasing deer
Or lion hunts. And at the entrance, Cecrops,
His daughters near him, wreathed himself in coils
Of serpents—this a gift which had been given
By some Athenian. Then in the center   1165
He put the golden mixing bowls. A herald
Then went and announced that any Delphian
Who pleased was free to attend the feast. And when
The tent was full, they wreathed their heads with
   flowers
And ate the food spread in abundance till

Desire was satisfied. When they had done   1170
With eating, an old man came in and stood
Among the guests, and threw them into laughter
With his officious antics. He poured out water
From jars to wash their hands, or burned
The ooze of myrrh, and put himself in charge   1175
Of golden drinking cups. And when the flutes
Came in together with the bowl which all
Had now to drink, he said, "Enough of these
Small cups, we must have large; the company
Will then be all the sooner in good spirits."   1180
And now they busied themselves with passing gold
And silver cups; but he, as though he meant
To honor his new master, offered him
A chosen cup of wine, and put in this
A fatal poison which they say our mistress   1185
Had given, to have an end of this new son.
And no one knew. But when like all the rest
He held his cup, one of the slaves let fall
Some phrase of evil omen. He had been reared
Among good prophets in the temple, and knew   1190
The sign and ordered them to fill another.
The first libation of the god he emptied
On the ground and told the rest to pour
As he had done. A silence followed when
We filled the sacred bowls with Byblian wine   1195
And water. While this was being done, there came
Into the tent a riotous flight of doves—
They haunt Apollo's shrine and have no fear.
To slake their thirst, they dipped their beaks into
The wine the guests had poured and drew it down   1200
Their well-plumed throats; and all but one were not
Harmed by the god's libation. But she had perched
Where Ion poured his wine and tasted it.
At once her feathered body shook and quivered,
She screamed strange cries of anguish. All the band   1205
Of guests looked on amazed to see her struggles.
She died in her convulsions, her pink claws

And legs relaxed. The son the god foretold
Then stretched his uncloaked arms across the table,
And cried, "Who planned my death? Tell me, old man,   1210
Since you were so officious; you handed me
The drink." He held the old man by the arm
And searched him instantly, so that he might
Convict him in the act. His guilt was proved
And he revealed, compelled against his will,   1215
Creusa's plotting with the poisoned drink.
　　The youth bestowed by Loxias collected
The guests, went from the tent without delay,
And took his stand before the Delphian nobles.
"O rulers of the sacred city," he said,   1220
"A foreign woman, daughter of Erechtheus,
Has tried to poison me." The lords of Delphi
By many votes decided that my mistress
Be put to death, thrown from the rock, for planning
The murder of a sacred person there
Inside the temple. Now all the city looks   1225
For her whom misery advanced on this
Unhappy path. Desire for children caused
Her visit here to Phoebus, but now her life
Is lost, and with her life all hopes.

Chorus

　　There is no escape, we are doomed,
　　No escape from death.   1230
　　It has been made clear,
　　The libation of Dionysian grapes
　　Mingled for murder with blood drops
　　From the swift-working viper,
　　Clear that in sacrifice to the gods below   1235
　　Our lives are set for disaster.
　　They will stone my mistress to death.
　　What winged flight can I take,
　　Down to what dark caverns of the earth
　　Can I go to escape the stones of destruction?   1240
　　By mounting a chariot

327

Drawn by horses with speedy hooves,
Or the prow of a ship?

There is no concealment, unless a god wishes
To withdraw men from sight.   1245
O unhappy mistress, what sufferings
Wait for your soul? Shall we not,
For the will to do harm to our fellows,
According to justice, suffer ourselves?

(Creusa rushes in, wildly agitated and despairing.)

Creusa
They are in pursuit, my friends, they want to butcher
    me;   1250
By the judgment of the Pythian vote my life is forfeit.

Chorus Leader
Yes, we know in what distress you are, unhappy woman.

Creusa
Where can I find refuge then? For I have evaded them
By a trick, just left the house in time to save my life.

Chorus Leader
Where, but at the altar?

Creusa
                      What advantage will that give me?   1255

Chorus Leader
God defends the suppliant.

Creusa
                      Yes, but the law condemns me.

Chorus Leader
They must seize you first.

Creusa
                      And here my bitter rivals come,
Pressing on with sword in hand.

Chorus Leader

Sit at the altar now.
For if you die sitting there, your killers will be made
Guilty of your blood. Now destiny must be endured.　　1260

(*Creusa retires quickly to the altar at the back of
the stage. She has hardly had time to sit there
before Ion, sword in hand, comes in at the
head of a group of armed men, closely followed by a crowd of Delphians. For some
time he is not aware that Creusa is
at the altar.*)

Ion

O Cephisus, her bull-shaped ancestor,
What viper or what serpent glancing out
A deadly flame of fire did you beget
In her, this woman who will balk at nothing,
Match for the Gorgon drops with which she tried　　1265
To poison me! Take hold of her and let
Parnassus' top, when like a quoit she bounds
From rock to rock, comb out those perfect tresses.
　　Luck favored me before I went to Athens
To fall a victim to a stepmother.　　1270
For here, among my friends I learnt to measure
Your mind, your menace, and your enmity.
But if I had been trapped inside your house,
You would have sent me straight to death.

(*He suddenly catches sight of Creusa cowering
at the altar. He strides up to her.*)

The altar will not save you, nor Apollo's　　1275
House, since my greater pity is reserved
For myself and my mother. For although
She is not here, my thought of her is constant.

(*He appeals to the people with him.*)

You see her treachery—how she can twist
One scheme upon another! She has fled
To cower at the god's own altar, hoping   1280
Thus to avoid her penalty for wrong.

Creusa

I warn you not to kill me—and I speak
Not only for myself but for the god
Who guards this place.

Ion

What can you have in common with the god?

Creusa

My body is his to save, a sacred charge.   1285

Ion

You tried to poison me and I was his.

Creusa

No longer his; for you had found your father.

Ion

I belonged to Phoebus till my father came.

Creusa

But then no more. Now I belong to him.

Ion

Yes, but I had the piety you lack.   1290

Creusa

I tried to kill the enemy of my house.

Ion

I did not march upon your land with arms.

Creusa

You tried to set Erechtheus' house in flames!

Ion

What fiery flame, what torches did I carry?

Creusa
> You hoped to force possession of my home.   1295

Ion
> My father's gift—the land he gained himself.

Creusa
> How can Aeolians share Athenian land?

Ion
> Because he saved it, not with words, but arms.

Creusa
> An ally need not own the land he helps!

Ion
> You planned my death through fear of my intentions?   1300

Creusa
> To save my life in case you ceased intending.

Ion
> Childless yourself, you envied my father's child.

Creusa
> So you will snatch those homes without an heir?

Ion
> Had I no right to share my father's state?

Creusa
> A shield and spear, these are your sole possessions.   1305

> *(Ion loses his temper.)*

Ion
> Come, leave the altar and the shrine of god.

Creusa

> *(Her moral indignation yielding to spite.)*

> Go, find your mother and give her advice.

Ion

While your attempted murder goes unpunished?

Creusa

Not if you wish to kill me in the shrine.

> (*She grasps the wreaths on the altar
> as if in supplication.*)

Ion

What pleasure can the god's wreaths give to death?   1310

Creusa

I shall thus injure one who injured me.

Ion

O this is monstrous! The laws of god for men
Are not well made, their judgment is unwise.
The unjust should not have the right of refuge
At altars, but be driven away. For gods   1315
Are soiled by the touch of wicked hands. The just—
The injured man, should have this sanctuary.
Instead both good and bad alike all come,
Receiving equal treatment from the gods.

> (*The Pythian Priestess now enters from the temple.
> She is old and very dignified, wearing long white
> robes fastened by a golden girdle at the waist;
> on her head is a wreath of bay leaves and
> the riband or fillet which is the sign of
> her office. She is carrying a cradle
> wrapped in bands of wool.*)

Priestess

O stop, my son. For I, the prophetess   1320
Of Phoebus, chosen by all the Delphians
To keep the tripod's ancient law, have left
The seat of prophecy to pass these bounds.

> (*Ion greets her with great respect.*)

Ion

Dear mother, hail! Mother in all but name.

Priestess
    Then let me be so called. It pleases me.   1325

Ion
    You heard how she had planned to murder me?

Priestess
    I heard—but your own cruelty is sinful.

Ion
    Have I no right to kill a murderer?

Priestess
    Wives are unkind to children not their own.

Ion
    As we can be ill used by them.   1330

Priestess
    No. When you leave the temple for your country—

Ion
    What must I do? What is your advice?

Priestess
    Go into Athens, with good omens.

Ion
    All men are pure who kill their enemies.

Priestess
    No more of that.—Hear what I have to say.   1335

Ion
    Then speak. Your message could not be unfriendly.

Priestess
    You see the basket I am carrying?

Ion
    I see an ancient cradle bound with wool.

Priestess
I picked you up in this, a newborn child.

Ion
What do you say? This tale is new to me.   1340

Priestess
I kept it secret. Now I can reveal it.

Ion
How have you kept it from me all these years?

Priestess
The god desired to hold you as his servant.

Ion
And now he does not wish it? How can I know?

Priestess
Revealing your father, he bids you go from here.   1345

Ion
Why did you keep the cradle? Was that an order?

Priestess
Apollo put the thought into my mind.—

Ion
What thought? Tell me. I want to hear the end.

Priestess
To keep what I had found until this time.

Ion
And does it bring me any help?—or harm?   1350

Priestess
The swaddling clothes you wore are kept inside.

Ion
These clues you bring will help to find my mother.

Priestess
Which now the god desires—though not before.

Ion
This is indeed a day of happy signs!

> *(She offers him the cradle.)*

Priestess
Take this with you—and now look for your mother.   1355

Ion

> *(Taking the cradle.)*

Throughout all Asia, to Europe's boundaries!

Priestess
That is your own affair. I reared you, child,
For Phoebus' sake, and these restore to you,
Which he wished me to take and keep, although
Without express command. Why he so wished   1360
I cannot say. There was no man who knew
That I had these or where they were concealed.
And now farewell. I kiss you as my son.

> *(She embraces him. She turns and takes a few
> steps toward the temple entrance. Then she
> faces him again, to prolong her farewell
> with a few last words of advice.)*

As for the search, begin it as you ought:
Your mother might have been a Delphian girl   1365
Who left you at the temple; inquire here first,
And then elsewhere in Greece. Now you have heard
All that we have to say—Apollo, who had
An interest in your fate, and I myself.

> *(She leaves the stage through the temple door.)*

Ion

> *(Putting his hands to his face.)*

O how the tears well from my eyes whenever
My mind goes back to the time when the woman   1370

Who gave me birth, the child of secret love,
Disposed of me by stealth, and kept me from
Her breast. Instead, unnamed, I had a life
Of service in Apollo's house; and fate
Was cruel, though the god was kind. I was
Deprived of my dear mother's love throughout
The time I might have lain content and happy, 1375
Held in her arms. My mother suffered too;
She lost the joy a child can bring.

And now
I will resign the cradle as a gift 1380
To god to ward away unpleasant news.
If by some chance my mother were a slave,
To find her would be worse than ignorance.
O Phoebus, to your shrine I dedicate—
And yet, what does this mean? It is against 1385
The god's own wish; he has preserved for me
My mother's tokens. I must have the courage
To open it. I cannot shun my fate.
O sacred bands and ties which guard my precious
Tokens, what secret do you hide from me? 1390

(He unties the bands of wool from the cradle.)

A miracle! See how the cradle's covering
Is still unworn; the wicker is not decayed,
Yet years have passed since they were put away.

*(Creusa is trembling with excitement, her eyes
riveted upon the cradle.)*

Creusa
But what is this I see—beyond my hopes? 1395

Ion
Silence. You were my enemy before.

*(Creusa controls her excitement with a great effort
and gradually raises herself to a standing position
by the altar. The crowd of Delphians, her own*

*women, and Ion all gaze toward her in tense
silence.)*

Creusa

This is no time for silence. Do not try
To check me. In that cradle I exposed
You then, my son, a newborn child,
Where the Long Rocks hang over Cecrops' cave.   1400
I will desert the altar even though
I have to die.

(*She rushes away from the altar, runs up to Ion,
and throws her arms round his neck.*)

Ion

Seize her! God's madness has made her leap away
From the altar's images. Now bind her arms.

Creusa

Go on and kill me. I will not lose you,
The cradle, or the tokens it contains.   1405

Ion

O hypocrite to cheat me with a trick!

Creusa

Oh no! You have found one who loves you.

Ion

What, you love me?—And try a secret murder?

Creusa

You are my son: a mother must love her son.

Ion

Stop spinning lies.—For I am sure to have you.   1410

(*Decides to trick her.*)

Creusa

O do so then! That is my aim, my son.

337

Ion

This cradle—has it anything inside?

Creusa

It has the things you wore when I exposed you.

Ion

And can you give their names before you see them?

Creusa

I can; and, if I fail, consent to die.   1415

Ion

Then speak. Your audacity is strange indeed.

> (*He opens the cradle, standing far enough away
> from Creusa to prevent her seeing inside it.*)

Creusa

Look for the weaving which I did in childhood.

Ion

Describe it; girls do many kinds of work.

Creusa

It is unfinished, a kind of trial piece.

Ion

And its design—You cannot cheat me there.   1420

Creusa

There is a Gorgon in the center part.

Ion (*aside*)

O Zeus! What fate is this to track us down!

Creusa

The stuff is fringed with serpents like an aegis.

Ion

And here it is—found like an oracle!

338

Creusa

    The loomwork of a girl—so long ago.   1425

Ion

    And anything else? Or will your luck fail now?

Creusa

    Serpents, the custom of our golden race.

Ion

    Athene's gift, who bids you wear them?

Creusa

    Yes, in memory of Erichthonius.

Ion

    What do they do with this gold ornament?   1430

Creusa

    It is a necklace for a newborn child.

Ion

    Yes, here they are.

        (*Shows them. He is now anxious for her success.*)
        I long to know the third.

Creusa

    I put an olive wreath around you, from
    The tree Athene first planted on the rock;
    If that is there, it has not lost its green,   1435
    But flourishes because the tree is holy.

        (*Ion, quite convinced, throws himself
            into his mother's arms.*)

Ion

    O dearest mother, what happiness to see you,
    To kiss you, and know that you are happy!

Creusa

    O child! O light more welcome than the Sun.

—The god forgives me—I have you in my arms.   1440
    I have found you against all my hopes,
    Whom I thought underground in the world
    Of Persephone's shades.

Ion

    Dear Mother, yes, you have me in your arms,
    Who died and now have come to you alive.

Creusa

    O radiant heaven's expanse,   1445
    How can I speak or cry
    My joy? How have I met
    Unimagined delight, and why
    Am I made happy?

Ion

    There was no more unlikely chance than this,   1450
    To find that I am, after all, your son.

Creusa

    I am trembling with fear.

Ion

    That I am lost, although you hold me now?

Creusa

    Yes, since I had cast all hope away.
    But tell me, Priestess, from where
    Did you take the child to your arms?
    Whose hand brought him to Apollo's house?   1455

Ion

    It was the work of god. But as we have suffered
    Before, so now we must enjoy our fortune.

Creusa

    My child, you were born in tears,
    In sorrow torn from your mother.

But now I can breathe on your cheek,   1460
And am blessed with tender joy.

Ion

I have no need to speak. You speak for both.

Creusa

I am childless no longer,
No longer without an heir.
The hearth is restored to the home,
The rulers return to the land,
And Erechtheus is young once more;   1465
Now the house is delivered from night
And looks up to the rays of the sun.

Ion

Mother, my father should be here with me
To share the happiness I bring you both.

Creusa

My child, my child—   1470
How am I put to shame!

Ion

Yes?—Tell me.—

Creusa

You do not know your father.

Ion

So I was born before your marriage then?

Creusa

The marriage which gave you birth
Saw no torches or dancing, my son.   1475

Ion

A bastard son—My father? Tell me that.

341

Creusa

>Athene who slew the Gorgon,
>I call her to witness—

Ion

>Why this beginning?

Creusa

>By the rocks where the nightingales sing,   1480
>Apollo—

Ion

>Why name Apollo?

Creusa

>Became my lover in secret—

Ion

>Speak on; for what you say will make me happy.   1485

Creusa

>When the time passed, I bore you,
>The unknown child of Apollo.

Ion

>How welcome this news is—if it is true.

Creusa

>And these were your swaddling clothes;
>In fear of my mother I wrapped you   1490
>In them, the careless work of a girl
>At her loom.
>I gave you no milk,
>You were not washed with my hands,
>But in a deserted cave,
>A prey for the beaks of birds,   1495
>Delivered to death.

Ion

>O mother, what horror you dared.

Creusa

    Myself in the bondage of fear,
    I was casting away your life,
    But against my will.

Ion

And I attempted an impious murder.   1500

Creusa

    Fate drove us hard in the past,
    lust now oppressed us again.
    There is no harbor of peace
From the changing waves of joy and despair.   1505
    The wind's course veers.
    Let it rest. We have endured
    Sorrows enough. O my son,
    Pray for a favoring breeze
        Of rescue from trouble.

Chorus Leader

    From what we have seen happen here, no man   1510
    Should ever think that any chance is hopeless.

             (*A pause. Ion is afflicted with doubt.*)

Ion

O Fortune, who has already changed the lives
Of countless men from misery to joy,
How near I was to killing my own mother,
How near myself to undeserved disaster.   1515

                  (*Pause.*)

But do the sun's bright rays in daily course
Illumine such events as this—all this?

        (*Pause, as he turns to his mother.*)

It was so good at last to find you, mother,
And I can cast no blame upon my birth.
But there is something else I wish to say   1520

343

To you alone. Come here with me; my words
Are for your ear; your answer shall be hidden.

(*He draws her aside.*)

Now tell me, mother—are you not, deceived
As young girls are in love affairs kept secret,
Now laying blame upon the god, and say,   1525
Attempting to escape the shame I brought,
That Phoebus is my father, though in fact
He is no god at all?

Creusa

No, by Athene, Goddess of Victory,
Who in her chariot fought by Zeus' side
Against the Giant race, my son, your father
Was not a mortal, but the very god   1530
Who reared you, Loxias.

Ion

If this is true, why give his son to others,
Why does he say that Xuthus is my father?

Creusa

No, he does not; you are his son, a gift
Bestowed by him on Xuthus, just as a man   1535
Might give a friend his son to be his heir.

Ion

But, mother, does Apollo tell the truth,
Or is the oracle false? With some good reason
That question troubles me.

Creusa

Then listen. This is what I think, my son:
It is for your own good that Loxias   1540
Is placing you within a noble house.
Acknowledged as his son, you would have lost
All hope of heritage or father's name.
What chance had you when I concealed

The truth, and even planned your death in secret?
And so to help you he is giving you
Another father.   1545

Ion

My question cannot be so lightly answered;
No, I will ask Apollo in his temple
If I am his, or born of man.

> (*As he steps toward the temple, he sees the god-*
> *dess Athene appearing above it.*)

Ah!
What goddess shows her face above the temple
To look toward the sun? O mother, let us fly.   1550
We should not see the gods unless the right
Is given to us.

> (*All on the stage bow their heads to the ground*
> *and step backward from the temple.*)

Athene

No, stay. I am no enemy to flee,
But well-disposed in Delphi as in Athens.
I am Athene, whose name your city bears: 1555
I have come here in haste, sent by Apollo,
Who did not think it right to come himself
Before you, lest he should be blamed for what
Has happened in the past; he has sent me
To give his message:

> This woman is your mother,   1560

Your father is Apollo; the one you know
Received you as a gift, and not because
You are his son; and this was done with purpose,
To find you an established place among
A noble house. But when this plan he made
Was open and laid bare, he was afraid
Your mother's scheme of murder would succeed,
Or she be killed by you, and found some means   1565
Of rescue; but for this he would have kept

345

The secret longer and in Athens revealed
Creusa as the mother and himself
The father of his child. But I must end
My task and tell the purpose of my journey.
Now hear Apollo's revelations.   1570
               Creusa,
Go with your son to Cecrops' land, and then
Appoint him to the royal throne; for since
He is descended from Erechtheus, he has
The right to rule my land: and he shall be
Renowned through Greece. His sons, four branches
    from   1575
One stock, shall name the country and its peoples,
Divided in their tribes, who live about my rock.
The first shall be named Geleon, the tribe
Of Hopletes second, then Argades, and one   1580
Aegicores, the name from my own aegis.
At the appointed time, the children born
Of them shall colonize the Cyclades,
Possess the island cities and the coasts,
And thus give strength to my own land of Athens.
They shall live in the two broad plains of Asia
And Europe, which lie on either side the straits,   1585
Becoming famous under this boy's name,
Ionians. Moreover, you and Xuthus
Are promised children. First Dorus, whose name
Shall cause the Dorians to be hymned throughout   1590
The land of Pelops. Then Achaeus, king
Of that sea coast near Rhion, who shall mark
A people with his name.
             Apollo then
Has managed all things well. He made your labor   1595
Easy, so that your parents should not know;
And when the child was born and you exposed
Him in his swaddling clothes, he ordered Hermes
To take him in his arms and bring him here,
And would not let him die, but reared him.   1600
But tell no one that Ion is your son,

And Xuthus will be happy in his belief,
While you may go away, Creusa, sure
Of your own blessings.—Now farewell;
You are delivered of your present evil,
The future holds good fortune.   1605

Ion (ironically)

O Athene, child of mighty Zeus, we have received
What you say on trust. And I believe myself Apollo's
And Creusa's son—though that was credible before.

(To the end of the scene Ion stands in silence.)

Creusa

Listen to my tribute. Though before I gave no praise,
Now I praise Apollo. For the son he had neglected   1610
Is restored to me; and now this oracle, these doors,
Wear a friendly look, though they were hateful in the
        past.
Joyfully I cling to them and bid farewell.

Athene

I approve this change, this praise of him. The gods
        perhaps
Move to action late, but in the end they show their
        strength.   1615

Creusa

Son, now let us go.

Athene

                      Yes, go, and I will follow you.

Creusa

Welcome guardian of our journey, one who loves the
        city.

Athene (to Ion)

Mount the ancient throne.
            (Ion is silent. There is an embarrassing pause.)

Creusa

That is a worthy prize for me.

(*The actors slowly move off the stage in procession.
Athene disappears.*)

Chorus

(*To the temple.*)

O Apollo, son of Zeus and Leto, now farewell.

(*To the audience.*)

He whose house is pressed by trouble should respect
the gods,   1620
So preserving courage. For at last good men are
honored,
Evil men by their own nature cannot ever prosper.

(*Exeunt.*)

RHESUS

Translated and with an Introduction by

RICHMOND LATTIMORE

INTRODUCTION TO *RHESUS*

The ancient Argument, or Introduction, to *Rhesus* contains the following statement: "Some have suspected that this play is spurious, that is, not by Euripides. For it shows a character which is more like Sophocles. Nevertheless, it is recorded in the play-lists as a genuine play of Euripides; and the overelaborateness [? Greek *polypragmosyne*] with which elevation is striven for is in the manner of Euripides." Who these "some" were we do not know, but it seems plain that their suspicions were based on internal, not external, evidence. The play was officially credited to Euripides. Further, from the notes (*scholia*) on the text, line 529, we have the following: "Crates says that Euripides was ignorant of astronomy in this passage because he was still young when he presented *Rhesus*."

Thus we may say that, while *Rhesus* was firmly attested as a play by Euripides, there was a feeling that there was something peculiar about it, that it did not read, feel, sound like Euripides. Modern critics have generally shared the uneasiness which the writer of our Argument felt, though they have not shared, or even understood, his notion that it is "more like Sophocles." While in this brief unscientific introduction I can offer no full treatment,[1] the following characteristics may be noted.

1. The action is taken direct from the Tenth Book of the *Iliad*. Its chief events, the sortie of Dolon, the countermission

[1] Those who are curious about the "Rhesus question" are referred to C. B. Sneller, *De Rheso Tragoedia* (Amsterdam: H.J. Paris, 1949). This is full and thorough. There is an excellent briefer discussion in G. M. A. Grube, *The Drama of Euripides* (London: Methuen & Co., 1941), pp. 439-47.

of Odysseus and Diomedes, who kill Dolon, and the death of Rhesus, are all in Homer, though there are changes in emphasis, particularly in the importance of the part played by Athene, the importance of Rhesus for the Trojan cause, and the introduction of the Muse as Rhesus' mother. This is the only extant tragedy which takes its material straight out of the *Iliad*.[2] The regular practice of the tragic poets when they dealt with the heroes and stories of the Trojan War was to choose episodes which fell outside the scope of the *Iliad*, before its opening or, more frequently, after its close.

2. This is the only extant tragedy whose action all takes place at night. But this is dictated by the facts of the situation in Homer.

3. Fate and divine mechanics are used more baldly than elsewhere in tragedy.

"If Rhesus survives this day or night [but he will not] all will be well." This is a minor motive in Sophocles' *Ajax* and serves better as such than as a major motive, which it is here.

"If Rhesus fights tomorrow, Achilles, Ajax, and all the rest of the Greeks cannot stop him." Why on earth should we believe this? He might, of course, be played in a costume, with built-up boots, that makes him tower, giant-like, over Hector himself. But belief in Rhesus is plainly enforced because a god guarantees him (Athene, ll. 600-605). Athene also tells Odysseus whom to kill, whom not to kill, because it is or is not authorized or "fated" (ll. 633-36).

"If a man is too confident, even if that confidence is justified, or if others speak too well of him, he is doomed to destruction" (see ll. 342-87, 447-53). The tragic poets may sometimes say that men are puppets in the hands of the gods, but they do not elsewhere make them so in action. This machinery is bare.

2. The fragments of tragedy offer only one other certain case, the trilogy by Aeschylus which contained *The Myrmidons*, *The Nereids*, and *The Ransoming of Hector*. It is striking that here Aeschylus also departed from the usual convention in using the theme of homosexual love, which I have not found elsewhere in tragedy. If he repeated neither experiment, perhaps that means that this trilogy was not well received.

4. The iambics of *Rhesus* show resolution (three syllables for two) in 8.6 per cent of the lines, on my count.[3] It is well known that in the period of his extant plays Euripides indulged more and more freely in resolution as time went on. His earliest dated play, *Alcestis* (438 B.C.), shows resolution of 6.5 per cent. His latest, the posthumous *Bacchae* and *Iphigenia in Aulis*, have 37.5 per cent and 48 per cent respectively. The rate of increase is by no means constant, but we may say flatly that *Rhesus* cannot be a play written by Euripides after 415 and that it is probably far earlier. There is, however, one complication. *Rhesus* has trochees; it should not. All but one of the latest plays, beginning with *The Trojan Women* (415; iambic resolution 22.5 per cent), contain trochees. The only earlier play which has them is *Heracles*, which, on metrical and material grounds, can probably be put about 422-420 B.C. Its resolution rate is 19 per cent. No extant play with a resolution rate below that of *Heracles* has trochees, except *Rhesus*. It is thus a metrical anomaly, and this is the strongest piece of internal evidence against Euripidean authorship. On the other hand, the fragments of Euripides' lost *Phoenix* do contain trochees, and *Phoenix* is securely dated before 425. The forty iambic lines preserved show a resolution rate of only 2.5 per cent. The conclusion must be that Euripides, while he made a habit of using trochees only in his late period, did use them occasionally long before.

The kind of scene which would call for trochees (the "meter of running") is precisely the kind of scene where we find trochees in *Rhesus*: a scene of activity, the scene where Odysseus and Riomedes are caught by the Chorus (ll. 683-91). In general, the characteristics of this play, material and metrical alike, its rapid, realistic action, its failure to find a central hero or a central dramatic problem, can plausibly be explained by the fact that its author did what the dramatic

3. Statistical counts will vary because the scholar has some latitude in deciding whether certain feet, apparently of three syllables, might actually be run together and read as two. I also think it fairer to count proper names. Some do not. One can make mistakes, too. But the variations will not be significant.

instinct of the fifth century said he should not: he made a book of the *Iliad* into a drama, but the story did better as an episode in epic than as a self-contained tragic action.

This author may not have been Euripides. If he was not, it by no means follows that the play belongs to the fourth century. Some minor poet of the late fifth is as good a guess.

Against the negative evidence, we should set the testimony of Crates that this is an early work by Euripides. This is evidence too, and it is supported by much that is in the play: the character of Odysseus, the messengers' speeches, the combined lament, explanation, and prediction of the Muse (why doesn't she have a name?), and especially the way in which, while reproaching Athene for ingratitude, she contrives to glorify Athens. This is a regular bit of Euripidean *sophia*.

Scholars will continue to doubt, and scholars who honestly doubt must speak their minds. I now believe that *Rhesus* is the work of Euripides and probably done before 440 B.C.

CHARACTERS

Chorus of Trojan guards
Hector
Aeneas
Dolon
Shepherd
Rhesus, king of the Thracians
Odysseus
Diomedes
Athene
Alexander (Paris)
Charioteer of Rhesus
Muse, mother of Rhesus

The manuscripts as usual do not distinguish between the lines spoken or sung by the Chorus as a group and those to be spoken by the Leader alone. In other translations I have followed the text without trying to discriminate. Here, however, the Leader seems to me to have a more definite actor's part than elsewhere in extant tragedy, especially at the beginning. Lines 7-10, for example, should be spoken by a single actor, not by a group; and the speaker must be the officer or non-com in charge of the detail, who is *also* the Leader heading the Chorus. I have therefore used my judgment in guessing where lines are to be given to the Leader and where they should be given to the Chorus.

RHESUS

SCENE: *The Trojan position on the plain between the city and the shore. It is late at night. Hector lies asleep on a pile of leaves with other Trojans asleep around him. Enter, in haste, the Chorus of sentries, headed by an officer or corporal of the guard (the Chorus Leader).*

Leader

Go find where Hector is sleeping. Ho there,
is any of the king's bodyguard awake,
or his armor-bearers?
There is a fresh report he must hear
from those who keep this quarter of the night's   5
guard duty for the entire army.

(*Shaking Hector.*)

Sit up, or lean your head on your arm;
unclose your lids. Open your keen eyes.
Rise now from the piled leaves of your bed,
Hector. A report. You must hear it.   10

Hector

Who speaks? Enemy or friend? What is
the word? But speak.
Who comes here out of the night to find
where I sleep? Declare.

Leader

Sentries of the army.

355

Hector

What troubles you so?   15

Leader
Never fear.

Hector
Not I.
What is it? A night raid?

Leader

No, not that.

Hector

Then why
have you left your post to come here and waken
the camp, unless we must form by night?
Do you realize that the Argive spears   20
are there, close by
where we sleep this night in our armor?

Leader
Arm, arm, Hector, and run to where
the allied forces lie sleeping.
Wake them, tell them to take their spears in their hands. 25

(*To various members of the Chorus.*)

You, send true men to run to your company.
You there, put the curb chains on your horses.
Someone go to Panthoüs' son
or Europa's, lord of the Lycian men. Who will?
Where are those who are in charge
of sacrifices?   30
Or the light-armed captains?
Where are the Phrygian archers?
Archers! Have your hornbows strung, quickly.

Hector
What you report seems partly alarm,

356

partly to be comfort. All is confusion.   35
What is this? Has the whiplash of Cronian Pan
struck you to shivering panic? Speak, say,
what *are* you reporting? You have talked a great deal
without telling me one thing clearly.   40

Leader

The Argive army has lit its fires,
Hector, all through the darkness.
The positions of their ships are clear in the firelight.
But all their army has gathered in darkness
by Agamemnon's shelter, noisily.   45
They must wish to consult, to take
counsel, since never before was this sea-borne army
so utterly routed. Therefore
I, to forestall anything that may happen,
came to report it, so that   50
you will not say I failed to do my duty.

Hector

Good. You are timely, though you come to us in alarm.
I see these people mean to row away by night,
quietly, when I cannot see them, and make good
their flight. I know exactly what their night fires mean.   55
O God, you robbed me, robbed the lion of his spoil.
All prospered, till you halted me before I swept
the Argive army to destruction with this spear.
For if the flaring lanterns of the sun had not
shut down against us, I would never have stayed my spear   60
in its fortune, until I had fired their ships, and made my
      way
through their camp, killing Achaeans with this murderous
      hand.
I myself was all ready to keep up the fight,
to use the darkness and the powerful hand of god.
But these diviners, these educated men who know   65
the mind of heaven, persuaded me to wait for day.
Thus no Achaean (they said) would be missed on land.

357

But will they wait to be carefully slaughtered? No,
not they. The runaway slave is a great man by night.
Come, then. We must pass the order to our men, at once.   70
Have them wake and put on the armor that lies by.
So the Achaean, even while he jumps for his ship,
shall be stabbed in the back and drench the ladderways
with blood. And the survivors can be caught, and tied,
and learn to work the wheat fields in our land of Troy.   75

Leader

Too quick, Hector. You act before you understand.
We are not certain yet that they are running away.

Hector

For what cause did the Argives light their fires?

Leader

I do not know. I am suspicious of the whole matter.

Hector

If you fear this, you would be afraid of anything.   80

Leader

The enemy never lit fires like this before.

Hector

They never fled in such an awful rout before.

Leader

Yes. It was your work. Now consider what comes next.

Hector

There is only one order to give: arm and fight the enemy.

Leader

Here comes Aeneas in great haste   85
of foot, as one who has news for his friends to hear.

(*Enter Aeneas.*)

Aeneas

Hector, why has the night-guard of the camp come here

to where you were quartered? Is it panic? Here is talk
going on at night, and all the army is disturbed.

Hector

On with your armor quick, Aeneas.

Aeneas

Yes? What for?   90
Has someone come in to report the enemy
have made a surprise attack upon us in the dark?

Hector

No, no, they are withdrawing. They are boarding their
ships.

Aeneas

And what good reason do you have to believe this?

Hector

Their watch fires are illuminating all the night,   95
and I believe they will not wait until the dawn
but burn them so that by their light they can escape
on their well benched ships, to leave this country and go
home.

Aeneas

What will you do to stop them, then? Why are you
armed?

Hector

To fall upon them as they flee and board their ships,   100
to charge with our spears against them, and hit hard.
It would be shame, and more than shame, sheer cow-
ardice,
to let them, when they did us so much harm, escape
without a fight, when God has given them to our hands.

Aeneas

I wish you could make plans as well as you can fight.   105
But so it is: the same man cannot well be skilled

359

in everything; each has his special excellence,
and yours is fighting, and it is for others to make good
     plans,
not you. You heard how the Achaeans had lit their fires
and hope roused you to wish to lead the army on   110
across their deep moats in the time of night. Yet see,
suppose you do cross over the ditch, despite its depth,
and meet an enemy not withdrawing from our coast
as you think, but standing with spears faced to your
     attack,
you will have no free way to escape if they defeat you.   115
How will a beaten army cross the palisades?
How will your charioteers drive over the embankments
without smashing the axles of their chariots?
Then, even if you win, they have Achilles in reserve.
He will not sit by while you fire their ships, he will   120
not let you prey on the Achaeans, as you hope.
The man is hot, and he has massive strength of hand.
No, better, let us hold our army out of the way
of hard strokes; let them sleep at peace upon their
     shields;
but send one volunteer to scout the enemy.   125
So I think best. Then, if they really are in flight,
we can advance in force upon the Argive host.
But if this burning of their fires leads to some trick,
our scout will inform us what they are doing.
Then take our measures. This, my lord, is what I urge.   130

Chorus

This is what I think best. Change your mind and accept
     it.
I do not like it when the general uses power that is
unsure. What could be better
than that a swift-paced man should go to spy on their
     ships,
from close, and see what it means   135
when our enemies have fires burning where their prows
     are beached?

Hector

Have your way, then, since this is approved by all. Go,
    you,
and quiet our allies, let them sleep, since the whole
    army
might well be restless, hearing how we consult at night.
I will send a man to spy upon the enemy,   140
and if we find out that there is some stratagem,
you shall hear all, Aeneas, and be called to plan
with us; but if it is flight and they are casting off,
be ready for action when you hear the trumpet speak;
because I will not wait for you, I shall be there   145
among the Argives and their cables, now, tonight.

Aeneas

Send him with all speed. Now your plan is sound. And if
the need comes for it, I will be as bold as you.

                                              (*Exit.*)

Hector

Is there a Trojan, then, present at this council,
who volunteers to spy upon the Argive ships?   150
Who is there who would have his country in his debt?
Who speaks? I cannot, by myself, do everything
that must be done to help our city and our friends.

Dolon

I will do it. I willingly undertake this cast
of hazard. I will go and scout the Argive ships   155
and listen to everything they plan to do and bring
word back. On such conditions I accept the task.

Hector

You are well named, my crafty Dolon, and you love
your city well. Your father's house was bright in name
before. Now you have made it twice as bright.   160

Dolon

It is good to work and fight, but when I do, it also
361

is good to be rewarded. For in every work
a reward added makes the pleasure twice as great.

Hector

 True. I will not deny that what you say is fair.
 Name your price. Anything except my royal power.   165

Dolon

 I do not want your royal power, nor to rule a city.

Hector

 Marry a daughter of Priam. Be my brother-in-law.

Dolon

 I think it best not to marry above my station.

Hector

 I have gold to give, if that is what you will be asking.

Dolon

 We have it at home. We do not lack for anything.   170

Hector

 What would you have out of the treasures of Ilium?

Dolon

 Nothing. Catch the Achaeans, and then grant my gift.

Hector

 I shall. But do not ask for the leaders of their fleet.

Dolon

 Kill them. I will not ask for Menelaus' life.

Hector

 It is not the son of Oïleus you are asking me for?   175

Dolon

 Those well-bred hands would never work well in the
  fields.

Hector
Is there any Achaean you would have alive, for ransom?

Dolon
I told you before. We have gold aplenty in our house.

Hector
Well, you shall come and take your own pick from the
spoils.

Dolon
Take them, and nail them on the houses of the gods.   180

Hector
What prize greater than such things can you ask me for?

Dolon
The horses of Achilles.
                        Since I risk my life
on dice the gods throw, it must be for a high stake.

Hector
Ah. You are my rival, for I want those horses too.
They are immortal, born of an immortal strain,   185
who bear the fighting son of Peleus. The king
of the sea, Poseidon, broke them once and tamed them
and gave
them to Peleus, so the story goes. Yet I have raised
your hopes, and I will not be false. I give you them:
Achilles' horses, a great possession for your house.   190

Dolon
I thank you. Thus my courage shall have a reward
that will outshine all others in the land of Troy.
But you should not be jealous. There is much besides
for you, our best and greatest, to take glory in.

                (*Hector retires to the rear of the stage and rests.*)
Chorus

363

High is the venture, high are the honors you hope to
    capture.   195
Blessed will your name be called if you win. For here
is glorious work to be done.
It would have been bold to marry into the house of our
    kings.
May the gods grant that Right's eyes be on you,
as men now grant that all you deserve shall be yours.   200

Dolon

I am ready, once I have gone inside my house
and put upon by body the necessary gear.
From there, I shall take my way against the Argive ships.

Chorus

What costume will you wear in place of what you have
    on?

Dolon

One suited to my venture and my stealthy way.   205

Chorus

Some cleverness is to be learned from the clever man.
Tell me then, how do you mean to have your body
    arrayed?

Dolon

I shall put a wolfskin upon my back, fitted
so that the grinning jaws of the beast are on my head,
then, with the forepaws on my hands and the hind feet   210
upon my legs, shall imitate the four-footed tread
of the wolf, to puzzle the enemy who track me there
beside the ditch and by the bows of the beached ships.
Then when I reach the lonely stretch where no one is
I shall go upright. Thus my strategy is planned.   215

Chorus

May Hermes, son of Maia, bring you there and bring
you back, since Hermes is the friend of slippery men.
You know your business. All you need now is good luck.

Dolon

    I shall come safely back, but kill Odysseus first
    and bring his head to you, to give you solid grounds   220
    for saying Dolon won through to the Argive ships.
    Or maybe Diomedes—but my hand will not
    be bloodless when, before the day breaks, I come home.

                                    (*Exit.*)

Chorus

    Lord of Thymbraeum, lord of Delos, who stand
    upright in the Lycian shrine,   225
    Apollo, O shining presence, come with your bow
    armed, come in the night,
    lead, preserve, and guide on his way this man
    of battles, lend your strength to Dardanus' children,   230
    O power complete, who long ago
    founded the walls of Troy.

    Grant that he reach their shipsteads and come to spy
    on the spread army of Greece
    and turn and make his way back to the house of his
        father
    and the sacred hearth, in Troy;   235
    and grant, some day, he may mount the Phthian horse-
        chariot,
    after our chief has smashed the war strength of Achaea,
    and win the gift the sea god gave   240
    once to Peleus, son of Aeacus.

    Yes, for he alone dared go down to spy on their ships
    for our land and people. I admire
    his courage; for indeed few   245
    are found brave when the city
    is a ship riding a hard
    storm on the open
    water. There is still manhood alive in Phrygia   250
    and valor left still in her spears.
    What Mysian is there who holds
    scorn that I fight beside him?

What shall that man of Achaea be whom our stalking
    killer
will spear among the shelters as he goes   255
on fours in the pace of a lurking
beast? Might it be Menelaus!
Or might he kill Agamemnon
and bring the head back
as a gloomy gift for the arms of his evil sister   260
by marriage, Helen. For he
it was led the thousand ships
and the army here against Troy.

           (Enter hastily a shepherd. As he speaks, Hector
                          rises and comes forward.)

Shepherd

    My lord, I hope I can always bring my masters news
    as good as what I bring you now, for you to hear.   265

Hector

    What crude creatures these yokels are. They have no
        sense.
    You think it fitting to report about the flocks
    to the armed nobility? You have no business here.
    Do you not know where my house is, or my father's
        throne?
    Go there for your announcement that the sheep are
        well.   270

Shepherd

    We herdsmen are crude creatures, I will not say no.
    Nevertheless, I am the bringer of good news.

Hector

    Will you stop trying to tell me about what goes on
    in the farmyards? We have spears and fighting on our
        hands.

Shepherd

    But it is just such matters I report to you.   275

There is a man, with strength of thousands at his back,
who comes to fight for our country at your side.

Hector
> Where are the native plains that he has emptied of
> men?

Shepherd
> Thrace; and his father is called Strymon.

Hector
>   Do you mean
> that Rhesus has set foot on Trojan soil?   280

Shepherd
> You have it. So saved me half of what I had to say.

Hector
> How did he lose the carriage road on the broad plains
> to wander through the herds on Ida's mountainside?

Shepherd
> I do not know exactly. I can guess at it.
> It is no small thing to bring an army through the night   285
> when you know the plain is full of enemies in arms.
> We countrymen, who live where Ida runs to rock,
> and plant our hearth on the bare ground, took alarm, as
>   he
> came through the oak wood with its animals in the
>   night.
> Because this army of the Thracians streamed along   290
> with great clamor, and we, terror-stricken, ran away
> to the high pastures, fearing some Argives had come
> on a plundering expedition and to rob your folds.
> But then our ears made out their language; it was not
> anything Greek, and now we were no more afraid.   295
> I went and stood before the pathway of their king,
> hailed him, and questioned him aloud in Thracian
>   speech:
> "Who rides as general here, and of what father called

367

comes he in arms to fight by Priam's citadel?"
Then, having heard answers to all I wished to know,   300
I stood and watched. There I saw Rhesus like a god
upright behind his horses in the Thracian car.
The golden balance of a yoke inclosed the necks
of his young horses, and these were whiter than snow.
The buckler on his shoulders glowed with beaten plates   305
of gold, and as upon a goddess' aegis, the bronze
face of a gorgon on the horses' frontlet shields
glared, and with bells beat out a clashing sound of fear.
I could not reckon on an abacus the count
of all their army, so innumerable did it seem,   310
horsemen in numbers, numerous squads of buckler men,
many archers with unfeathered arrows, and, besides,
the light troops, in their Thracian costume, followed
    with them.
Such is the man who comes to fight for Troy. Neither
by flight, nor yet by standing to him with the spear,   315
will Peleus' son Achilles find escape from death.

Leader

When the gods change and stand behind the citizens,
our depressed fortune climbs uphill, and wins success.

Hector

Now that my spear is fortunate, and Zeus is on
our side, we shall be finding that we have many friends.   320
We can do without them. We want none who did not
    fight
our perils, past now, when the driving God of War
blew big upon our city's ship and wrecked our sails.
Rhesus has shown what kind of friend he is to Troy.
He is here for the feasting, but he was not there   325
with spear in hand to help the huntsmen catch the
    game.

Leader

Your grievance and complaint of friends is just. And yet,
accept those who, of their free will, will fight for us.

Hector

We have saved Ilium this long time. We are enough.

Leader

Are you so sure you have the enemy beaten now?   330

Hector

I am so sure. God's daylight, which is near, will show.

Leader

Look to the future. God often reverses fortunes.

Hector

I hate it in friends when they come too late to help.   333
As for this man, since he is here, let him be here   336
as a stranger guest at our table, but as no fighting man.   337
He has lost all the kind feelings of the sons of Troy.   338

Leader

Spurn allies, lord, and you gain peril and lose love.   334

Shepherd

If the enemy only saw him they would be afraid.   335

Hector

(*To Chorus.*)

You urge me faithfully.

(*To Shepherd.*)

You have given a timely report.   339
So, for the sake of what the messenger has said,   340
let golden-armored Rhesus come as our ally.

Chorus

Adrasteia: Necessity; Zeus'
daughter! Keep bad luck from my mouth.
For I will speak what is in my heart.
All I wish shall be spoken.   345
You are here, child of the River,
here, at long last now in the court of Friendship,

and welcome, since it was long, before
the Muse your mother and the grand-channeled
River-God sent you to help us.   350

This was Strymon, who with the Muse
melodious, in the clear shining
and watery swirl of their embrace
begot your youth and glory.
You come, a Zeus resplendent   355
for show, driving behind your dappled horses.
Now, O my country, my Phrygia,
now, with gods' will, we can claim the aid
of Zeus himself, Liberator.

Will it ever happen again that our ancient Troy   360
will know the day-long revelries,
the love pledge and companionship,
the strumming on the lyres and the wine cups circling,
passed to the right in sweet contention,
while on the open water the sons
of Atreus make for Sparta,   365
gone from the shores of Ilium.
O friend, could it only be
that with hand and spear you could do
this before you leave us.

O come, appear, lift and flourish your golden buckler,   370
slant it across the eyes
of Peleus' son, over
the split chariot-rail, feint with your feet, then
cast the twin javelins. None
who stands against you shall dance   375
ever again on the level lands
of Argive Hera. He shall die
here, by a Thracian death, a welcome
weight on this land, which will take him.

Great King, he comes, O great King.

(*Rhesus enters, with some of his following.*)

Gallant, O Thrace, 380
is this youngling you bred, a monarch to behold.
See the great force on his gold-armored body,
hear the brave noise of his clashing bells
that jangle on the shield rim.
A god, O Troy, a god, a real Ares 385
is this stallion sired by the singing muse
and Strymon, who comes to inspire you.

Rhesus

Great son of a great father, despot of this land,
O Hector, hail. On this late day I greet you,
and greet the good success that finds you so advanced 390
against the enemy's fortress. I am here to help
you knock their walls to rubble and to burn their ships.

Hector

O son of a melodius mother, one of the Nine,
and Strymon, the River of Thrace: it is my way
always to speak the truth. I have no diplomacy. 395
Long, long ago you should have come to help our struggle.
For all you have done, Troy could have fallen to Greek
arms.
This should not be.
You will not say it was because your friends never called
you
that you did not come, and did not help, and paid no
heed. 400
What herald or what aged representatives
did not reach you, to entreat you to our city's help?
What honorable gifts did we not send? For all
you did, you might as well have thrown us to the Greeks,
though you and we are non-Greek, one Barbarian blood. 405
Yet it was I who with this hand made you so great
and lord of Thrace, though you were but a small baron
before I swept Pangaeum and Paeonia,
fought with the Thracian bravest face to face, and broke

their lines of bucklers, made slaves of their people, turned   410
them over to you. You owe us much. You have spurned it
and to your friends in distress come with late relief.
Yet here are others, who are not our kin by blood,
who came long ago, and some of them have fallen and lie
buried in their mounds, who greatly kept faith with our
   city,   415
while others, in their armor, by their chariot teams,
have stood whatever cold winds or thirsty heat the god
sends, and still do endure it, without
sleeping, as you did, snug beneath the covers.
There, you may know that Hector speaks his mind.   420
I have my grievance, and I tell you to your face.

Rhesus

I am another such as you. I have a path
straight through arguments. I too have no diplomacy.
But I have been hurt more at the heart than you, more
   vexed
and shamed, not to be here in your country.   425
But see. There is a land neighbor to mine, its people
are Scythian, and as I was about to keep appointment
at Ilium, these attacked me. I had reached the shores
of the Euxine Sea, to put my Thracian army across,
and there the ground was sopped with Scythian blood,
   and Thracian   430
too, as the spearwork made commingled slaughter.
Such were the accidents that kept me from my march
to Troy's plain and my arrival as your ally.
Once I had beaten them, made hostages of their children,
and set a yearly tribute to be brought to us,   435
I crossed the sea gate with my ships, went on by land
over the intervening country, and so am here;
not, as you claim, because I stayed in comfort, not
because I slept at leisure in my golden house.
For I know well, I have endured them, those stiff winds   440
of ice that sweep Paeconia and the Thracian Sea.

Sleepless, and in this armor, I have come through these
and come to you behind my time, but timely still,
for here is the tenth summer of your years of war,
and *you* have made no progress, but day after day   445
you throw your dice against the hazard of Argive arms;
one single day of sunlight is enough for *me*
to storm their walls and burst upon their mooring-steads
and kill the Achaeans. On the next day after that
I am off for home, having disposed of your whole war.   450
Not one of your people needs to lift a single shield.
I will deal with these vaunted Achaeans and their spears,
and destroy them, even though I came behind my time.

Chorus

Hail, hail,
welcome your cry, welcome, you come from Zeus, only I
    pray   455
that Zeus keep away
the invincible Spirit of Envy from cursing your words.
For what man from Argos
did the sea-armament bring, before   460
or now, stronger than you? Say how
could even Achilles endure your spear?
How could Ajax endure it?
If I could only see, my lord, only see that day
when your spear hand   465
is bloody with retribution.

Rhesus

Now for my too-long absence I will make amends
thus (but may Adrasteia not resent my words):
when we have liberated this city of yours and when
you have chosen first spoils and devoted them to the
    gods,   470
I am willing to sail with you against the Argives, storm
and ravage the whole land of Hellas with our spears.
So let them learn what it is like to be attacked.

373

Hector
    If I could only get rid of my present troubles
    and rule a peaceful city as I did before   475
    I would be very grateful to the gods.
    As for the Argive country and the Greek domain,
    they are not so easy to devastate as you seem to think.

Rhesus
    Do they not say the greatest of the Greeks are here?

Hector
    They are great enough for me. I want no more.   480

Rhesus
    Then, once we have killed these, have we not done every-
        thing?

Hector
    Do not plan for ventures before finishing what's at hand.

Rhesus
    You seem content to be acted on, not to act.

Hector
    I have my own kingdom here, and it is large.
    Now, whether you want the left wing, or the right,   485
    or to be among the central allies, take your choice,
    and plant your shields, station your army where you wish.

Rhesus
    My wish, Hector, is to fight the enemy alone;
    but if you think it shame to take no hand in burning
    their beached ships, an end for which you fought so long, 490
    set me face to face with Achilles and his men.

Hector
    It is not possible to set your eager spears
    against him.

Rhesus
              The story was he sailed to Troy.

Hector

    He sailed. He is here. But angry
    with their generals, and takes no part in the fighting.   495

Rhesus

    Who is most famous in their army after him?

Hector

    Ajax, I think, is just as good, and Tydeus' son
    Diomedes. Then there is that talker, that big mouth,
    Odysseus, but his heart is brave enough, who has done
    more damage to our country than any single man.   500
    He it was who crept in the night to Athene's shrine
    and stole her image and took it to the Argive ships.
    There was a time the Argives sent him to scout us,
    and in a beggarman's miserable outfit, disguised,
    he got inside our walls and did us great mischief.   505
    For he killed the sentries and the gate guards and got free
    away. Constantly he is observed, under cover
    by the Thymbraean altar, near the city, watching
    his chance. A wicked planner, always on our hands.

Rhesus

    Why, no true man of spirit deigns to kill his man   510
    by stealth. One should go forward and attack direct.
    This man you speak of, crouching in thievish ambuscades
    and scheming stratagems, this man I will seize alive,
    impale him through the back where the road goes out the
        gates,
    and leave him there to feed the vultures.   515
    That is the kind of death that such a man should die
    for being a simple brigand and a temple robber.

Hector

    Well, it is night now, and time for you to bivouac.
    I will show you your place, apart from where the rest
    of the army is stationed. There your men can spend the
        night.   520

Should you want anything, the watchword is "Phoebus."
Learn it. Remember. Tell it to your Thracian force.

(To the Chorus.)

Now, you must go out in advance of our position,
keep a sharp watch, and be on the lookout for Dolon
who scouted the ships, for, if he is still alive,   525
he must be almost back now to the Trojan camp.

(Exeunt all principals. The Chorus have the stage to
themselves. There is some business of waking
men who lie asleep on the ground or
calling to imaginary persons off stage.)

Leader
  Whose is the watch now? Who relieves
  mine? The early constellations
  are setting. The Pleiades' sevenfold course
  rides high, and the Eagle soars in the center of heaven.   530
  Wake. What keeps you? Wake
  from your sleep, to your watch.
  Do you not see how the moon shines?
  Dawn is near, dawn   535
  is breaking now, here is the star
  that runs before it.

  Who was announced for the first watch?

First Soldier
  Coroebus, they say, Mygdon's son.

Leader
  Who was after that?

First Soldier
                           The Paeonian force   540
  relieved the Cilicians. Mysians relieved us.

Leader
  Then is it not time to go wake the Lycians

and relieve, take the fifth
watch, in our turn, as allotted?   545

Second Soldier

I hear. But perched above Simois
the nightingale,
the own-child-slayer in vociferous chant
sings her murderous marriage, sings her song and her
  sorrow.   550

Third Soldier

The flocks are pasturing on Ida
now. I can hear the night-murmuring
call of the shepherd's pipe.

Fourth Soldier

Sleep is a magic on my eyes.
It comes sweetest   555
to the lids about dawn.

Fifth Soldier

Why is the scout not here, that one
Hector sent to spy on their ships?

Sixth Soldier

I fear for him. He is long gone.

Fifth Soldier

Might he have stumbled into an ambush   560
and been killed?

Sixth Soldier

He might. It is to be feared.

Leader

My orders are to go wake the Lycians
and relieve, take the fifth
watch, in our turn, as allotted.

*(The Chorus file out, leaving the stage empty. Then
    enter, furtively, Odysseus and Diomedes.)*

377

Odysseus
> Diomedes, did you hear? Or was it a noise without   565
> meaning that falls on my ears? Some clash of armor?

Diomedes
> It was nothing, the jangle of iron on the harness
> against the chariot rails. But I was frightened too,
> at first, when I heard the clanking of the harness.

Odysseus
> Be careful. You might run into their sentries in the dark.   570

Diomedes
> I will watch how I step despite the darkness.

Odysseus
> If you do wake anyone, do you know what their watch-
> word is?

Diomedes
> I know it. It's "Phoebus." Dolon told me.

Odysseus
> Look!
> Here are some bivouacs of the enemy. But empty.

Diomedes
> Dolon spoke of this too. He said Hector should be
> sleeping   575
> here. And it is for Hector that this sword is drawn.

Odysseus
> What can it mean? Is there an ambush set up some-
> where?

Diomedes
> He may have gone to work some stratagem against us.

Odysseus
> Hector is bold, very bold, now that he is winning.

Diomedes

What shall we do now, Odysseus? We hoped to find 580
our man asleep, but we've failed.

Odysseus

We must go back to our mooring-place as quick as we
can.
Whatever god it is who grants him his success
is watching over him now. We must not force Fortune.

Diomedes

But should we not look for Aeneas? Or for that Phrygian 585
we hate worst of all, Paris? Cut his head off?

Odysseus

How, without deadly peril, can you find these men
in the dark, and here among our enemies?

Diomedes

But it is shameful to go back to the Argive ships
without doing our enemies the least damage. 590

Odysseus

How can you say you have done no damage? Did we not
kill
Dolon, who scouted our ships? Do we not carry his
armor
here, our spoils? Do you think you can rout their whole
army?

Diomedes

You are right. Let us go back. May we only succeed!
        (*The voice of Athene is heard, but, though visible
        to the audience, she is not visible to the characters.*)

Athene

Where are you going? Why do you leave the Trojan
camp
595
biting your very hearts for disappointed spite
because the god will not allow you to kill their Hector

379

or their Paris? Have you not heard of the ally,
Rhesus, who has come to Troy in no mean circumstance?
For if he survives this night and is alive tomorrow,   600
not even Achilles, and not Ajax with his spear,
can keep him from destroying all the Argive fleet,
smashing, demolishing your walls and storming in
to fight with level spears.
Kill him, and all is won. Let Hector bivouac   605
in peace, nor try to murder him.
His death shall come, but it shall come from another
   hand.

Odysseus
   Athene, mistress, for I recognized your voice
   and way of speaking that I know so well, and know
   how you are always with me and watch over me,   610
   tell me, where is this man sleeping whom you bid us
   attack? Where is his station in the Trojan camp?

Athene
   He is camped right here and has not joined the main
      army.
   Hector gave him this place to sleep, outside the lines,
   until this night passes and day comes, and by him   615
   are picketed the horses from the Thracian
   chariots, so white that you can see them through the
      dark
   gleaming, as if they were the wings of swans on water.
   Kill their master and bring these home to your camp,
   spoils of surpassing splendor, for no place on earth   620
   contains a team of chariot horses such as these.

Odysseus
   Diomedes, yours be the work of killing Thracians—
   or let me do it, and you look after the horses.

Diomedes
   I will do the killing, you manage the horses.

You are the experienced one, the quick improviser.   625
One ought to place a man where he can do most good.

Athene
  Alexander is here, I see him, coming our way
  in haste. He must have heard from some of the guards
  confused rumors about the presence of enemies.

Diomedes
  Does he have others with him or is he by himself?   630

Athene
  He's alone. He seems to be making for where Hector
          sleeps,
  so he can report to him the presence of spies in the
          camp.

Diomedes
  Well, should he not be killed and his account settled?

Athene
  No. You must not go beyond what has been destined for
          you.
  There is no authority for you to kill this man.   635
  You came here, bringing their destined death to certain
          others.
  Do it. Dispatch. Now to this man I shall pretend
  I am his Cyprian ally, standing beside him
  in all perils. I'll hold him here with rotten lies.
  This I have said. But though my victim stands close by   640
  he's heard and knows nothing of what's in store for him.

        (Diomedes and Odysseus vanish as Alexander [Paris]
                                        appears.)
Paris
  Hector, my general, my brother, Hector I say,
  are you sleeping? How can you sleep? Waken, will you?
  Here is some enemy got close inside our lines;
  someone has come to rob us, or to spy on us.   645

Athene

> Fear not. Here is your faithful Aphrodite
> watching over you. Your war is my war. I do not forget
> your favor and your kindness to me. I am grateful,
> and now, to your Trojan army in its high succcess
> I come, bringing a friend and mighty man of war,   650
> the Thracian, child of that divine maker of melodies,
> the Muse herself; the River Strymon is named his father.

Paris

> Always you are in truth the good friend of my city
> and me. I think the best thing I ever did
> in my life was to judge you first and win you to my city.   655
> What brings me here—there are wild rumors flying
>   about
> among the sentries, nothing clear. Achaean spies
> said to be among us. One man reports but has not seen
>   them;
> another saw them coming but knows nothing else
> about it. This is why I came to Hector's quarters.   660

Athene

> Never fear. There's nothing wrong in the camp.
> Hector is gone to give the Thracians a place to sleep.

Paris

> I trust you. I always believe what you say. I'll go
> and keep my station, free of this anxiety.

Athene

> Go, for your interests are always on my mind,   665
> and all my purpose is to see my friends succeed.
> Oh, you will learn soon how I shall take care of you.

> *(Paris goes. Athene calls inward to Odysseus and*
> *Diomedes.)*

> You two, in there. You are too bold. You, I am calling
> you, son of Laertes, put your sharp sword away.

Our Thracian captain's down.   670
We have his horses, but the enemy are aware
and coming at you. Now is the time for speed, speed,
to run for where the ships are moored. What keeps you?
The enemy are upon you. Save your lives.

(*From one side Odysseus and Diomedes, from the
other the Chorus of Trojan sentries, come cau-
tiously on, and run into each other, to their
mutual surprise, as Athene vanishes.*)

First Soldier
There they go, there!

Second Soldier
Shoot, shoot.   675

Third Soldier
Spear them.

Fourth Soldier
Who is it? Look! That's the man I mean.

Fifth Soldier
They have come to rob us in the night, and they have
roused the camp.

Leader
This way all.   680

Sixth Soldier
Here they are. We have them fast.

Leader
What's your regiment? Where do you come from? Who
are you?

Odysseus
Nothing for you to know. You have done an evil day's
work.
You shall die.

Leader
> Tell me the watchword, will you, before you get this
> > spear stuck through your chest.

Odysseus
> Stop. There's no danger.

Leader
> Bring him here. Now, everyone, strike him. 685

Odysseus
> Was it you killed Rhesus?

Leader
> No. You tried to kill him. We'll kill *you!*

Odysseus
> Hold hard everyone.

Leader
> We will not.

Odysseus
> Hold. You must not kill a friend.

Leader
> What's the watchword?

Odysseus
> Phoebus.

Leader
> I acknowledge it. Down spears all.
> Do you know where the men have got to?

Odysseus
> Yes, I saw them go this way.

> (*He points. As the Leader and his men start in that
> direction, Odysseus and Diomedes slip out on the
> opposite side.*)

Leader
   On their trail, then, everyone.

Seventh Soldier
                    Should we raise a general alarm?   690

Leader
   No. It would be bad to disturb our friends with an alarm
      in the night.

> (*All go off, but almost immediately begin to return,
>   singing the following ode as they re-enter sev-
>   erally.*)

Chorus
   Who was the man who was here?
   Who is it so hardy that he shall boast
   that he escaped my hand?
   Where shall I find him now?   695
   What shall I think he can be,
   that man who came on fearless foot through the dark
   across the stations of our ranks and our guards?
   Some Thessalian
   or some dweller in a seaside Locrian city?   700
   One whose living is made on the scattered islands?
   Who was it? Where did he come from? What country?
   Which god does he acknowledge as god supreme?

First Soldier
   Was this the work of Odysseus after all? Or whose?

Second Soldier
   If we are to judge by past deeds, who else?   705

First Soldier
   You think so?

Second Soldier
                I must do.

First Soldier
   He has been bold against us?

Third Soldier
  Bold? Who? Whom are you praising?

First Soldier

                                    Odysseus.

Third Soldier
  Never praise him, that thief, that treacherous fighter.

Chorus
  He came once before   710
  into our citadel, bleary eyed
  and huddled in a disguise
  of rags, his sword hand
  hidden under his clothes,
  begging his bread he crept in, a wretched vagrant,   715
  dirty, unkempt, foul.
  and much evil he spoke
  against the royal house of the sons of Atreus
  as if he had hated all the lords of their host.
  I wish he had died, died as he deserved   720
  before he ever set foot on the Phrygian shore.

Leader
  Whether it was Odysseus or not, I am afraid.
  We are the picket, and Hector will hold us to blame.

First Soldier
  With what charge?

Leader
  With curses.

First Soldier
  For doing what? What do you fear?   725

Leader
  Because they got through us.

First Soldier

                        Who did?
                        386

Leader
Those men who got into the Phrygian camp tonight.

Thracian Charioteer (*within*)
Oh god. Disaster.

Leader
Listen!
Silence. Keep your places all. Perhaps someone is in our
nets. 730

Charioteer
Halloo, help!
Disaster and ruin of the Thracians.

Leader
This is one of our allies in pain or terror.

Charioteer (*entering*)
Halloo!
I am hurt, I am done. And you, lord of the Thracians,
how hateful that day you saw Troy,
what an end to your life. 735

Leader
You must be one of our allies, but who? My eyes
fail me in the dark. I cannot clearly make you out.

Charioteer
Where can I find some chief of the Trojans?
Where is Hector himself?
Drowsing somewhere, sleeping under arms? 740
Is there none in command to whom I can report
what happened to us, what someone has done
and got clean away, vanished, leaving plain to see
the hurt he inflicted on the Thracians?

Leader
Some mishap has come to the Thracian force, it seems 745
from what this mans says.

Charioteer

The army is shattered, the king is killed
by a traitor's stroke,
and oh, my own wound hurts   750
deep and bleeds. Shall I die? Must both
Rhesus and I be basely killed
in Troy, which we came to help?

Leader

There is no mystery in ill news he reports
now; it is plain that some of our allies are killed.   755

Charioteer

There has been wickedness done here. More than
    wickedness;
shame too, which makes the evil double its own bulk.
To die with glory, if one has to die at all,
is still, I think, pain for the dier, surely so,
but grandeur left for his survivors, honor for his house.   760
But death to us came senseless and inglorious.
When Hector with his own hand led us to our
    quarters
and gave us the watchword, we lay down to sleep, worn
    out
with the fatigue of our long march. No one kept watch
in our contingent for that night, nor were our arms   765
stacked out in order, nor were the goads in place beside
the yokes of the horses, since our king had been assured
that you were masters of the field and your pickets
    threatened
their anchorage; so we dropped in our tracks, and grossly
    slept.
Yet my own heart was restless, and I woke again   770
to give some fodder to the horses, thinking we must
harness them for the dawn's fighting, so I heaped their
    food
lavishly. Now I see two fellows stealing through our
    camp

in the dim dark, but when I started in their direction
they dodged away and made off.   775
I called out and warned them to stay away from the
    camp.
I thought some of the allies had gone out to steal
from us.
        No reply.
                I did not give it another thought.
I went back to where I had been, and slept again.
But now there came an apparition to my sleep.   780
Those horses, that I trained and drove as charioteer
at Rhesus' side, I saw them, as one sees in a dream,
but wolves had got astride their backs and rode them
    now,
and stabbed and gored their backs and rumps with
    goads, and the mares
went wild with terror, bucking and fighting, snorting   785
from flared nostrils.
I started up to drive those savage beasts away
from the mares, for the dream's terror had awakened me.
As I raised my head I heard a moan such as men make
when they die, and a jet of hot fresh blood splashed me.
    It came   790
from my master, who had been murdered, and died hard.
I leapt upright, but there was no spear in my hand,
and as I looked about and fumbled for a weapon
somebody coming close up slashed me hard in the side
with a sword. I took and felt a cut from the blade   795
that ripped me deep.
I fell on my face. He and the other man seized the team
and car, mounted, galloped away, and escaped.
Ah.
I am faint from my wound, I cannot stand.
I know what happened, for I saw it, but do not   800
understand in what way these men could have been
    killed
nor what hand killed them. I can guess.
My guess is that our friends were the ones who hurt us.

Leader

O charioteer of that unfortunate Thracian king,
do not be angry with us. The enemy did this.   805
And here is Hector in person, who has heard the news
and comes, I think, in sympathy for your misfortune.

(*Hector enters hastily.*)

Hector (*to the Chorus*)

You are responsible for a disaster. How did it happen
that these marauders sent out by the enemy
got past you and made havoc in our camp? Disgraceful!   810
Why did you neither head them off as they came in
nor catch them as they went out? Someone will pay for
this,
and who but you? I hold you responsible. You had the
watch.
Now they are gone, untouched, and much amused, no
doubt,
with the feebleness of the Trojans, and of me, their
leader.   815
I tell you now—father Zeus be witness to my oath—
death by flogging or by the headsman's ax awaits you
for your part in this. Else, say Hector is a weakling.
Say he is nothing.

Chorus

No, no!   820
We came to you, lord, defender of the city, we did,
we came (it must have been these),
we told you their fires were burning beside the ships.
Since then, all through the night's vigil   825
our eyes have not deadened, they have not slept,
by the springs of Simois we swear it. O my lord,
do not be angry with us. None of all this
that has happened is our fault.
If again, in the course of time, you prove we have said or
done   830
anything wrong, then bury us
alive in the ground. We will not protest.

Charioteer (to Hector)

You are Barbarian, so are we. Why do you parry
my charge by threatening these men? Why make a
    Greek
lawyer's speech here?
You did this.
            We Thracians,   835
the wounded and the dead, will not be satisfied
with anyone else. It would take you a long and artful
    speech
to convince me that you have not been killing your
    friends.
You coveted those horses. For their sake, you murdered
your own allies, whose coming you had begged so hard.   840
They did come. They are dead. When Paris shamed
    hospitality
he was better than you—you murderer of your friends
    and helpers.
Never tell me it was one of the Argives
got through to destroy us. Who could slip through the
    Trojan lines
without detection and reach us?   845
You and the whole of the Phrygian army lay between.
Who of your own particular allies is dead,
or wounded, by those enemies you speak of? We
who lay beyond are wounded, some, while others fared
    worse
and do not look any longer on the light of the sun.   850
I tell you plain. I do not think this was any Achaean.
Who could pick a path through the enemy in the dark
and find where Rhesus lay—unless they were directed
by a god? They would not even know
of his arrival. Your defense is artificial.   855

Hector

We have had the help of our allies through all the time
that the Achaean army has been on our shores,

and not one word of complaint has come from any of
  them
of ill treatment. You would be our first. I hope
no greed for horses ever makes me kill my friends   860
to get them. This is more of Odysseus. What man else
among the Argives could have planned and done it?
I fear him. The thought, too, racks my mind,
he might have chanced to meet Dolon and killed him.
  Dolon
has been gone for a long time, and there's no sign of
  him,   865

Charioteer

  I don't know what "Odysseuses" you're talking about.
  I do know we're hurt, and it was no enemy did it.

Hector

  Since you cannot think otherwise, you must think this.

Charioteer

  O land of my fathers, how can I reach you, and there
    die?

Hector

  No dying. Too many have died already.   870

Charioteer

  I have lost my masters. Where shall I turn me?

Hector

  My own house will take you in and make you well.

Charioteer

  How shall the hands of his murderers take care of me?

Hector

  This man keeps saying the same thing. He will not stop.

Charioteer

  Perish the murderer. I do not mean you,   875

you need not protest. The Spirit of Justice knows who
   did it.

Hector

Take him up. Help him into my house,
then look after him carefully, so that he will not
be complaining any more.

                You go to the forces on the wall,
to Priam and the elders. Tell them it is time   880
to bury these dead beside the highway where it leaves
our city.

      (*Some soldiers [not the Chorus] lift the Thracian
      charioteer and carry him out, while others leave
                    to deliver the last message.*)

Chorus

After our high success, does the god
now change Troy's luck, bring us back, to suffer
new losses? What does he plan?
    (*The Muse appears above, holding in her arms the
                      body of Rhesus.*)

But see, see,   885
my King, over your head, what goddess
hovers, carrying aloft in her arms
the man lately slain?
A pitiful sight. It fills me with fear.

The Muse

Behold me, Trojans, and fear not. I am the Muse,   890
one of the Nine and prized among the poets, who stand
before you. I have seen the death of my dear son
so sadly slain by the enemy. His killer, treacherous
Odysseus, some day shall be punished as he deserves.

With my own song of mourning   895
I mourn you, my child. Oh, you hurt
your mother when you went
that day to Troy,
a cursed, wretched way.

393

I would not have had you go, but you went.   900
Your father restrained you, but you broke away.
I mourn you, my child, dear,
dearest head, I mourn you.

Chorus

I, too, as much as ever one can grieve
who has no kinship with the dead, grieve for your son.   905

The Muse

Perish the scion of Oeneus.
Perish the son of Laertes.
He made me childless, who had
the best child in the world.
Perish the woman who forsook   910
her Greek home for a Phrygian bed.
She, dearest son, she is your true destroyer,
she, who made the unnumbered cities
empty of the brave.
Philammon's son, who live and die your many lives   915
and deaths, you have struck back and wounded me deep,
O Thamyris.
Rude violence did all. It brought you down. The quarrel
of the Muses, too, made me bear this unhappy son;
for as I waded through the waters of the Strymon,
the River-God was on me, I was in his arms   920
and conceived. It was when we Muses, all arrayed
with instruments, went to the gold-soiled mountain-mass
of Pangaeus, and the high contest of melody
with that great Thracian singer, and we blinded him,
Thamyris, who had vilified our craft of song.   925
When you were born, in shame over my maidenhood
and before my sisters, I flung you into the great waters
of your father, and Strymon gave you into the care
of no mortals, but the maiden nymphs of his own springs
who nursed you to perfection and then sent you forth,   930
child, to be king of Thrace and first of mortal men.
There in the bloody valors of your land's defense

I never feared your death.
Only to Troy I warned you you must never go
knowing what waited you there, but Hector's embassies   935
and the repeated conclaves of the men of state
persuaded you to move to the defense of friends.

Athene! You alone are guilty of this death.
Odysseus and the son of Tydeus were your agents,
they could have done nothing. Never think I do not
    know.   940
And yet I and my sister Muses make your Athens
great in our art, and by our presence in the land;
and it was Orpheus, own blood cousin to this man
you have slain, who first instructed your people in the
    rites
of mystery and secrets revealed; last, it was we   945
the sisters who with Phoebus educated
Musaeus, your great and respected citizen,
so he surpassed our other pupils.
Here is your gratitude. I hold my son in my arms
and mourn him.
            I need no advocate, Athene.

Chorus

Hector, that Thracian charioteer with his mad charge   950
that we plotted Rhesus' murder is proved wrong.

Hector

I knew that well. It took no divination
to see the hand of Odysseus in this warrior's death.
And as for my part, when I saw the Greek army camped
on our shores, what should I do but send my heralds out   955
to our allies and ask them to come and help?
I sent heralds. This man was in my debt. He came to
    help.
But do not think I am unmoved by his death.
I am even ready to make him a great funeral mound
and burn the glory of innumerable robes.   960
He was my friend. He came to help. His loss is mourned.

The Muse

Rhesus will not go to the black meadow in the earth.
So much at least I claim from the infernal bride,
the daughter of Demeter, goddess of the fields,
that she remit his life. She is in debt to me   965
for her ordaining of the Orphics' revelations.
For me he will be as one dead, with no more light
in his eyes, for the rest of time. He will not come again
to where he looks upon his mother any more.
Hidden deep in the caves among the silver mines   970
he shall live on, a human Spirit underground,
where Bacchus' medium under the Pangaean horn
is housed, a holy god to the initiate.
The load of grief that I must bear is lighter
than that of the sea goddess. Her son too must die.   975
I with my sisters first shall dirge your death, my son,
then mourn Achilles, on Thetis' day of sorrow.
Pallas, who killed you, cannot save him.
Apollo's quiver holds the shaft which means his death.

O making of children, hapless work, sorrow of mankind,   980
the man who reasons well
will live his life through childless and not risk the chil-
    dren
whom some day he must bury.

(*The Muse disappears.*)

Leader

Rhesus is in his mother's hands, and she will mourn
    him.
Hector, your work lies now before you. It is dawn.   985
It is time. What would you have us do?

Hector

About your business. Tell the allies to arm with speed,
and yoke their horses to the chariots,
then, when full armed, await the call of the Tyrrhenian
trumpet. For I am confident we can overrun

the camp and walls of the Achaeans, fire their ships,   990
and that this sunlight that begins to climb
brings us of Troy our day of liberty.

Leader

Obey the King. Let us march, well armed,
in good order, give the word
to the allies. Who knows? The god who is on our side   995
might grant us the victory.

THE SUPPLIANT WOMEN

Translated and with an Introduction by

FRANK WILLIAM JONES

INTRODUCTION TO
THE SUPPLIANT WOMEN

This play, which may be dated between 420 and 415 B.C., deals with the aftermath of the war stirred up against Eteocles, a son of Oedipus, by his brother Polynices, who had quarreled with him over the kingship of Thebes after their father's death. Aeschylus, in *Seven against Thebes*; Sophocles, in *Antigone* and *Oedipus at Colonus*; and Euripides, in *The Phoenician Women*, present other aspects of this story of rival brothers. Euripides here concerns himself not with the rights and wrongs of the dispute, but with the sufferings war brings to civilians. The play is best understood as a plea against inhumanity, especially in wartime. It is similar, in this respect, to Euripides' *The Trojan Women*, with the addition of a scene or two in favor of democracy, suggesting that the basic decencies of life have a better chance of being observed under popular than under autocratic government. And yet eloquent praises of peace (ll. 476-93) are put into the mouth of an antidemocratic person. Historically, this may reflect the war-weariness of the time; artistically, it shows that Euripides, like Shaw, lets all his parties have their say and say it well.

The action of the play is primarily ethical and political. Individual feelings take a minor role. Aethra, as her son points out (l. 292), has nothing to gain or lose by supporting the plea of the mothers of the seven warriors who fell in the attempt on the Theban throne. Theseus, at first reluctant to do anything for the pathetic Adrastus, overcomes his dislike of that ineffective person to the extent of defending his cause by force. It is evident that Euripides is holding Theseus up as an example of civic virtue, which he sees as flexible but not pliant —ready to change, for the better, under the influence of moral and religious arguments.

With Aethra and Theseus, models of principled moderation, Adrastus and Evadne provide an effective contrast. Both of them are capable of being carried away by feeling: Adrastus by guilt and shame, Evadne by love and grief. And both of them shock and repel better-balanced people: Adrastus irritates Theseus, Evadne horrifies her father and even the chorus, who interrupt their grief over their fallen sons to express amazement at Evadne's suicide (ll. 1072, 1076). Here Euripides' pity for humanity finds noble expression. He sees how war, and other extreme situations, bring out the essence of every individual: self-reproach in Adrastus, fanatical loyalty in Evadne, filial devotion in the sons of the Seven. And he also feels deeply the futility and cruelty of war, which keeps breeding new wars from old (ll. 1142-49), kills the noblest men, and lets Adrastus survive. With the morbid timidity of this king's actions and attitudes—for example, in lines 765-69— we may contrast the excellences he sees in his fallen companions (ll. 856-917). Yet even Adrastus redeems himself, somewhat, in the course of the action: his utterances become less hysterical and self-pitying, and he speaks out as an advocate of peace (ll. 949-54). He represents, in his fashion, the type of tragic hero who learns by suffering.

The intervention of Athene, at the end of the play, may seem pointless to modern readers. The passage possibly refers to an alliance of Athens with Argos, about 420 B.C. At any rate, Euripides here leaves the territory of philanthropic principle and talks hard political sense. Or perhaps he is suggesting that one is not much use without the other.

Lines 176-83 present some difficulty. It is likely that the poet is here defending himself against charges that he broke the decorum of tragedy by presenting paupers and slaves as serious personages. In lines 180-83, he is perhaps implying that sad scenes in a man's plays do not mean that he leads a sad life. The passage as a whole has little to do with what Adratus is saying. Perhaps it was interpolated from another play, or lines linking it with Adrastus' main point have been lost. The opening of Theseus' answer (ll. 195-200) does not refer directly to anything Adrastus has said. It may be aimed at pessimistic implications of lines 176-79, which present life as perpetual conflict between wealth and poverty. These implications were perhaps more clearly worked out in the correct text. Whatever Adrastus said, Theseus thought he was questioning the motives or the very existence of the gods, on the ground that human life has more bad than good in it.

Lines 1026-30 are obscure in the original. Evadne seems to be inveighing against marriage, perhaps to fortify her resolve to die with the man she loves; but her picture of a happy home life belies her embittered intent. Either Euripides is being very subtle here or the text is corrupt.

The translation follows Gilbert Murray's text as edited by T. Nicklin (Oxford, 1936). At line 763 there is a lacuna, which I have ventured to fill with a question from Adrastus, as Nicklin suggests. But lines 844-45 of the Oxford text appear as lines 858-59 in this translation. If Theseus said (as he does in the text) "I saw the deeds . . . by which they hoped to take the city," it would mean that he had witnessed the attack of the Seven against Thebes. This is unlikely, and since the words would come much more properly from Adrastus at this point, I have transferred them to him.

CHARACTERS

Aethra, mother of Theseus
Theseus, king of Athens
Adrastus, king of Argos, and leader of the Theban adventure
A Herald from Thebes
A Messenger from Thebes
Evadne, widow of Capaneus, who fell in the Theban adventure
Iphis, her father
Athene
Chorus: Mothers of the Seven against Thebes
A group of sons of the fallen fighters

THE SUPPLIANT WOMEN

SCENE: *The temple of Demeter, at Eleusis, near Athens.*

Aethra

    Demeter, enshrined in this land Eleusis,
    And you who tend the goddess' temple,
    Bless me and bless Theseus my son
    And the city of Athens, and Pittheus' land,
    Where in prosperous halls my father reared me,   5
    Aethra, and wed me to Pandion's son
    Aegeus, as Loxia's oracle bade him.

    So I pray as I look upon these women
    Burdened with years, who left their homes in Argos
    To fall with suppliant branches at my feet   10
    In dreadful loss: their seven noble sons
    Are dead at Cadmus' gates, and they are childless.
    Adrastus, lord of Argos, led the men
    To claim for his son-in-law, exiled Polynices,
    A share of Oedipus' inheritance.   15
    They perished in the struggle, and their mothers
    Desire to bury them; but those in power
    Spurn what the gods hold lawful and refuse
    Even to grant removal of the bodies.
    The burden of these women's need for me   20
    Adrastus also bears: look where he lies,
    With tearful face mourning the grievous doom
    Of the expedition that he sent from home.
    He stirs me on to make my son his champion,

Employing either words or force of arms   25
To take the corpses and give them burial.
Only this he asks of my child and Athens.

My visit was for sacrifice
That the land be fruitful; I left my house
For this sanctuary, where soonest   30
The corn-ear bristles above the ground.
Now with a bondless bond of leaves
I stay by the sacred hearth of the Two,
Demeter and Kore, as pity moves me
For these gray, childless mothers of sons,   35
And I revere their holy garlands.
I have sent a herald to town, to summon
Theseus, that either he drive from the land
These people and the distress they bring,
Or free them from their suppliant needs—
A pious action for the gods.   40
It is proper for women, if they are wise,
Always to get things done by men.

Chorus

I appeal to you
From aged mouth:
Old, I fall at your knee.
Free my children—   45
Left by lawless men
To body-slackening death,
Food for mountain beasts!
See the piteous
Tears at my eyelids
And wrinkled tearing of hands   50
At hoary flesh
Because I could not lay out
My dead sons in my house
Or see their tombs of earth!

Gracious lady, you too have borne a son,
In blessing of the bed   55

406

For your husband: now to me
Grant a part of your loving-kindness,
In recompense for grievous pain
From the death of those I bore:
Prevail, we beg, upon your son   60
That he go to Ismenus and bring to my hands
The bodies of youthful dead that long for the tomb.

Not for holy rites but in need I came
To fall and pray at the goddess'
Fire-receiving altars;
Justice is ours, and you have power—   65
For you are happy in your child—
To take away my trouble.
My plight is pitiful: I beseech
Your son to bring to these poor hands
The corpse, my son's sad limbs, for my embrace.   70

(*The temple attendants begin to chant.*)

And now the strife of wailing, wailing!
Cry against cry, clashing of priestesses' hands!
Let blows resound together!
Moan in the strain
Of the dance that Hades loves!   75
Bloody the white fingernail
Along the cheek, and stain the skin!
To mourn the dead
Brings honor to those who live.

Insatiable delight of wailing,
Abounding in labor, carries me away,
As from a towering rock   80
Cool water flows
Unceasing ever: I wail,
For to bear the death of children brings
A labor of lament to women.   85
Would that in death
I might forget these griefs!

(Enter Theseus, attended.)

Theseus

    What were those wails I heard, and breast-beating,
    And dirges for the dead? Here, from the temple,
    The echoes came. Alarm takes hold of me:
    My mother has been long away from home;   90
    I come to find her; has she met with trouble?

    Aha! What's there? I see strange things to talk of!
    My aged mother sitting by the altar,
    And foreign women with her, all awry
    In forms of woe: from age-dimmed eyes they shed   95
    Piteous tears to earth; their hair is shorn,
    The robes they wear are not for festivals.
    Mother, what does this mean? Yours to reveal,
    And mine to listen. I expect some ill.

Aethra

    These women, child, are mothers of the sons—   100
    Seven commanders—who died at Cadmus' gates;
    And now with suppliant boughs they watch and wait,
    Circled around me, as you see, my son.

Theseus

    And that one, groaning bitterly at the door?

Aethra

    They say he is Adrastus, lord of Argos.   105

Theseus

    And the boys beside him? Children of the women?

Aethra

    No, they are sons of the warriors who fell.

Thesus

    Why do they stretch out suppliant hands to us?

Aethra

    I know; but let them have the word, my son.

Theseus
    I call on you, hidden beneath your cloak!   110
    Leave off your wailing, bare your head and speak:
    Nothing goes far that does not pass the tongue.

Adrastus
    O glorious victor king
    Of the land of the men of Athens,
    Theseus: I come as suppliant
    To you and to your city.

Theseus
    What do you seek, and what is your need?   115

Adrastus
    You know of my ruinous campaign.

Theseus
    Your passage through Greece was hardly silent.

Adrastus
    In it I lost the chiefs of Argos.

Theseus
    Such are the doings of wretched war.

Adrastus
    I went to the city in quest of the dead.   120

Theseus
    To bury them, counting on Hermes' heralds?

Adrastus
    And now the slayers will not let me.

Theseus
    What are their grounds? Your demand is sacred.

Adrastus
    No grounds. They are bad at being winners.

Theseus
  So you come to me for advice—or what?   125

Adrastus
  I want you to bring back Argos' sons.

Theseus
  And where stands Argos? Are her boasts vain?

Adrastus
  Defeated, finished. We come to you.

Theseus
  By your sole will or that of all the city?

Adrastus
  All we sons of Danaus beg you to bury our dead.   130

Theseus
  Why did you go with seven bands to Thebes?

Adrastus
  To please the men who married my two daughters.

Theseus
  To which of the Argives did you give your children?

Adrastus
  The bond I formed was not among my kind.

Theseus
  To strangers, then, you wedded Argive girls?   135

Adrastus
  Yes: Tydeus, and Polynices, of Theban stock.

Theseus
  How did you come to want them for your kin?

Adrastus
  Puzzling riddles of Phoebus lured me on.

410

Theseus
What words of Apollo meant marriage for the maidens?

Adrastus
That I give my daughters to a boar and a lion.   140

Theseus
And how did you unravel the god's pronouncement?

Adrastus
The pair of exiles came to my door at night—

Theseus
What pair? You speak of two at once: explain.

Adrastus
Tydeus and Polynices—and fought each other.

Theseus
To them, as being beasts, you gave your girls?   145

Adrastus
Yes, for I fancied two wild creatures fighting.

Theseus
Why had they left the borders of their countries?

Adrastus
Tydeus in guilt of shedding kindred blood.

Theseus
And what brought Oedipus' son away from Thebes?

Adrastus
A father's curse: that he should kill his brother.   150

Theseus
Then voluntary flight was wise of him.

Adrastus
True; but those remaining wronged the absent.

Theseus
You mean his brother robbed him of his goods?

Adrastus
That is the case I went to judge; and lost.

Theseus
You consulted the seers, and watched their victims burn?   155

Adrastus
Ah! You pursue me to my weakest point.

Theseus
The gods, it seems, did not approve your mission.

Adrastus
It also flouted Amphiaraus' will.

Theseus
So lightly you ignored divinity?

Adrastus
Unruliness of youthful men confused me.   160

Theseus
You followed strength of heart, not strength of mind.

Adrastus
That course has ruined many generals.
O Lord of Athens! Crown of power in Hellas!
I am ashamed—a gray-haired man who once
Was king, and fortunate—that now I fall
To earth and clasp your knee; and yet I must   165
Submit to my disaster. Save my dead!
Take pity on my woes, and on these mothers
Of fallen sons! Old age brings childlessness   170
For them, and movement burdens aged limbs,
And yet they venture here, to a land of strangers—
Not to attend Demeter's mysteries,
But wishing burial of the dead whose hands,

In manly duty, should have buried *them*.   175
The sight of poverty is wise for wealth;
The poor should gaze with envy on the rich,
To learn the love of goods; untroubled men
Are well advised to look at wretchedness.
The poet bringing songs into the world   180
Should labor in joy. If this is not his mood,
He cannot—being inwardly distressed—
Give pleasure outwardly. That stands to reason.
You may well ask: "Why pass by Pelops' land,
And seek to lay this task of yours on Athens?"   185
In fairness, I would make this answer. Sparta
Is fierce; her ways are artful; and the others
Are small and weak. Yours is the only city
With strength enough to undertake the task:
She sees what misery is and has for leader,   190
In you, a good and youthful shepherd; ruin
Has come to many states for lack of such command.

Chorus

I make the same request of you as he does:
Theseus! be pitiful to my wretchedness.

Theseus

I have heard such arguments before, from others,   195
And fought them hard. Somebody said that life
Holds more of worse conditions than of better;
But I oppose that school, for I believe
That there are more good things than bad for mortals;
If there were not, the light would not be ours.   200
I praise the god who set our life in order,
Lifting it out of savagery and confusion.
First he put wits in us, and then gave language,
Envoy of words, to understand the voice;
And fruits of earth to eat, and for this food   205
Watery drops from heaven, to quench our thirst
And nourish the yield of the land; providing also
The fortress winter, against the sun-god's fire,

And commerce over sea, that by exchange
Each country may obtain whatever it lacks.   210
Things without mark, not clearly visible,
Are brought to light by seers, observing fire
And reckoning from birds and the folds of entrails.
Now, if all this is not enough for us—
So well equipped for living, by God's gift—   215
Are we not pettish? But intelligence
Seeks power more than divine; our minds grow haughty,
Until we think we are wiser than the gods.
That is your kind of folly, it would seem.
First, bowing to Phoebus' words, like one who thinks   220
The gods exist, you gave your girls to strangers:
A mating of fair with foul, to hurt your house!
Wrongdoers' bodies should not be joined to the just;
A wise man will ally his family
With well-regarded people. Sickness spreads: 225
A man may do no wrong; yet, if he suffers
From the same ill as one marked out for ruin,
God fells them both at once.
                                       Then, when you took
All Argos with you on that expedition,
The seers spoke omens but you slighted them,   230
Flouted the gods, and laid your city low.
You were led astray by glory-loving youngsters,
Promoters of unjust wars, who spoil the townsmen.
One of them wants to be a general;
Another to seize the power and riot in it;   235
A third is set on gain. They never think
What harm this brings for the majority.
The classes of citizens are three. The rich
Are useless, always lusting after more.
Those who have not, and live in want, are a menace,   240
Ridden with envy and fooled by demagogues;
Their malice stings the owners. Of the three,
The middle part saves cities: it guards the order   245
A community estabishes.
                         And so

I am to be your ally? What fine words
Will make my citizens favor that? Farewell!
You planned your actions poorly. Take what comes:
Wrestle with fate alone, and let me go.

Chorus

He blundered. That is natural in the young,   250
And should be pardoned in him. We have come
To you, my lord, as healer of these ills.

Adrastus

In choosing you, my lord, I did not think
That you would sit in judgment on my woes,
Or estimate and punish any action   255
I may have lacked the skill to execute;
I only wanted help. If you refuse it,
I have no choice but to accept your will.
Now, aged dames, go forth: lay on that spot
The verdant twigs, and turn the leaves face down,
Calling to witness gods and earth and sunlight   260
And Demeter, goddess, bearer of the torch,
That prayers to the gods availed us nothing.

Chorus

O King, you are of Pelops' line, and we are from his
      country:
The same ancestral blood is ours. How can it be
That *you* forsake this cause, and drive out of your land 265
Old women who have gained nothing that is owed them?
We pray you not to do this. Beasts have rocks for refuge;
Slaves, the altars of the gods; city huddles with city
When storms come. Nothing mortal prospers to the end   270

—Woman of sorrows! Leave Persephone's sacred
      ground;
Go up to him and put your hands about his knees;
Beg him to bring my sons' dead bodies—Oh, the grief!
Lads who were lost to me under the walls of Cadmus.

—Alas! these poor old hands: take them, guide them,
  support them.   275

—Friend! Honor and glory of Hellas! I touch your
    beard;
Here at your knees I fall and seek your hand in my woe.

—If you would shelter a wanderer, pity me—   280
Suppliant for my children, piteously lamenting.

—Child! I appeal to you: do not leave boys your age
Unburied in Cadmus' land, to gladden the wild beasts!

—I fall and clasp your knees: see the tears at my eye-
    lids!
I beg you, bring to fulfilment the burial of my children! 285

Theseus
  Mother: you hold your fine-spun cloak to your eyes.
  You are weeping. Why? Is it because you hear
  The groans of misery coming from these women?
  Somehow, they pierce me too. Lift your white head:
  No more tears, at Demeter's sacred hearth!   290

Aethra
  Alas!

Theseus
    Their troubles should not make you moan.

Aethra
  Poor women!

Theseus
    You do not belong to them.

Aethra
  Child! May I speak, for the city's good and yours?

Theseus
  Many wise things are said even by women.

416

Aethra
> I shrink from showing what I have in mind. 295

Theseus
> It is shameful to hold back words that might help your
> kin.

Aethra
> I would not now be still, and afterward
> Blame myself for a silence wrongly kept;
> Or fear that women's well-meant words are wasted,
> And in that dread let my good will be lost. 300
> My child I bid you: first, look to the gods;
> For if you slight them you will fall. Intentions
> Otherwise good can be wrecked by that one fault.
> If you were asked to launch an enterprise
> For men who had not been wronged, then certainly 305
> I would say nothing. But you must be told
> How greatly it would honor you (so much
> That I am not afraid to advise it, child!)
> If cruel men, who would deny the dead
> The rights of burial and their funerals,
> Were forced to grant this, by your hand, and stopped 310
> From violating what all Greece holds lawful.
> The power that keeps cities of men together
> Is noble preservation of the laws.
> It will be said that, lacking manly strength,
> You stepped aside in fear when you had a chance 315
> To win a crown of glory for the city—
> That you chose to hunt wild boars, a mean pursuit,
> And when it was time to take up helmet and spear
> And drive the task through, then you proved a coward.
> That must not be. Remember, child: you are mine. 320
> Do you see, if ever your fatherland is mocked
> For lack of resolution, how she stares
> Straight at the mockers, with a Gorgon eye?
> She thrives on strenuous action. States that work
> In stealth and darkness wear a somber look 325

417

To match their caution. Child, will you not help
The dead, and these poor women in their need?
Your setting forth is just; I do not dread it.
Yes, Cadmus' people now are uppermost;
But soon their dice will fall another way.   330
Of that I am certain. God reverses all.

Chorus

O best-loved lady! Nobly you have spoken,
For him and me, making a double joy.

Theseus

Mother, what I have said about this man
I still consider right. I spoke my mind   335
On the designs that led him to his ruin.
But I also see the truth of what you tell me:
That it is not in keeping with my ways
To run from risk. By many noble deeds
I have made myself a byword to the Greeks: 340
They count on me to punish wickedness.
I am unable to decline a task.
What then will hostile persons say of me
If you, my parent, you who fear for me,
Must urge me first to undertake this labor?   345
Forward, then; I shall go and free the dead.
Persuasion first: if that does not succeed,
Then force of arms will gain my end. The gods
Will not be jealous. I desire the city
With all its voices to approve this plan.   350
It will approve because I want it to:
But if I state my reasons, I shall have
More favor from the people, whom I made
Sole rulers when I set their city free
And gave them equal votes. So I shall take
Adrastus to support my argument
And go to all the citizens assembled,   355
Convince them that this must be done, pick out
A group of young Athenians, and return.
Then, resting on my weapons, I shall send
To ask the bodies of the dead from Creon.

Matrons: remove my mother's ritual garlands.
I must conduct her to the house of Aegeus,   360
Clasping her loving hand. A wretched child
Is he who does not return his parents' care.
Noblest of gifts! By granting it, he earns
Back from his children what he gives his parents.

Chorus
    Argos, my fatherland, pasture of horses: 365
    You heard him speak, you heard from the king
    Words that the gods hold sacred,
    Words that mean greatness for Greece and Argos.
    May he go to the end of my woes, and beyond;
    Carry the mother's murdered idol   370
    Away, and then make friendship
    Firm with the land of Inachus.

    A work of piety brings honor and glory to cities
    And earns thanks that last forever.
    What dare I hope from the city? Will it truly gain   375
    A pledge of friendship, and graves for my sons?

    City of Pallas! A mother begs you to prevent
    The desecration of human law.
    You revere right, look down on crime, and are ready
    Always to help ill-fated men.   380

Theseus (to an Athenian herald)
    The skill you have as bearer of proclamations
    Has given constant service to me and the city.
    Now you must cross Asopus and Ismenus' water
    And tell the stately ruler of the Cadmeans this:
    "Theseus asks you, by your grace, to bury the dead. His
        country   385
    Neighbors yours, and he believes the request is worth the
        granting.
    Do this and you will have all of Erechtheus' folk for
        friends."
    If they consent, commend them and hasten back.

419

If they refuse, deliver a second message:
"Welcome my band of revelers, men who carry shields!"   390
A ready task-force waits, under review,
Here and now at the sacred Fount of the Dance.
The city, when it saw I willed this effort,
Was ready to accept it, even glad.

But who comes here, to interrupt my words?   395
I cannot tell for sure; he seems to be
A Theban herald. Stay a while. His coming
Might change my plans, and you would be released.

(*Enter a Herald from Thebes.*)

Herald
What man is master in this land? To whom
Must I give the word I bring from Creon, ruler   400
In Cadmus' country since Eteocles
Fell at his brother Polynices' hand
Beside the seven-mouthed gates?

Theseus
                    One moment, stranger.
Your start was wrong, seeking a master here.
This city is free, and ruled by no one man.   405
The people reign, in annual succession.
They do not yield the power to the rich;
The poor man has an equal share in it.

Herald
That one point gives the better of the game
To me. The town I come from is controlled   410
By one man, not a mob. And there is no one
To puff it up with words, for private gain,
Swaying it this way, that way. Such a man
First flatters it with wealth of favors; then
He does it harm, but covers up his blunders   415
By blaming other men, and goes scot-free.
The people is no right judge of arguments;

Then how can it give right guidance to a city?
A poor man, working hard, could not attend   420
To public matters, even if ignorance
Were not his birthright. When a wretch, a nothing,
Obtains respect and power from the people
By talk, his betters sicken at the sight.   425

Theseus
What bombast from a herald! Waster of words,
If it is argument you want—and you yourself
Have set the battle going—listen. Nothing
Is worse for a city than an absolute ruler.
In earliest times, before there are common laws,   430
One man has power and makes the law his own:
Equality is not yet. With written laws,
People of few resources and the rich
Both have the same recourse to justice. Now
A man of means, if badly spoken of,
Will have no better standing than the weak;   435
And if the lesser is in the right, he wins
Against the great. This is the call of freedom:
"What man has good advice to give the city,
And wishes to make it known?" He who responds   440
Gains glory; the unwilling may hold their peace.
For the city, what can be more fair than that?
Again, when the people is master in the land,
It welcomes youthful townsmen as its subjects;
But when one man is king, he finds this hateful,
And if he thinks that any of the nobles   445
Are wise, he fears for his despotic power
And kills them. How can a city become strong
If someone takes away, cuts off new ventures
Like ears of corn in a spring field? What use
To build a fortune, if your work promotes   450
The despot's welfare, not your family's?
Why bring up girls as gentlewomen, fit
For marriage, if tyrants may take them for their joy—
A grief to parents? I would rather die

421

Than see my children forced to such a union. 455
   These are the darts I shoot at what you say.
What have you come to ask of this, our country?
You talk too much; you would regret your visit
Had not a city sent you. Messengers
Should state their mission promptly, then return. 460
I hope that henceforth, to my city, Creon
Sends a less wordy messenger than you.

Chorus
   When fortune favors bad men, how they revel!
   They act as if their luck would last forever.

Herald
   Now I shall speak. On what has been debated, 465
You may hold your views; I the opposite.
   I and the whole Cadmean people say
Adrastus must not pass into this land.
If he has entered it, you must strip off
His sacred ritual wreaths and drive him out 470
Before the sun-god's flame is down. His dead
Must not be removed by force; the Argives' city
Is no concern of yours. Do what I say
And you will steer your city's course in calm.
If you refuse, there will be much rough water
For us, for you, and for our allies: war. 475
Think now: do not let anger at my words
Goad you to puffed-up answers. Your city is free;
That does not make it powerful. Hope has driven
Many cities against each other; she stirs
An overreaching heart; she is not to be trusted. 480
When the people vote on war, nobody reckons
On his own death; it is too soon; he thinks
Some other man will meet that wretched fate.
But if death faced him when he cast his vote,
Hellas would never perish from battle-madness. 485
And yet we men all know which of two words
Is better, and can weigh the good and bad

They bring: how much better is peace than war!
First and foremost, the Muses love her best;
And the goddess of vengeance hates her. She delights   490
In healthy children, and she glories in wealth.
But wickedly we throw all this away
To start our wars and make the losers slaves—
Man binding man and city chaining city.
And you would help our enemies in death,
Bringing away for burial men who fell   495
By their own pride? Do you not think it right
That thunderbolts made smoke of Capaneus,
The one who thrust the ladders at the gates
And swore to sack the city whether God
Willed it or not? The bird-interpreter,
Was he not swallowed by a gulf that opened   500
Around his four-horse chariot? There they lie,
The other squadron-leaders, by the gates;
Rocks have pounded the framework of their bones.
Now boast a greater mind than Zeus, or grant
That the wicked are justly punished by the gods.   505
Wise men should cherish children first, then parents,
Then fatherland—and that they ought to strengthen,
Not enervate. A bold leader or sailor
Brings peril; the man who knows when not to act
Is wise. To my mind, bravery is forethought.   510

Chorus
    Zeus the punisher was enough. No need
    For you to gloat like this over their doom.

Adrastus
    You miserable wretch—

Theseus
              Silence, Adrastus!
    Restrain yourself. Do not give precedence
    To your words over mine. This challenge comes   515
    To me, not you; and I must answer it.

423

(*To the herald.*)

I am not aware that Creon is my master,
Or even more powerful than I. How then
Can he compel Athens to do his bidding?
If we serve him, the world runs backward! I   520
Did not begin this war: I was not with them
When they went to Thebes; I only think it just
To bury their dead. I mean no harm to the city,
No man-destroying struggles: I uphold   525
The law of all the Greeks. Is that unfair?
Yes, certainly the Argives did you wrong,
But they are dead. You fought them off with honor,
To their disgrace; and now the case is closed.   530
Come! Let the dead be covered by the ground,
And let each part regain the element
From which it came to light: the spirit, air;
The body, earth. The flesh is only ours
To dwell in while life lasts; and afterward   535
The giver of its strength must take it back.
Do you think to hurt Argos, not burying her dead?
You are mistaken. All Hellas is concerned
When anyone tries to strip the dead of their due
And keep them from the tomb. If that were law,   540
Brave men would turn cowards. And yet you come
To threaten me with frightful words. Do you dread
The corpses? If they are hidden in earth, what then?
Will they overthrow your country from the grave,
Or beget children in the womb of earth   545
Who will avenge them some day? Fears like these
Are base and vain, a waste of breath to speak.
Fools! Be instructed in the ills of man.
Struggles make up our life. Good fortune comes   550
Swiftly to some, to some hereafter; others
Enjoy it now. Its good luxuriates.
Not only is he honored by the hapless
In hope of better days, but lucky ones
Exalt him too, fearing to lose the wind.

Aware of this, you should not take it hard   555
When moderately wronged, or do a wrong
So great as to hurt your city. That is why
You ought to grant the bodies of the fallen
To us, who wish to do them reverence.
If you choose otherwise, my course is clear: 560
To go and force their burial. Never the Greeks
Shall have this news to tell: that ancient law,
Established by the gods, appealed to me
And Pandion's city, only to be shattered.

Chorus
Courage! Keep alive the light of justice,
And much that men say in blame will pass you by.   565

Herald
May I make a speech that is short and plain?

Theseus
Say what you like: you are far from still.

Herald
You will never take Argos' sons from my country.

Theseus
Now hear me, if you will, in turn.

Herald
I listen; I must grant your due.   570

Theseus
I shall bury the dead away from Thebes.

Herald
First you must risk a clash of shields.

Theseus
I have come through many other trials.

Herald
Did your father make you a match for all?

425

Theseus
Offenders, yes; I do not crush virtue.   575

Herald
You and your city have busy habits.

Theseus
Much effort, much prosperity.

Herald
Go, and be caught by a Sown Man's spear!

Theseus
What martial fury can come from a dragon?

Herald
Feel it and know it. You are still young.   580

Theseus
You cannot rouse my mind to wrath
By boasting. Take the foolish words
You brought, and leave the country. Talk
Will gain us nothing.

(*The Theban Herald goes out.*)

Forward, every man   585
Who fights on foot or from a chariot!
Let cheek-pieces rattle, flecking the horses' mouths
With foam as they gallop toward the Theban land!
I march on Cadmus' seven gates; I bear
Sharp iron in my hand and act as herald   590
In my behalf. Adrastus, I command you,
Stay here; do not attach your fate to me.
I shall lead the army, guided by my god,
As a new campaigner with a new intent.
Only one thing I need: to have with me
The gods who honor justice. That support   595
Gives victory. Human excellence means nothing
Unless it works with the consent of God.

426

(*Exeunt Theseus and attendants; Aethra.*)

Chorus

Pitiful mothers of lost commanders!
Yellow fear sits on my heart.

—What new word is this you bring?   600

—How will the mission of Pallas stand the test?

—By fighting, did you say, or exchange of words?

—I pray that good will come of it!
But what if it ends in slayings by Ares,
Battles, din of beaten breasts throughout the city?   605
Then, alas! What could I find to say,
I, who caused it all?

—The man who glories in his luck
May be overthrown by destiny;
In that hope I rest secure.

—Then you believe in gods who stand for justice.   610

—Of course; what other beings make things happen?

—I see much else in the way they treat us.

—That is because you are crushed by fear
From the past. But justice has called for justice, blood
    for blood;
The gods, who hold in their hands the end of all,
Now give men rest from pain.   615

—How might we leave the sacred fount of the goddess
And reach the plains with the beautiful towers?

—If one of the gods would give you wings,   620
—On the way to the two-rivered city.

—You would know, then you would know how our
    friends are faring.

427

—What destiny, what turn of fate, I wonder,
Is waiting for this country's mighty lord?   625

—Again we call on gods invoked already:
Here is the foremost hope of the frightened.

—O Zeus, who fathered a child for the heifer
Of Inachus, mother of old,
Favor this my city and help its cause.   630
Your image, the city's mainstay, has been outraged;
And I would make it ready for the pyre.

(*Enter a Messenger from Thebes.*)

Messenger

Women, I bring much news that you will welcome.
I have come through to safety after capture   635
In the battle which the seven companies
Of fallen masters fought by Dirce's stream.
I am here to tell of Theseus' victory.
To spare you long inquiry: I was a servant
Of Capaneus, whom Zeus's flaming bolt   640
Riddled to ashes.

Chorus

                    Oh, with joy we greet
Your news of coming home, and hear the word
You bring of Theseus! If Athens' army too
Is safe, then all you have to tell is welcome.

Messenger

Safe; and it did what should have been achieved
By Adrastus with the Argives whom he marched   645
From Inachus against the Cadmean city.

Chorus

How did the son of Aegeus and his comrades
Set up the trophy to Zeus? Speak: as a witness,
You can give joy to those who were not there.

Messenger

A brilliant ray of sunlight, straight and clear,   650

428

Was striking the ground as I stood by Electra's gate,
Where a watchtower gave a sweeping view. I saw
Three forces marshalled. Infantry with armor
Extended toward high ground: the Ismenian hill,   655
I was told. The king, that famous son of Aegeus,
And his men from old Cecropia held the right;
The left wing, spear-armed Coast men, took positions
Beside the spring of Ares. Cavalry massed   660
On the end of each wing, in equal groups; and chariots
Stood at the foot of Amphion's sacred mound.   665
Cadmus' men, posted before the walls, had put
The corpses, ground of conflict, at their rear.
Horsemen faced horsemen; chariots stood ready,
Equipped to battle four-horse chariots.
Then Theseus' herald spoke these words to all:
"Silence, my men; silence, Cadmean troops.
Listen: we come to take the dead. We wish   670
To bury them, and so uphold the law
Of all the Greeks. It is not our desire
To shed more blood." Creon gave no command
To answer this, but stood in silence, ready.
Then the charioteers began the combat.   675
Driving their chariots toward and past each other,
They set their fighters down, in line of battle.
While these crossed swords, the drivers turned their
    horses
Back to support their men. When Phorbas, captain   680
Of Athens' horsemen, and the overseers
Of Theban cavalry saw the chariots throng,
They threw their forces into the tide of war.
As witness, not from hearsay—I was close
To the battleground of chariots and riders—   685
I know the many horrors there, but not
Where to begin. With the dust that rose toward heaven?
How thick it was! Or men tossed up and down,
Caught in the horses' reins? Or streams of blood   690
From men who fell, or were thrown head first to earth
When cars were shattered, leaving life beside

Wreckage of chariots? When Creon saw
Our mounted forces winning, he took his shield   695
And moved to keep his allies from despair.
Then all the middle of the field was spattered
As men slew and were slain; and the word passed,   700
Shouted aloud among them: "Strike! Thrust back
The spear at Erechtheus' sons!" But Theseus'
       fortunes
Were not to fall by terror. Snatching up
His shining arms, he charged at once. Fiercely
The host that grew to men from dragon's teeth
Opposed us, pushing our left wing back; but theirs   705
Lost to our right and fled. The scales of war
Stood even. Then our general earned praise;
Not seeking only to follow up advantage,
He hurried to his forces' breaking-point,
Shouting so loud that he made the earth resound: 710
"Hold, lads, against these dragon men's stiff spears,
Or else farewell to Athens!" That stirred courage
Throughout the Cranaid army. Then he seized
His Epidaurian weapon, a terrible club,
And swung it right and left, dealing his blows   715
On heads and necks together; the wooden blade
Mowed off and snapped their helmets; turning to flee,
They could hardly move their feet. I shrieked and danced
And clapped my hands. The Thebans made for the gates.   720
Then there were cries and groans throughout the city
From young and old; frightened, they thronged the
       temples.
Now Theseus might have gone inside the walls;
But he held back, declaring that his purpose
Was not to sack the town but claim the dead.   725
    That is the kind of general to elect:
One who puts forth his strength in time of trouble,
Hates arrogant men, and when he prospers, still
Striving to reach the topmost rung of the ladder,
Loses the wealth he might enjoy in calm.   730

Chorus
   Now, having seen this day, surpassing hope,
   I believe in gods. The lesser share of evil
   Seems to be mine now; Thebes has paid the price.

Adrastus
   Zeus! Who dares call us hapless mortals wise?
   You dangle us; whatever you want, we do.   735
   Argos, we thought, was irresistible:
   We were so many, young, and strong of arm!
   Eteocles would have come to terms; his claims
   Were fair; but we refused, and lost.   740
   The winner then, malignant folk of Cadmus,
   Ran riot like a pauper newly rich;
   But now their rioting brings them down, in turn.
   O you who try to shoot beyond the mark!
   O witless mortals! Richly you deserve   745
   Your many woes; you listen not to friends,
   But to your interests. Cities! You might use
   Reason to end your troubles; but with blood,
   Not words, you ruin your affairs.—Enough!   750

                        (*To the messenger.*)

   I would like to know how you reached safety;
   Then I will ask my other questions.

Messenger
   When the city shook in turmoil of war,
      I went through the gates where the troops came in.

Adrastus
Do you bring the dead for whom they fought?

Messenger
Yes, the heads of the seven great houses.   755

Adrastus
But the mass of the fallen—where are they?

431

Messenger
Buried near Cithaeron's folds.

Adrastus
This side, or that? By whom were they buried?

Messenger
At Eleutherae's shady ridge. By Theseus.

Adrastus
Those he did not bury—where have you left them?   760

Messenger
Close by. Speed makes all roads short.

Adrastus
Did it pain the servants to bring them out of the carnage?

Messenger
No one who was a slave had charge of that.

Adrastus
Did Theseus welcome the task?

Messenger
                              You would have said so
If you had seen his loving salute to the dead.

Adrastus
And did he wash the victims' stains himself?   765

Messenger
He even spread the couches and covered the bodies.

Adrastus
That was a dreadful burden, bringing shame.

Messenger
How can our common ills be shameful to us?

Adrastus
Oh, how much rather had I died with them!

Messenger

Your laments are vain, and make these women weep.   770

Adrastus

Yes. It was they who taught me. Now I cease.
Let me lift up my hand when I meet the dead,
And speak, in long and tearful chants of Hades,
To friends by whom I am left to mourn alone.
There is one expense no mortal can recover: 775
A human life. For money, there are ways.

(*The Messenger goes out.*)

Chorus

Part well, part ill—this turn of fate.
For city and soldiers who went to war,   780
Glory and honor redoubled;
For me, to look upon my children's bodies—
A bitter, lovely sight, if ever I see it
And the day despaired of,
Greatest pain of all.   785
Would that old Time, father of days,
Had left me unwed all my life.
What need had I of children?
Once, I thought, I could not bear the sorrow   790
Of being kept away from wedlock. Now—
In loss of dearest children—
Its evil is plain to see.

(*Attendants enter, bearing the corpses
of the fallen chiefs.*)

The woeful sight has come: my fallen children's bodies!   795
  Oh, to join them in death and go down to Hades to-
    gether!

Adrastus

Mothers! Wail for the dead who lie on the ground!
Wail in answer when you hear my moans!   800

433

Chorus
  Children! I bid you now in death
  A bitter farewell for loving mothers.

Adrastus
  O grief, O grief!

Chorus
                  For my own woes I cry.   805

Adrastus
  We have borne

Chorus
              the most tormenting evil.

Adrastus
  O Argive city! Do your folk not see my downfall?

Chorus
  They see me too in my wretched state, barren of children.   810

Adrastus
  Bring on the bloodstained bodies of the doomed—
  Champions in struggle, foully slain by the foul.

Chorus
  Give me my children to take in my arms;   815
  My hands are ready for that embrace.

Adrastus
  You have and hold

Chorus
                  burden enough of woes.

Adrastus
  Alas!

Chorus
      No word for the parents?

Adrastus
    Hear me.

Chorus
                    You groan with your pain and mine.   820

Adrastus
    I wish the Theban columns had struck me down in the
        dust.

Chorus
    Would that my body had never been yoked to a hus-
        band's bed.

Adrastus
    O wretched mothers of children!   825
    Behold, a sea of troubles.

Chorus
    Our nails cut furrows down our cheeks;
    We have poured dust over our heads.

Adrastus
    Oh, Oh, alas, alas!
    Swallow me, earth!
    Hurricane, tear me apart!   830
    Blaze of Zeus's fire, swoop down upon me!

Chorus
    Bitter the wedding you saw,
    Bitter the word of Phoebus;
    A Fury, bringer of grief,
    Has abandoned Oedipus' house and come to yours.   835

                    (*Enter Theseus and Athenian soldiers.*)
Theseus

                                        (*To an Argive captain.*)

    During your long lament before the army
    I would have asked you this, but I refrained

From speaking then, and now I let it pass;   840
Here is Adrastus.

(*To Adrastus.*)

These are men whose spirit
Has brought them fame. What is their lineage?
Speak, from your greater knowledge, to the young
Among our citizens; you have understanding.   845
One thing I ask not, or you'd laugh at me;
Beside whom every warrior stood in battle,
Or from what foe he took a spear-wound. Vain
To tell or hear such tales—as if a man   850
In the thick of combat, with a storm of spears
Before his eyes, ever brought back sure news
On who was hero. I can neither ask
Such questions nor believe those who make bold
To answer them. When you stand against the foe,   855
It is hard enough to see what must be seen.

Adrastus

Hear, then. By granting me the privilege
Of praising friends, you meet my own desire
To speak of them with justice and with truth.
I saw the deeds—bolder than words can say—
By which they hoped to take the city. Look,
That handsome one, through whom the lightning passed,   860
Is Capaneus. A man of means, he never
Flaunted his wealth but kept an attitude
No prouder than a poor man's. He avoided
People who live beyond their needs and load
Their tables to excess. He used to say
That good does not consist in belly-food,   865
And satisfaction comes from moderation.
He was true in friendship to present and absent friends;
Not many men are so. His character
Was never false; his ways were courteous;
His word, in house or city, was his bond.   870

436

Second I name Eteoclus. He practiced
Another kind of virtue. Lacking means,
This youth held highest honors in Argos' land.
Often his friends would make him gifts of gold,   875
But he never took them into his house. He wanted
No slavish way of life, haltered by money.
He kept his hate for sinners, not the city;
A town is not to blame if a bad pilot
Makes men speak ill of it. Hippomedon,   880
Third of the heroes, showed his nature thus:
While yet a boy he had the strength of will
Not to take up the pleasures of the Muses
That soften life; he went to live in the country,
Giving himself hard tasks to do, rejoicing   885
In manly growth. He hunted, delighted in horses,
And stretched the bow with his hands, to make his body
Useful to the city. There lies the son
Of huntress Atalanta, Parthenopaeus,
Supreme in beauty. He was Arcadian,
But came to Inachus' banks and was reared in Argos.   890
After his upbringing there, he showed himself,
As resident foreigners should, not troublesome
Or spiteful to the city, or disputatious,
Which would have made him hard to tolerate   895
As citizen and guest. He joined the army
Like a born Argive, fought the country's wars,
Was glad when the city prospered, and took it hard
If bad times came. Although he had many lovers,
And women flocked to him, still he was careful   900
To cause them no offense. In praise of Tydeus
I shall say much in little. He was ambitious,
Richly endowed, and wise in deeds, not words.
From what I have told you, Theseus, you should not
    wonder
That these men dared to die before the towers.   910
To be well brought up develops self-respect:
Anyone who has practiced what is good
Is ashamed to turn out badly. Manliness

437

Is teachable. Even a child is taught
To say and hear what he does not understand; 915
Things understood are kept in mind till age.
So, in like manner, train your children well.

Chorus
O my child, to an evil fate I bred you!
I carried you in my womb
And felt the pangs of birth; 920
Now, alas! Hades holds my burden,
And I have none to cherish me in age,
Though I bore a child, to my sorrow.

Theseus
And what of Oicles' noble son? His praises 925
Are uttered by the gods, who bore him off
Alive, with his chariot, into the depths of earth.
I too, in all sincerity, might honor
Oedipus' son: I speak of Polynices.
He was my guest, after leaving Cadmus' city, 930
Till he chose Argos for his place of exile.
Now, do you know what I wish to do with the fallen?

Adrastus
This only I know—to obey your orders.

Theseus
Capaneus, struck by Zeus's fire—

Adrastus
You will bury apart, as a sacred corpse? 935

Theseus
Yes. One pyre for all the others.

Adrastus
Where will you place his single memorial?

Theseus
Beside this shrine I will build the tomb.

Adrastus
The slaves may look to that labor now.

Theseus
And I to the rest. Bearers, move on.   940

(*The attendants take up the biers.*)

Adrastus
Sorrowful mothers! Draw near your children!

Theseus
Adrastus! That was not well said.

Adrastus
Why? Must the parents not touch their children?

Theseus
To see their state would be mortal pain.

Adrastus
Yes; corpse-wounds and blood are a bitter sight.   945

Theseus
Then why would you add to the women's woe?

Adrastus
I yield.

(*To the women.*)

You must be brave, and stay where you are.
Theseus is right. When we put them to the fire,
You will take home their bones. O wretched mortals,
Why do you slaughter each other with your spears?   950
Leave off those struggles; let your towns take shelter
In gentleness. Life is a short affair;
We should try to make it smooth, and free from strife.

Chorus
Blest no more with children, blest no more with sons,   955
I have no share in happiness

439

Among the boy-bearing women of Argos.
And Artemis, who watches over birth,
Would have no word for childless women.
Life is a time of woe;   960
I am like a wandering cloud
Sent hurtling by fierce winds.
Seven mothers, we gave birth to seven sons
Who gained the heights of fame in Argos;   965
But that has brought us suffering.
And now, without a son, without a child,
Most miserably I grow old,
Neither a living creature
Nor one of the dead, my fate
Somehow apart from both.   970

Tears are left to me; sad
Memorials of my son are in my house:
Locks of his hair, and wreaths for mine, in mourning,
Libations for the vanished dead, and songs   975
Unwelcome to golden-haired Apollo.
At every dawn I shall wake to weep
And drench the folds of my dress at the breast with tears.

Already I can see the vaults   980
Of the sacred tomb of Capaneus,
And Theseus' memorials to the dead, outside the
    temple.
And close at hand I see Evadne,
Famous wife of him who died by lightning,   985
Daughter of Iphis the king.
Why has she climbed that path
To stand on a lofty rock
That towers above this shrine?

(*Enter Evadne.*)

Evadne
Over what blaze, what gleam did sun and moon   990

440

Drive their chariots through the air
Where the light-bringers ride,
On that dark day when Argos' city   995
Built towers of song and greetings
For my wedding and the bridegroom,
Bronze-armored Capaneus? Alas!
To you I come, wildly running from home!   1000
I shall enter the glow of the pyre and share your grave,
Making Hades my release
From the weary weight of life
And the pain of being.   1005
This is the sweetest death: to die with loved ones dying,
If God should so decree.

Chorus
You see the pyre; you stand above and near it;
It is a treasure-house of Zeus. There lies   1010
Your husband, victim of the lightning-flash.

Evadne
Yes; where I stand I see my end; may fortune
Guide the leap of my feet to glory.   1015
From this rock I shall dive
Into the flames. My body will mingle
In fiery glow with my husband,   1020
His loved flesh close to mine.
So shall I come to Persephone's halls,
Resolved never to cheat your death by living
Upon this earth. Daylight, wedlock, farewell!   1025
Away with Argive marriages
Shown to be true by children!
Out of my sight,
Devoted man of the house, drawn to your noble wife
By steady winds of love!   1030

Chorus
Your father, aged Iphis, comes upon
Strange words, unheard-of, that will hurt to hear.

441

(Enter Iphis.)

Iphis

O women of sorrows! To my sorrowful age
My family has brought a double grief.   1035
I have come to take my dead son home by ship—
Eteoclus, who fell to the Theban spear—
And to seek my daughter, wife of Capaneus,
Who sped from my house in longing to die with her
    husband.
In former days, she was watched at home; beset   1040
By present troubles, I dismissed the guards;
And she has gone. I think she must be here;
If you have seen her, tell me.

Evadne

                                Why ask them?   1045
I am here on a rock above his pyre, my father—
Lightly poised, like a bird, for a flight of doom.

Iphis

My child, what wind has blown you here? What errand?
Why did you slip from home and come to this land?

Evadne

You would be angry if I told my plans;   1050
I do not wish you to hear about them, Father.

Iphis

What? Is it not right that your father should know?

Evadne

You would not be an able judge of my intent.

Iphis

For whom have you put on this finery?

Evadne

My dress has glory in its meaning, Father.   1055

Iphis
You are not like one in mourning for her husband.

Evadne
No, I have made myself ready for something new.

Iphis
And yet you appear beside a tomb and a pyre!

Evadne
I come to celebrate a victory.

Iphis
I beg you, tell me over whom you won it.   1c 6c

Evadne
Over all women on whom the sun looks down.

Iphis
In Athena's skills, or in the ways of prudence?

Evadne
In valor: I shall lie with my husband in death.

Iphis
You speak in sickly riddles. What is this?

Evadne
I rush to the pyre of fallen Capaneus.   1065

Iphis
My daughter! Do not speak that word to many.

Evadne
I want it known by everyone in Argos.

Iphis
I shall not suffer you to do this thing.

Evadne
No matter; I am beyond the reach of your hand.

443

My body falls! a release not dear to you 1070
But to me and the husband who will burn with me.

(*She leaps into the pyre.*)

Chorus

Woman! Terrible the deed you brought to pass!

Iphis

Daughters of Argos! I am ruined, doomed.

Chorus

Having borne this heavy woe,
Alas! you will grieve to see 1075
Her wildly daring deed.

Iphis

The world holds no more miserable man.

Chorus

What suffering is yours! A part of Oedipus' doom
Has befallen you, old sire, and me and my poor city.

Iphis

In grief I ask: Why cannot mortals be 1080
Twice young, then reach old age a second time?
If anything goes wrong at home, we right it
By afterthoughts; but not so with a life.
If youth and age came twice, a double life 1085
Would be our lot, and we could set things right
No matter what mistakes were made. When I saw others
With families, I became an adorer of children
And sorely longed for some to call my own.
If I had come to this experience
With children, and known what it is for a father to lose
them, 1090
Never would I have reached the point of woe
Where now I stand: to have started into life
A noble youth, and then be robbed of him.
And now, in my wretchedness, what shall I do?

444

Return to my house, to see the emptiness 1095
Of many rooms, and a hopeless round of living?
Or shall I go where Capaneus once dwelt?
What a delight that was, when I had this child!
But now she is no more—she who would draw 1100
My cheek to her lips and clasp my head in her hands.
To an old father, nothing is more sweet
Than a daughter. Boys are more spirited, but their ways
Are not so tender. Quickly, take me home
And give me to the dark, to starve until 1105
My aged frame is wasted and I rot.
What will I gain by touching my child's bones?
O harsh old age! How hateful is your reign!
How I hate those who want to stretch life out,
Counting on meats and drinks and magic spells 1110
To turn the stream aside and stave off death.
When useless to the world, they ought to die:
Away with them! Let them leave it to the young.

(*The ashes of the fallen chiefs are brought in.*)

Chorus

Look, look! Alas! They are bringing
The bones of my children who perished.
Attendants, take them from a weak old woman. 1115
Grief for my children has robbed me of my strength.
I have been alive for many lengths of time
And many woes have made me melt in tears.
What greater pain could mortals have than this: 1120
To see their children dead before their eyes?

Boys

Sorrowful mothers! Out of the fire
I bring, I bring my father's limbs;
A weight not weightless, so great is my grief 1125
As I gather my all in a little space.

Chorus

Alas, alas! Who do you bring

445

Tears for the mother whom the fallen loved?
A little heap of dust instead of bodies   1130
Once glorious in Mycenae?

Boys

You are childless! childless! and I,
Having lost my unhappy father, will dwell
An orphan in a house of loss,
Cut off from the father who gave me life.

Chorus

Alas, alas! Where is the labor   1135
Spent on my children? Where, the reward of childbirth,
A mother's care, sleepless devotion of eyes,
The loving kiss on the face?

Boys

They have gone, they are no more. Alas, my father!
They have gone.   1140

Chorus

                    The air holds them now,
Crumbled to dust in the fire;
They have winged their way to Hades.

Boys

Father, I beg you, hear your children's cries!
Shall I ever set my shield against your foes,
Making your murder engender death? May that day
      come!   1145
If God is willing, justice will be done
For our fathers.

Chorus

                    This evil sleeps not yet.
I am grieved; I have had enough
Ill chance, enough of woe.

Boys

Some day Asopus' gleam will welcome me   1150

As I march in the bronze armor of Danaus' sons
On a campaign to demand revenge for my fallen father.
Still I seem to see you, Father, before my eyes—

Chorus
Planting your kiss, so loved, upon my cheek.

Boys
But your encouraging words   1155
Are borne away on the air.

Chorus
He left woe to us both: your mother,
And you, whom grief for your father will never leave.

Boys
I bear so great a burden that it has destroyed me.

Chorus
Come, let me lay the dear dust close to my breast.   1160

Boys
Oh, piteous words! I weep
To hear them; they pierce my heart.

Chorus
Child, you have gone: never again
Shall I see you, idol of your beloved mother.

Theseus
Adrastus! Women of the race of Argos!   1165
You see these youths, holding in their hands
The bodies of their fathers, noble men
Whom I took up for burial. To them
I and the city now present the ashes.
You, who behold what you have gained from me,   1170
Must keep this act in grateful recollection,
And tell your children constantly to honor
This city, handing down from son to son
The memory of answered prayers. Zeus

And the gods in heaven know the kindnesses 1175
Of which we thought you worthy. Go in peace.

Adrastus

Theseus, we are aware of all the good
You have done the land of Argos, in its need
Of benefactors, and our gratitude
Will never fade. We have been nobly treated
By you, and owe you action in return.

Theseus

How can I be of further service to you? 1180

Adrastus

By faring well, as you and your city deserve.

Theseus

We shall; and may you have the same good fortune.

(Athene appears, ex machina.)

Athene

Theseus, hear what I, Athene, tell you.
There is a duty that you must perform
To help the city now. Do not intrust 1185
These bones to the boys, to take to the land of Argos,
Releasing them so lightly. First exact
An oath, in compensation for the efforts
You and the city have made. Adrastus here
Must swear—he has authority, as king,
To take an oath on behalf of all the land 1190
Of Danaus' sons. And this shall be the oath:
"Argos will never move against this country
In hostile panoply. If others try
To invade it, she will hinder them by arms."
If they forsake the oath and come, then pray
That the Argive land may fall again to ruin. 1195
Now hear me name the vessel for the blood
From the rite you must perform. You have
Inside your house a tripod with feet of bronze.

After destroying Ilium's foundations
Long years ago, Heracles, going forth
On another labor, bade you place that vessel   1200
On the altar of Apollo. Over it
You must cut the throats of three sheep, and inscribe
The oath on the hollow of the tripod; then
Present it to the god who has charge of Delphi,
To be preserved in memory of the oath
And as witness to it in the eyes of Hellas.
The sharp-edged knife, with which you execute   1205
The sacrifice and deal the death-wound, you must bury
Deep in the earth, here, beside the seven
Pyres of the fallen. Then, if the Argives ever
Move on the city, the knife, revealed, will work
Fear in their hearts, and an evil journey home.
When this is done, you must send the dead from the
      land,   1210
And dedicate a shrine of the Isthmian goddess
Beside the triple crossroads, where the bodies
Were purified by fire. These are my words
To you. To the sons of the Argives, I proclaim:
When you are men you will sack Ismenus' city,
Avenging the murder of your fallen fathers.   1215
You, Aigialeus, will take your father's place
As a young campaigner, and you, the son of Tydeus
From Aetolia, named Diomedes by your father.
You must no sooner get your beards than march
A mighty force of bronze-clad Danaids   1220
Against the Thebans' seven-mouthed walls. Your com-
      ing
Will bring them sorrow—true-bred lion-cubs
That you are, sackers of cities! This shall befall:
Hellas will know you as the Sons of Sons,
A theme of future song. So great will be   1225
Your expedition, favored by the gods.

Theseus
   I shall obey your orders, Queen Athene!

You have corrected me; I err no more.
Yes, I shall bind this man to me by oath.
Only, I pray you, set me in the right path;   1230
So long as you mean kindly to the city,
Our life will be secure to the end of time.

Chorus

Now let us go, Adrastus, and give our word
To this man and his city, who have labored
On our behalf in ways that deserve all honor.

MODERN LIBRARY GIANTS

A series of sturdily bound and handsomely printed, full-sized library editions of books formerly available only in expensive sets. These volumes contain from 600 to 1,400 pages each.

THE MODERN LIBRARY GIANTS REPRESENT A
SELECTION OF THE WORLD'S GREATEST BOOKS